NATURAL
MENOPAUSE

NATURAL MENOPAUSE

The Complete Guide
Revised Edition

SUSAN PERRY

KATE O'HANLAN, M.D.

PERSEUS BOOKS

Reading, Massachusetts

Library of Congress Cataloging-in-Publication Data
Perry, Susan (Susan L.)
    Natural menopause : the complete guide / Susan Perry, Kate
O'Hanlan.—Rev. ed.
        p.   cm.
    Includes bibliographical references and index.
    ISBN 0-201-47987-7 (alk. paper)
    1. Menopause—Popular works.   I. O'Hanlan, Kate.   II. Title.
RG186.P47   1996
612.6'65—dc20   96-27094
                                                      CIP

Perseus Books is a member of the Perseus Books Group

Cover design by Suzanne Heiser
Text design by Anna George
Set in 11-point Goudy Old Style by Pagesetters, Inc.

    6 7 8 9 10   02010099

Find us on the World Wide Web at
http://www.perseusbooksgroup.com

To my sisters, Deborah and Jean,
as we begin together our journey
through the third season of life,

and to my daughter, Erin,
who will one day follow us.
-S.P.-

To my wonderful friends who are my patients at the
Albert Einstein College of Medicine Hospital
and at the Stanford University Hospital.
Your smiles and hugs and the lessons you have shared
with me as you live and struggle with your cancer
are my constant source of strength.

And to Léonie, I thank you for the support
and love at home.
-K.A.O'H.-

Contents

Acknowledgments

Writing a book is a journey of sorts. Like most good journeys, it leads you along unexpected paths and introduces you to new ideas and interesting people. We would like to thank the many wonderful people whom we met during the writing of this book and who helped us in so many different ways.

First we would like to thank the dozens of women who spoke to us so openly about their experiences with menopause. Their voices are heard throughout the book and helped to shape what we wrote.

We would also like to thank the many scientists and researchers who gave us their time and expertise, especially Sonja McKinlay; Sidney M. Wolfe, M.D.; John La Rosa, M.D.; Arthur Balin, M.D.; Louise Brinton; Catherine DeLorey; Kathleen MacPherson; Deb Boehm; and Patricia Hausman. A special thanks goes to Virginia Morgan of the National Institute on Aging and to Cindy Pearson of the National Women's Health Network. Thanks also to Judy Lutter and the Melpomene Institute for opening up their research files to us.

For Susan, the writing of this book would not have been possible without the help of many supportive friends. She would like to begin by thanking Ann Redpath for her untiring friendship and invaluable editorial advice. Thanks also to Lynne Burke and Andrea Matthews for their encouragement and for the long hours they spent digging up research at the University of Minnesota's medical library. In addition, Susan would like to thank Clare Rosen, Carol Harrison, Joe Alper, Ann Waters, Kim Olson, Jerry Bono, and Jim Young for their unwavering support and encouragement.

Kate would like to thank Lynne Randall, Lynn Thogerson, and Janet Callum at the Feminist Women's Health Center in Atlanta, Georgia, who started her on the path of feminist medicine in 1980. She also thanks Dr. George C. Lewis and Dr. Lorna Rodriguez-Rodriguez, both of whom are friends and colleagues on this path. Thanks also to Susan Perry for her courage, intelligence, and clarity.

Finally, we both would like to thank our agent, Heide Lange, for working yet another miracle, and our editor, Nancy Miller, for her editorial guidance and strong commitment to the book.

NATURAL
MENOPAUSE

Introduction to the Revised Edition

In the few short years since the first edition of *Natural Menopause* was published, a great deal of new information has been uncovered about midlife women and their journey through menopause. On the medical front, there have been many new studies concerning everything from the safety and efficacy of hormone replacement therapy to the possible connection between estrogen and Alzheimer's disease. New drug treatments and diagnostic techniques for osteoporosis have also been introduced, while others have been discarded.

In addition, much more is now known about the benefits of natural approaches to menopause, especially in the areas of exercise and diet. Ancient herbal therapies for hot flashes and other signs of menopause are being scientifically examined. Researchers are also studying the possible benefits of soy and other foods containing estrogen-like substances known as phytoestrogens. Some scientists believe phytoestrogens may not only bring women relief from hot flashes, but may also protect them against heart disease, breast cancer, and other diseases.

We have included the very latest information on all these topics and more in this revised edition of *Natural Menopause*. The updating of the book has been an often exhausting process, for menopause has become a "hot" topic, with new studies being published continuously. Yet even with all this new information, many issues remain controversial, especially the question of whether a woman should use hormone replacement therapy. As in our earlier edition, we present you with the very latest information about the pros and cons of taking hormones, but we don't make the decision for you. Only you—with your physician's help—can decide how you want to undertake your journey through menopause. We hope, however, that we have given you enough information to make a knowledgeable decision, and we encourage you to listen to your body and keep up-to-date on new research as it becomes available.

Introduction

Menopause is the invisible experience. People don't want to hear about it. But this is the time when everything comes good for you—your humor, your style, your bad temper.

—Germaine Greer

Although it is a natural and universal phase of life for women, menopause is fraught with mystery and myth. For many women, just thinking about menopause brings on a sweaty hot flash. They dread the thought of it. They have heard tales of its physical discomforts—hot flashes, night sweats, painful intercourse, and so on. They have also been told of its great toll on the emotions—how hormones run wild during the menopausal years, causing a woman (so the story goes) to act like the Wicked Witch of the West one moment and the teary-eyed Cowardly Lion the next.

In fact, history's best-known psychiatrist, Sigmund Freud, described the menopausal woman as "quarrelsome, peevish, and argumentative, petty and miserly . . . sadistic and anal-erotic." Helene Deutsch, a well-known disciple of Freud, referred to menopause as "partial death" and wrote that overcoming its psychological problems was "one of the most difficult tasks of a woman's life."

In more recent years, the popular press has contributed to this dismal image of menopause. In his best-selling book, *Everything You Always Wanted to Know About Sex, But Were Afraid to Ask*, psychiatrist David Reuben declared that after menopause a woman becomes "not really a man but no longer a functional woman" and lives "in the world of intersex." In another best-selling book, *Feminine Forever*, gynecologist Robert Wilson warned that "no woman can be sure of escaping the horror of this living decay."

5

Even as late as 1989, another gynecologist warned in his book that menopause could lead to "aggressiveness" and "antisocial" behavior. No wonder so many women are apprehensive about making the passage through menopause!

Fortunately, for the vast majority of women, menopause does not live up to these negative characterizations. In fact, studies have shown that menopause is feared most by younger women—those who have not yet encountered it. Once women reach midlife and actually experience menopause, most report that it creates no major crisis or disruption in their lives.

That is not to say that menopause is an unimportant event in a woman's life. Indeed, for most women, menopause carries significant meaning; it marks an important point of passage, and thus often becomes a time for deep reflection, for taking on new interests, and for realizing new dreams. Nor can the physical effects of menopause be discounted or trivialized. Hot flashes, for example, are not, as was once believed, the psychosomatic imaginings of neurotic middle-aged women. They are very real.

Still, menopause—hot flashes and all—does not throw most women into an emotional or physical crisis. During their menopausal years, women do not lose their minds, their intelligence, or their interest in sex. Nor does their femininity decay and wither away, leaving them, as one prominent gynecologist put it, "a caricature of their younger selves at their emotional worst."

In what is perhaps the most comprehensive study of its kind to date, researchers Sonja M. McKinlay and John B. McKinlay of the New England Research Institute in Watertown, Massachusetts, interviewed more than 2,300 women several times over a period of five years as the women approached and passed through menopause. Their goal was to find out what menopause means to healthy women and how it affects their physical and psychological health. All the women interviewed were between the ages of 45 and 55 at the onset of the study.

The McKinlays found that only 3 percent of the women expressed regret during or after menopause about the physical changes associated with menopause, such as hot flashes and menstrual irregularities. Few lamented the end of menstruation; many, in fact, expressed relief that they would no longer have to be concerned with contraception, menstruation, and pregnancy.

The study also revealed that the depression experienced by some women during the menopausal years is due not to physiological changes, as has been long believed, but to other midlife events, such as problems with children, parents, and husbands.

What expectations you bring to menopause will depend greatly on your own sense of worth and identity. Research has shown that the better a woman feels about herself and her life, the easier time she will have with the passage through menopause.

Of course, this doesn't mean that all women who find the transition through menopause distressing have self-esteem problems. For sound biological reasons, some women do have a more difficult time with hot flashes and other menopausal complaints—just as some women have more trouble with menstrual cramps or with premenstrual syndrome. It's important that all women feel their experience with menopause is validated, no matter what it is. No woman should be made to think that she is somehow inferior, either physically or mentally, for finding menopause to be a struggle.

We also need to recognize that women who undergo menopause suddenly, as a result of surgery, radiation therapy, or chemotherapy, have a much different experience than women who go through menopause naturally. Generally speaking, menopause is more difficult for women who enter it abruptly as a result of surgical removal of the ovaries or other medical treatment. They tend to have more severe hot flashes and are more likely to report being depressed or in poor health. For these women, the passage through menopause can be very intense and disruptive.

Whether you experience menopause naturally or as the result of surgery, you will find it to be a uniquely individual experience. In fact, the only universal statement that can be made about menopause is that menstruation stops. All the other particulars of the experience, including the intensity and frequency of hot flashes, vary from woman to woman.

You will also find that, contrary to the dire predictions of Freud and others, menopause does not signal an end to your mental prowess, your sexuality, or your sanity. In fact, it need not be viewed as an end at all, but as the beginning of a new and liberating chapter in your life. As one 42-year-old woman puts it: "I'm looking forward to the calm, to having my body quit playing tricks on me."

•   •   •

In her short story "The Long Distance Runner," Grace Paley walks us through a kind of menopausal experience. The female protagonist takes up running at midlife and in the process explores her past and gathers new insights and energy for her future. Paley uses running as a metaphor for the personal growth so many women experience during their menopausal years:

"I . . . didn't begin my run till the road opened up somewhere along Ocean Parkway. I was a little stiff because my way of life had used only small movements, an occasional stretch to put a knife or teapot out of reach of the babies. I ran about ten, fifteen blocks. Then my second wind came, which is classical, famous among runners, it's the beginning of flying. . . ."

It is hoped that this book will help you find that second wind or, as anthropologist Margaret Mead called it, that "postmenopausal zest."

This is a practical book. It describes the physical and emotional changes you can expect as you pass through your menopausal years and explains which ones are a direct result of menopause and which ones are just a natural part of aging. It deals with the importance of exercise and proper diet during the menopausal years and the need for adequate rest and stress reduction. It takes you through the great hormone debate, informing you about the pros and cons of hormone treatment so that you can decide for yourself whether that is a road you wish to run down. And it debunks the great myth that menopause marks the end of a woman's sexuality.

The book also includes the thoughts of dozens of women around the country about their experiences coping with menopause and other midlife changes. Their comments teach us that although our bodies are sometimes out of our control, we are still in charge of how we accept life's changes.

"Have you known it to happen much nowadays?" asks Paley's long distance runner. "A woman inside the steamy energy of middle age runs and runs. She finds the houses and streets where her childhood happened. She lives in them. She learns as though she was still a child what in the world is coming next."

As we approach menopause, most of us wonder about what in the world is coming next. What we find as we pass through menopause is that what comes next is really quite remarkable.

1

WHAT IS MENOPAUSE, AND WHEN CAN I EXPECT IT TO HAPPEN?

Most people would consider the old phrase "change of life" a euphemism for the medical term "menopause," but I, who am now going through the change, begin to wonder if it isn't the other way round. "Change of life" is too blunt a phrase, too factual. "Menopause," with its chime-suggestion of a mere pause after which things go on as before, is reassuringly trivial.

—Ursula K. Le Guin
"The Space Crone,"
Dancing at the Edge of the World

In a survey asking women what was the worst thing about menopause, most said, "Not knowing what to expect." One woman added, "You wish someone would tell you—but you're too embarrassed to ask anyone."

You think you should just *know*.

In past generations, many women were too embarrassed to discuss menopause, even with other women friends. Today, thanks in large part to the rise of the women's movement, menopause is talked about more openly. Self-help menopause discussion groups have sprung up in the United States and around the world, as women have recognized the need to come together and share their menopausal and other midlife experiences.

Still, many women remain in the dark about the details of menopause. One survey, for example, found that most women think the average woman experiences menopause at age 45, when the actual average age is between 50 and 51. Also, most women significantly overestimate the length of time the average woman experiences hot flashes, believing it to be five years rather than two.

This chapter looks at the basic biological facts about menopause—in other words, at what causes it to happen. It also takes a look at when you can expect to experience menopause and the factors that may speed up or delay its arrival.

•   •   •

"What is meant by menopause? I don't know if I'm in it. I think I am, but I don't know."

•   •   •

COMING TO TERMS

In simplest terms, menopause is the final end to menstruation. You know it has happened when you have not had a menstrual period for one year.

But, of course, menopause is not a simple event. The biological changes that trigger it are very complex. Nor does menopause happen overnight. It's part of a longer life transition—a period of some ten to fifteen years—during which a woman's reproductive system gradually changes.

Most of us use the word *menopause* to describe this entire transitional period, during which a woman goes from having regular menstrual cycles to not having any cycles at all. In strict biological terminology, however, menopause refers only to the date of the final menstrual period. Physicians use another term—the *climacteric* (kly-MAC-ter-ic)—to describe the ten to fifteen years during which the ovaries gradually stop producing eggs and large amounts of hormones.

Menopause and climacteric, therefore, are not synonymous—at least, not in the medical literature.

Another popular term for the climacteric is *change of life*. This is a useful term, for it encompasses the emotional and intellectual changes, as well as the physical ones, that are often going on during this important time in a woman's life.

PREDICTING YOUR LAST PERIOD

Most of the experts will tell you that the average woman has her last menstrual period around her fifty-first birthday. That doesn't mean, however, that most women experience menopause when they are 51, only that half of all women stop menstruating before they turn 51 and half stop menstruating afterward.

THE MEDICALIZATION OF MENOPAUSE

Derived from the Greek words for *month* and *cessation*, the term *menopause* was first used in 1872. By that date, Western medicine viewed menopause as a medical crisis that had the potential of causing a variety of diseases, from diarrhea to diabetes. The crisis was deemed greatest for women who had acted indiscreetly in the past. Such indiscretions included getting too much education, having too much sex, attempting to use birth control, or even being insufficiently devoted to husband and children. As a prescription for menopause, doctors recommended a quiet lifestyle centered on the family.

Sometimes more drastic measures were taken. Leeches were often put on a woman's ears or on the nape of her neck to cure menopausal complaints. Another popular remedy was an oophorectomy, or surgical removal of the ovaries. Such an operation was considered especially helpful in curing menopausal depression and "disorderliness."

Not all nineteenth-century physicians, however, shared their peers' negative views of menopause. One trend-breaker dared to refer to menopause as "a period of increased vigor, optimism, and even of physical beauty." Another physician publicly criticized his medical colleagues for subjecting women to unnecessary oophorectomies, stating in a medical journal that he had "yet to see a woman made better in health by the removal of her ovaries."

By the middle of the twentieth century, the medical profession switched from looking upon menopause as the cause of disease and began to think of it as a disease itself—a deficiency disease, like diabetes. This gave doctors the exclusive right to diagnose menopause and to treat its symptoms with estrogen, the hormone women were said to be lacking.

Today, many women are beginning to question the medicalization of menopause. Just as women have in recent years insisted on a more natural approach to childbirth, so they are insisting that menopause be treated as a natural event, not a medical crisis or deficiency disease. They are reclaiming the experience as a healthful part of their lives and are celebrating it as the onset of maturity.

In the United States, the statistics break down as follows: 10 percent of women experience natural menopause (as opposed to menopause brought on by surgery or other medical procedures) by age 38, 30 percent by age 44, 50 percent by age 49, 90 percent by age 54, and 100 percent by age 58.

So if you stop menstruating before your forty-fifth birthday, don't be alarmed. Menopause happens that early to about a third of all women.

And don't be surprised if you are still menstruating well into your early fifties. Many women follow that pattern as well.

• • •

"I think there was part of me that was thinking, 'Menopause? That's something your mother goes through!' I was embarrassed to tell my friends. I was embarrassed to tell anybody because I was so young."

• • •

INFLUENTIAL FACTORS

There's no way of predicting exactly when your menopause will occur. Although researchers have searched, they have found no conclusive link between the age a woman's periods stop and the age her periods began. The age at which your mother experienced menopause *may* have something to do with it, although researchers are not sure. Nor does where you live or whether or not you took birth control pills or how old you were when your first or last child was born seem to influence the timing of menopause.

It seems most likely that the age at which we experience menopause—like the age at which we begin to menstruate—is determined by our individual genes. In other words, each of us has an internal biological timer that is programmed before birth to set off the hormonal events that trigger both the start and the end of menstruation.

Researchers have, however, discovered several factors that appear to cause that timer to slow down or speed up a bit:

- *Smoking.* In general, smokers tend to experience menopause earlier than nonsmokers. Scientists are not sure why this is so, but they suggest that it is linked to the fact that smoking decreases secretion of estrogen from the ovaries. Studies have shown that smokers have lower levels of estrogen in their bloodstream, and, as we will see shortly, estrogen and other hormones play a major role in the reproductive system.

    Some studies indicate that the more cigarettes you smoke, the earlier you are likely to experience menopause.
- *Income and education.* The lower a woman's income and the less education she has had, the earlier she is likely to experience menopause. These factors may be linked to smoking, however, for smokers tend to have lower incomes and less education than nonsmokers.
- *Weight.* According to one study, women who weigh more than about 130

pounds tend to experience menopause at a later age than women who weigh less than that. This may be because estrogen can be made in body fat as well as in the ovaries. Thus, women with extra fat on their bodies may have an excess supply of estrogen that can delay the onset of menopause.

- *Twins.* Women who have given birth to twins appear to begin menopause about a year earlier than other mothers. Just why this is so is not yet clear.

THE MISSING SEASON OF LIFE

One of the earliest references to the menopause can be found in the Talmud, the ancient commentaries on Jewish law and tradition. According to the Talmud, if a woman misses three periods she is old, but if her periods restart, she becomes young once again.

This idea of equating menopause with old age makes sense only when you consider that during the period of time when the Talmud was written (third to fifth century A.D.), the average life span for women was 23 years. Disease, poor nutrition, hard physical work, and childbirth usually put women in their graves long before menopause arrived. Even as late as 1900, European and American women had an average life expectancy of only about 45 years, which meant that they often died before experiencing menopause.

Today, women living in developed countries can expect to survive well into their seventies. That means a full third of our lives will occur after our childbearing years are over. The experience of menopause, therefore, comes not when we are "old," but at midlife, when we still have many active and productive years ahead of us.

Western society, however, continues to associate menopause with being old. As psychotherapist Rita Ransohoff points out in her book *Venus After Forty*, which explores the myths and fantasies about female sexuality after 40, Western culture makes little distinction between a middle-aged and an older-aged woman. As an example, Ransohoff points to the word *hag*. In a standard dictionary a hag is "an evil and ugly old woman endowed with supernatural powers." But in a dictionary of slang *hag* is also used to describe a middle-aged woman!

The myths of our culture divide the lives of women into only three seasons: childhood (spring), reproductive adulthood (summer), and old age (winter). "[This] leave[s] no room for the ripeness and fullness of maturity that is personified by women after their childbearing years are past," declares Ransohoff. "I believe the human imagination has room for a new image—a fourth season—a true picture of a middle-aged woman."

PREMATURE MENOPAUSE

Menopause that occurs before the age of 35 is considered premature. An early menopause can be the result of a variety of factors:

- *Surgical removal of the ovaries.* This is by far the most common cause of premature menopause. The ovaries are usually removed because they have been destroyed by ovarian tumors, pelvic inflammatory disease, or cancer. Both ovaries must be removed, however, for menopause to occur; a single ovary, or even a portion of an ovary, can continue to produce eggs and hormones for as long as if both ovaries were still present.
- *Radiation therapy.* If the ovaries receive significant doses of radiation, such as those used to treat various cancers, menopause may occur.
- *Tubal ligation.* In very rare cases, a tubal ligation done for sterilization purposes may bring on menopause by cutting off the blood supply from the uterus to the ovaries and causing them to stop functioning.
- *Mumps.* Some studies suggest that, in a small number of women, a bout with mumps may lead to premature menopause. Scientists believe the infection spreads to the ovaries, causing irreversible damage.
- *Autoimmune reaction.* Sometimes, for reasons not yet clear, a woman's body may start making antibodies that attack her ovaries, eventually destroying her supply of eggs. Frequently, women to whom this happens have a specific autoimmune disease, such as lupus or rheumatoid arthritis, but for many other women, there is no clear explanation as to why their ovaries cease to function.

LATE MENOPAUSE

Menopause that occurs after the age of 55 is considered late or delayed. Having regular periods into your late fifties can be perfectly natural, particularly for women who are overweight and thus producing extra amounts of estrogen. However, be sure to alert your health care provider to the fact that you are continuing to menstruate. Factors other than a late menopause may be causing the bleeding, such as an abnormal growth in the uterus. A uterine overgrowth can lead, in some instances, to a cancer, which is why you'll want to have it carefully diagnosed—and why you should be having regular gynecological check-ups even if you consider yourself long past your reproductive years.

A late menopause can increase your risk of both uterine and breast cancer. Researchers believe that the extra risk is due to the prolonged exposure to estrogen without the release of an egg and the completion of

---

THE STAGES OF MENOPAUSE

The medical community has divided the climacteric, or "change of life," into the following stages. Your doctor may refer to them when describing your health.

- *Premenopause*. Sometimes this stage is defined as all the years when menstrual cycles are regular—in other words, all the reproductive years preceding the change of life. At other times, it is defined as the beginning years of the climacteric—usually after age 40—when menstrual periods may become irregular. Because of these conflicting definitions, you should ask your doctor to be more specific if he or she tells you that you are premenopausal.
- *Perimenopause*. The period approximately two years before and two years after the final menstrual period. This is the time when women notice the most physical changes, such as irregular periods and hot flashes.
- *Menopause*. Your final menstrual period. Determining the date of menopause can be done only retroactively, after you have been free of menstrual bleeding for a full year.
- *Postmenopause*. The months and years that follow your final menstrual period. It overlaps with the perimenopausal stage.

---

the menstrual cycle. The risk of cancer of the uterus is two times greater for women whose menopause occurs after age 50. Similarly, the risk of cancer of the breast is two times greater for women whose menopause occurs after age 55.

If you continue to menstruate well into your fifties, take extra care to do monthly breast self-exams. You should also be sure you have an annual Pap test, pelvic exam, and mammogram.

THE CAUSE OF MENOPAUSE

To understand why menopause occurs—and how and why it affects you—you must first have a basic understanding of your endocrine system. That's the system that regulates those all-important chemicals in your body known as hormones. Such knowledge can be reassuring when you're hit with one of the telltale signs of menopause, such as a hot flash or an on-again-off-again menstrual period. You'll know that what you're experiencing has a physiological basis—and that it's not just "in your head." In addition, if you arm yourself with the bodily facts about menopause, you will be in a more knowledgeable position to discuss with your physician any kind of medical treatment he or she may prescribe.

•　　•　　•

"Actually, I didn't have any feelings about menopause. I was raised in a family where you just didn't talk about those things. My mother had a hysterectomy; I don't even know how old she was when she had it. I would imagine she was probably in her middle forties. But we just never discussed it, so I didn't have any feelings toward menopause one way or the other."

•　　•　　•

A Tale of Three Glands

The endocrine system consists of a number of small glands located throughout the body. These glands release powerful chemicals called *hormones* that travel via your bloodstream to other organs within your body. The hormones act as messengers, telling specific cells to act in specific ways. Without such messages, your internal organs—including those that make up your reproductive system—would not be able to get on with their daily activities.

The reproductive system gets its major messages from three endocrine glands—the hypothalamus, the pituitary, and the ovaries. Both the hypothalamus, which is about the size of a walnut, and the pituitary, which is about the size of a small pea, are located in your brain. The ovaries rest on either side of the uterus, just below the funnel-shaped openings of the Fallopian tubes.

The *hypothalamus* is the master gland, serving as the controlling link between the brain and the endocrine system. It regulates many of the inner workings of the body, from body temperature to water retention, and controls such basic drives as hunger, thirst, and sex. It also plays a dominant role in reproduction, directing the monthly menstrual cycle. The hypothalamus also responds to stress and trauma, which is why some women experience irregular periods or may even temporarily stop menstruating during times of physical or emotional stress.

The *pituitary* acts as the go-between for the hypothalamus, translating messages from the master gland to the separate endocrine glands throughout the body. When, for example, the hypothalamus signals the pituitary to get the menstrual cycle going, the pituitary quickly responds by releasing two of its own hormones, which have a direct influence on the ovaries.

The *ovaries* are the main manufacturers of women's sex hormones, the two most important of which are estrogen and progesterone. Both of these hormones play an important role in the physical and emotional lives of women.

A Typical Month in the Life of Your Hormones

At the beginning of the cycle, the hypothalamus sends a chemical signal to the pituitary to secrete two substances, known as follicle-stimulating hormone (FSH) and leutinizing hormone (LH). At first, FSH dominates. It stimulates several eggs within the ovaries to begin to grow. As the eggs develop, the tissue surrounding them, or *follicles*, produce the hormone *estrogen*, which directs the lining of the uterus to thicken in order to prepare for the possibility of the implantation of an embryo and its growth into a fetus.

Gradually, one egg dominates and continues to grow, while the others wither away. When the estrogen reaches a certain peak level—about twelve days into the cycle—the hypothalamus sends another message to the pituitary to curb its production of FSH and emit a surge of LH. This surge of LH causes the developed egg to be released from the ovary—an event known as *ovulation*. The egg usually enters the Fallopian tube, where it may or may not become fertilized.

At the site where the egg falls away from the ovary, something quite amazing now happens. The scar tissue forms a new, temporary gland called a *corpus luteum* (meaning "yellow body"). This gland continues to produce estrogen in lower levels and also begins producing a second hormone, *progesterone*, to further help the uterus prepare for a fertilized egg. The progesterone, whose name means "for pregnancy," stimulates cells in the uterine lining to secrete nutrients that will nourish the egg if it should become fertilized.

If an egg does not become fertilized and an embryo is not formed, the corpus luteum degenerates and gradually stops secreting progesterone and estrogen. Without hormonal messengers telling them to grow or to secrete nutrients, the cells of the uterine lining wither and die. When the cells dissolve, some of the blood vessels supplying them leak. This flow of blood is known, of course, as *menstruation*.

Just before the menstrual flow begins, however, the low levels of

17

estrogen and progesterone alert the hypothalamus to the need to get the cycle started again. The master gland sends its messenger to the pituitary once more, and the appropriate hormones begin their monthly rhythmic performance.

And so it goes, month after month, for more than thirty years of a woman's life. With the exception of pregnancy—and until menopause— the cycle is rarely broken.

●   ●   ●

"It's made me think about my mother going through menopause. I wasn't told a whole lot about it, by either of my parents. Except I remember my mother being upset sometimes and my dad saying, 'Oh, your mother's going through the change of life.' I wished we had talked about it, because I have so many questions that were never answered. Now I think about how mothers aren't really telling their daughters about it."

●   ●   ●

Why the Cycle Changes at Menopause

So what happens at menopause to bring the menstrual cycle to a final, if somewhat bumpy, halt? Scientists are not sure about all the complex factors involved, but the most important one is quite simple: the ovaries simply run out of eggs.

The depletion of eggs is not an overnight phenomenon. In fact, it begins even before you are born. Your ovaries contain the most egg follicles—several hundred thousand—when you are a 7-month-old embryo. By birth, fewer than half of those follicles remain; the others have simply dissolved and disappeared. When you begin to menstruate a dozen or so years later, your ovaries contain only about 75,000 eggs—many fewer than at birth but still a generous number, considering that only a few hundred will be needed during the next few decades for ovulation. After that, the decline of eggs is slower but steady. By age 40, a woman's ovaries contain only a few thousand eggs. By the time a woman reaches 50, most of those eggs are gone, and the few that remain are no longer sensitive to the chemical messages sent to them from the pituitary.

With fewer and fewer eggs, the production of estrogen and the cyclic release of progesterone become erratic or less intense. This confuses the hypothalamus, which signals the pituitary to release ever-increasing amounts of FSH and LH to the ovaries in a desperate attempt to arouse the egg follicles to produce more estrogen and to ovulate. FSH levels, in particular, climb dramatically—as much as fifteen times higher than they were earlier—and they remain at high levels for two to three years after menopause. Eventually, even extraordinary amounts of FSH are not enough to stimulate the few remaining egg follicles to produce significant amounts of estrogen. Without adequate levels of estrogen, the lining of the uterus does not thicken in preparation for an embryo. No ovulation occurs, and menstruation stops. This is the menopause.

A NEW HORMONAL BALANCE

Contrary to common belief, women do not completely cease producing estrogen in their bodies after menopause. Your body made estrogen when you were a small child, long before you began menstruating, and it continues to make it after your periods have stopped—only at lower and more stable levels.

After menopause, the body makes most of its estrogen by converting a hormone called androstenedione into estrogen. The androstenedione comes from two sources: the ovaries and the *adrenal glands*, two crescent-shaped glands located just atop the kidneys. The adrenal glands are best known for secreting the hormone adrenaline when the body is under stress or confronted with danger.

•　　•　　•

"It seems to me that there are subjects that women are taught to keep secret, events we learn to cover up rather than celebrate. I think in my family it was more true that we didn't talk about things than that we did. I think that's why my mother found hot flashes to be so embarrassing—because it made public something she thought she shouldn't be talking about. I mean, she couldn't hide them—she became absolutely drenched—but she felt as though she should because it was an embarrassment to be going through menopause."

•　　•　　•

The ovaries and adrenal glands release their supplies of androstenedione into the bloodstream. The hormone then makes its way to fat cells throughout the body, where it is converted into estrogen. Other tissues, such as the liver and kidney, also appear to aid in the conversion.

HELPING YOUR ADRENAL GLANDS
PRODUCE ESTROGEN

A steady and stable supply of estrogen from your adrenal glands can help ease your physical transition through menopause. The amount of estrogen in postmenopausal women varies greatly. Some women have much higher levels than others. You can theoretically help your adrenal glands produce a healthful supply of estrogen after menopause by exercising and keeping at least some (but not too much!) body fat on your body. Exercise appears to speed up the conversion of androstenedione into estrogen, and having a little body fat provides more cells in which the conversion can take place. The key here is a *little* body fat: Your body weight in fat should not drop below 15 percent, but neither should it go much above 25 percent. Too much weight can be just as risky for your health as too little.

Diet is also important for ensuring healthy adrenal glands. You need to make sure you get enough nutrients (especially vitamins B and C) and that you avoid excessive amounts of foods, such as coffee, alcohol, and sugar, that may place extra stress on the adrenals.

For more information about the importance of exercise and diet during the menopausal years, see chapters 7 and 8.

TESTS FOR DETERMINING
WHETHER YOU ARE NEARING MENOPAUSE

Measuring blood levels of estrogen is not considered useful for determining a woman's menopausal status because estrogen levels in the blood fluctuate widely. A more accurate test is to measure the blood level of FSH, the hormone secreted by the pituitary gland that makes ovarian follicles grow. As noted earlier, FSH levels tend to rise dramatically around menopause, directly as a result of decreased levels of estrogen.

In addition, cells from the wall of the vagina can be studied under a microscope to help determine whether a woman is near or past menopause. Estrogen carries a message to these cells to grow thick and lush and strong. When estrogen levels fall, as they do during menopause, the cells that make up the vaginal wall gradually thin considerably—and look much different under a microscope.

Cells to examine are obtained through a vaginal smear—a procedure similar to the Pap smear except that the specimen is taken from the vaginal wall rather than from the cervix. This test reflects the effects on the vaginal lining of all estrogens from any source.

Blood tests and vaginal smears are usually done only if a woman appears to be experiencing signs of premature menopause and if she wants confirmation from her physician that this is indeed what is happening.

• • •

"All I want to do is survive menopause without killing someone!"

• • •

MAKING THE TRANSITION

Your body makes some truly remarkable changes during the menopausal years. A full understanding of these changes can help you approach menopause with acceptance and perhaps even a sense of wonder, rather than apprehension.

Above all, remember that menopause is not a medical event, but a natural biological transition—just one of several in a woman's life.

"Perhaps, with education and proper perspective, we can look forward to the day when people will stop viewing menopause as a crisis, or even as 'the change,' and see it more appropriately as 'yet another change,'" writes Dr. Kathryn McGoldrick, former editor in chief of the *Journal of the American Medical Women's Association*. "For living is constant change. That is its essence and its promise."

2

HOT FLASHES AND OTHER SIGNS OF MENOPAUSE, AND WHAT YOU CAN DO ABOUT THEM

My mother is both the toughest woman in the East and the least depressed person I have ever met. She has never complained of an ache or pain. She fights endless battles in the conduct of her business. She has never asked for help from anyone. I recently asked her if she remembered going through menopause. Indeed, she did. Was it painful? Had she become sad? "I don't know," she answered. "I never notice my body. I don't have time to think of such things."
—Avodah K. Offit, M.D.

Now that you understand all the hormonal churnings going on inside your body as you approach and pass through menopause, you can better understand the signs most clearly associated with menopause, most notably erratic periods, hot flashes, and vaginal dryness.

Medical professionals usually refer to these signs as menopausal *symptoms*. That term, however, implies that menopause is some kind of disease or illness, rather than a natural life passage. Many women, therefore, prefer the term *signs*.

Throughout medical history, there have been many signs attributed to menopause, everything from headaches to heart palpitations to hysteria. Many of these signs, however, have more to do with the natural aging process or with medicine's often sexist attitudes toward "female complaints" than with the hormonal changes of menopause.

The scientific evidence available today supports three signs of menopause: menstrual cycle irregularities, hot flashes, and a thinning and drying of the vaginal and urinary tissues. Even these three signs, however, are not universal among women. Many women who are significantly overweight, for example, do not experience hot flashes or drying of the vagina because substantial amounts of estrogen continue to be produced in their fat cells.

•   •   •

"Last summer I started getting hot flashes. I knew something was wrong. I had had irregular periods for quite some time before that. I wouldn't have a period for four or five months and then I would get one that was really heavy, and then I'd skip again. It was erratic like that for about two years. But I thought, 'I'm only 37. I can't be going through menopause.' Well, I was wrong. I was."

•   •   •

This chapter examines how and why menopause can cause such changes in our bodies. It also looks at all the steps women can take to ease any discomfort these changes may bring.

CHANGES IN THE MENSTRUAL CYCLE

A change in the menstrual cycle is usually the first sign that menopause is approaching. That change can take many forms. You may notice that your periods are more frequent or that they are more spread apart. You may even skip periods, sometimes for several months in a row. The length of your period—the actual days you are menstruating—may also change, becoming either shorter or longer. In addition, you may experience either a lighter or heavier flow of menstrual blood.

Most women—about 80 percent—experience some kind of change in their menstrual cycle prior to menopause.

All of these changes reflect the hormonal instability that is going on within your body as you approach menopause. Shortened cycles, for example, are the result of the extra high amounts of FSH that occur before menopause. The extra FSH causes the egg follicles in your ovaries to develop more rapidly, which can shorten your cycle by several days. In addition, as you approach menopause, your body's monthly production of progesterone occurs over a shorter, yet more intense, time frame, resulting in earlier bleeding—and a shortened cycle.

Changes in the menstrual cycle are usually first noticeable about seven years before menopause. If you are a woman who has been closely in tune with her cycles, however, you may notice more subtle changes long before then. Most women's menstrual cycles, for example, gradually become shorter as they grow older, from an average of 27.8 days at age 20 to 26.2 days at age 40—or a difference of about a day and a half.

Right before menopause, however, the cycles usually lengthen and lighten as estrogen production becomes sporadic and ovulation happens less frequently.

Heavy Periods

Heavy menstrual bleeding can be both annoying and troubling, especially for women who experienced only mild periods during their twenties and thirties. If you begin to experience more bleeding during your periods than in past years, try to keep in mind that some amount of heavy bleeding is normal and common during the years leading up to menopause. It is usually the result of prolonged secretion of estrogen without ovulation; the ovaries are more resistant to FSH stimulation during the menopausal years. As a result, the lining of the uterus becomes extra thick and releases unusually high amounts of blood when it is shed. As you proceed toward menopause and your estrogen levels drop, heavy menstrual bleeding will become less and less of a problem. In the meantime, however, you may want to try some of the self-help tips on page 25.

For some women, however, heavy bleeding before menopause can become debilitating, drastically curtailing activities for a day or two each month. "I would have one or two days of phenomenally heavy bleeding every month," remembers Clare, who started experiencing heavy menstrual periods in her late thirties. "I'd end up having to take a book into the john and sit there, sometimes for an hour or more, because I could put in two tampons and wear a pad and I would still bleed through everything. It was almost like projectile bleeding."

Persistent heavy bleeding can be accompanied by other symptoms, such as dizziness, chills, and a general sense of weakness. It can also lead to a deficiency of iron, resulting in "anemia," or low concentration of the oxygen-bearing red blood cells. If you have heavy periods, it's important to have a diet rich in iron (see chapter 7). You may also choose to take a vitamin supplement that contains iron. If you suspect you are anemic—most notably, if you feel tired all the time—you should check it out with your health care provider. You'll need to take a blood test, and if the test indicates anemia, you'll need to undergo testing to determine the cause. Other causes of anemia are stomach ulcers, poor diet, and some intestinal cancers.

Never assume, however, that the heavy vaginal bleeding you are experiencing is related to impending menopause. The bleeding may be the symptom of a condition that requires medical attention. It may be a benign condition, such as vaginitis (a vaginal infection or inflammation), cervicitis (inflammation of the cervix), or cervical or endometrial polyps (noncancerous growths that protrude from the cervix or from the lining of the uterus). Fibroids (benign muscular outgrowths of the uterine wall) can also cause heavy menstrual bleeding.

• • •

"One month I just didn't get a period. Then, about two months later I began to have an odd sort of spotting. So I went to the doctor and he performed a D&C. He told me I was clean as a whistle and that was the end of it. Another four months went by with nothing, no bleeding, and then I was away at my son's graduation out east. I was sitting on the bed in the motel room and suddenly I had a flood of blood. It was really quite dramatic. I'm happy to say I didn't have to clean those sheets. There was lots of warm sticky blood. It ended as quickly as it came, and then I was done. I felt fine; I looked fine. About four months after that I had one little spotting period. Then nothing else. I was about 54."

• • •

Unusually heavy vaginal bleeding can also be a symptom of a much more serious condition, such as endometrial hyperplasia (an overthickening of the lining of the uterus) or cancer of the cervix, uterus, or ovary. For this reason, you should report any heavy or prolonged bleeding promptly to your physician so that its cause can be determined. Early detection is

---

SELF-HELP TIPS FOR HEAVY BLEEDING

Some women have found that making a few positive changes in their health habits has helped them control heavy menstrual bleeding. Here are some of these self-care tips:

- *Exercise*. Regular strenuous exercise lowers the body's production of the pituitary hormones FSH and LH, which in turn lowers the amount of estrogen produced by the ovaries. In addition, women who exercise regularly tend to be thinner and leaner. With fewer fat cells, they have a smaller secondary source of estrogen.
- *Avoid alcohol*. Heavy drinking can cause fewer blood platelets to form. With fewer platelets, blood does not clot as well and may flow more profusely during menstruation.
- *Avoid hot showers or baths on days of heavy blood flow*. Heat increases bleeding by dilating blood vessels.
- *Avoid aspirin*. It also increases blood flow by inhibiting the clotting ability of blood platelets.
- *Have your blood checked regularly for signs of anemia*. If your hemoglobin—the part of your blood that carries oxygen—is low, eat more iron-rich foods and take iron supplements (see chapter 7).
- *Have your blood checked for signs of a dysfunctional thyroid gland*. Abnormally low or high levels of the thyroid hormone can cause heavy or irregular bleeding.

especially important for the successful treatment of cancer. Although most causes of heavy bleeding are benign, such bleeding is often the only early sign of a malignancy. Your physician will put you through a battery of tests to determine the cause of the bleeding. These tests will likely include an endometrial biopsy and a blood test. If the bleeding is found to have a hormonal cause, your physician may recommend progesterone therapy. How much progesterone you take and for how long will depend on how heavy your bleeding is and the result of the endometrial biopsy. However, your aim should be to take the smallest effective dose for the shortest time possible.

Be alert to pressure from your physician to have surgery for the bleeding. Before agreeing to a hysterectomy, you should always get a second or even a third opinion. You can also contact one of the women's health groups listed in the Resources section of this book for information and counseling about hysterectomies. Other, less drastic, options may be more appropriate for your situation.

Irregular Periods

It is not unusual for periods to become more frequent and irregular as menopause approaches. But such bleeding—even if it is slight—can also be the symptom of a serious health problem, such as cervical or uterine cancer. For that reason, you should keep a menstrual calendar (see the box on page 29) and report any irregular bleeding or spotting to your physician immediately.

Skipped Periods

As you approach menopause, you will most likely experience some missed periods. This is because there will be some months when your ovaries do not release an egg. When you don't ovulate, you will not produce progesterone; nor will your uterus shed its lining on a regular basis.

A missed period during the change of life is often a cause of concern for women, who may mistake it as a sign of pregnancy. How can you tell the difference? By looking for other bodily changes. A missed period that is accompanied by tenderness in the breasts and feelings of nausea is a strong indication of pregnancy. If the missed period, however, is accompanied by hot flashes and dryness in the vagina, it is more likely a sign of menopause. When in doubt, of course, you should consult your health care provider.

•   •   •

"Every once in a while I'll hear someone who hasn't gone through menopause yet joke about it and say something like, 'Gee, I'm so warm I feel like I'm having a hot flash.' There's part of me that gets real angry because I feel like saying, 'You don't even know what it is. You don't know how miserable it is. You don't know what it's like to be sitting in a meeting of all men with a $400 suit on and feel a flash coming on. There's no amount of willing you can do to make it stop. There's nothing you can do.' "

•   •   •

Because of fluctuating pituitary hormones, women who are nearing menopause are more likely than younger women to show a false positive on many in-home pregnancy tests. So don't make any assumptions about pregnancy until you have had further tests done at your doctor's office.

What You Can Do about Heavy or Irregular Periods

You can't keep your menstrual cycles from becoming irregular as you approach menopause, but you can keep from panicking about it. Remember, irregular periods are normal during this time of life. Unfortunately, some women become so confused and frightened about changes in their menstrual cycles that they become easily led into unnecessary hysterectomies to "cure the bleeding problem." In fact, almost one-fourth of all hysterectomies done in the United States are done to control abnormal, prolonged bleeding.

If the sole cause of your heavy bleeding is menopause-related hormonal changes, prescribing a hormonal regimen will usually make hysterectomy unnecessary. Taking iron supplements and low doses of hormones is far safer than having a hysterectomy. And remember—the bleeding stops after menopause. If fibroids are the source of the bleeding, a hysterectomy should be done only when there are significant symptoms from the fibroids, such as painful pressure on the bladder or rectum, *and* when other treatments, such as D&Cs and hormonal tablets, have failed to resolve the problem. (A D&C, or *dilation and curettage*, is minor surgery in which the inside of the uterus is scraped to get a sample of the uterine lining. D&Cs used to be done only in operating rooms and under general anesthesia, but now they are often done in physicians' offices, causing only minimal discomfort for most women.)

Rapidly growing fibroids (ones that double in size during a six-month period) may require a hysterectomy because, even though they are rare, a tumor or cancer may be the cause. The growth of a fibroid can be tracked with sonograms, or ultrasound tests, that use sound waves to provide visual images of internal organs. Your physician will also want to do an endometrial biopsy to help rule out the possibility of a malignancy and to determine future therapy.

Keeping track of your periods may help alleviate some of your concerns about irregular periods (see the following box). If you are experiencing heavy menstrual bleeding, you can take some self-help steps to

---

TRACKING YOUR PERIODS

Many women find it helpful to keep track of their menstrual periods as they approach menopause. They can then follow the irregularities in their periods more closely, and be alert to signs of possible problems.

To track your periods, simply buy or make a monthly calendar. Use a star to indicate the first and last days of each period and jot down whether the bleeding on each day was light, moderate, or heavy (L, M, or H). In addition, make a note of any spotting (S) or bleeding (B) that occurs at other times of the month. Also, note any remarkable mood fluctuations. Many women recognize that their periods are about to begin when they experience these premenstrual mood changes.

If you notice any of the following patterns, you should bring them to the attention of your gynecologist. Although these are usually temporary, normal signs of menopause, they may also signal a potential problem.

- Heavy or gushing blood flows.
- A period that lasts extra long.
- Periods that occur more frequently than every twenty-one days. (Be sure to count the days from the first day of your menstrual period to the first day of your next menstrual period, *not* from the last day of your menstrual period to the first day of the next.)
- Bleeding between periods.
- Cramping during periods, especially if you do not usually experience cramping while menstruating.
- Bleeding that begins again after you have been free of menstrual periods for about twelve months. Once a woman has gone at least one year without a period, subsequent bleeding may be an early sign of a cancer.

---

ease the flow of blood (see the box on page 26). But remember: Heavy and irregular or prolonged bleeding can be a sign of a more serious underlying health problem. You should report it to your physician as soon as possible.

HOT FLASHES

Most women—up to 85 percent in some studies—experience hot flashes at some time during their menopausal years. In fact, hot flashes are almost as inevitable as menopause itself. Hot flashes can begin when your menstrual periods are still regular or after they have started to become irregular. The flashes usually stop about one to two years after the final menstrual period; however, some women experience them for much longer periods of time—sometimes up to ten years after menopause.

What Is a Hot Flash?

A flash may be just a passing feeling of warmth in the face or upper part of the body, or it may be a drenching sweat followed by chills. Often, a hot flash is preceded by an "aura"—an inexplicable but clear sense that the flash is coming. Feelings of anxiety and tension may precede the flash by moments, or such physical sensations as dizziness, nausea, or tingling in the fingers may be noted. Some women report heart palpitations before and during hot flashes.

•   •   •

"I never had hot flashes. The only thing I remember is a little tremulousness one time. I was very thin at the time, but I think it was more related to my hormones realigning themselves. But I'm a believer in letting nature take its course—unless you have a real problem. So it came and went, came and went, and then it never came back."

•   •   •

Although hot flashes are perfectly harmless, they can be frightening if you are not aware of what is going on. Some women understandably mistake the heart palpitations and feelings of suffocation that sometimes accompany severe flashes as symptoms of a heart attack. Sometimes, hot flashes *can* be a sign of a circulatory problem or other illness. It's there-fore a good idea to report them to your health care provider when you first begin to experience them. If, however, your periods have been irregular or nonexistent for several months and you are in your forties or fifties, that sudden flushing of the face and pulsing of the heart you are experiencing is probably nothing more—and nothing less—than a hot flash.

What Causes a Hot Flash?

Just what causes all the physical sensations of a hot flash is still not totally understood. Scientists believe, however, that hot flashes are caused by changes in the hypothalamus, the master gland in the brain that regulates a host of bodily tasks, including body temperature and the monthly ebb and flow of sex hormones.

Chapter 1 discussed how the hypothalamus directs the sex hormones. Here's how it regulates body temperature: When the body is too warm, the hypothalamus sends a chemical message to the heart to pump more blood and tells tiny blood vessels just under the skin to dilate, or expand, to let off the heat and thus cool the body. It also causes the skin to perspire, which lowers body temperature even more.

Around the time of menopause, however, the hypothalmus begins triggering the cooling response at inappropriate times. It is as if the body's thermostat has been reset to a lower temperature. Room temperatures that once felt quite comfortable may now seem stifling hot; 70 degrees suddenly feels like 90 degrees or more. To release the unwanted heat, the body takes the necessary steps to cool itself—dilating the blood vessels and perspiring for a few minutes. In other words, it initiates a hot flash.

During a hot flash, skin temperature often rises 4 to 8 degrees Fahren-heit, but, surprisingly, internal body temperature falls.

A hot flash, however, is not the same as being overheated. One team of researchers tried to induce hot flashes in premenopausal women by warming them with hot water bottles and blankets. Although the women became hot and sweaty, they did not experience the changes in heart rate and blood pressure typical of a true hot flash.

Scientists are not sure exactly what causes the temperature-regulating function of the hypothalamus to fluctuate so around menopause, but they believe it has something to do with declining estrogen levels. Indeed, studies have shown that the more abrupt the drop in a woman's estrogen levels, the more severe her hot flashes. Women who experience menopause as the result of surgical removal of their ovaries, for example, are more likely to have severe flashes than are women who go through menopause gradually. And thin women tend to have a more difficult time with hot flashes than heavy women, who produce estrogen in their fat cells even after menopause and thus experience a more gradual decline of the hormone.

The most striking evidence for a relation between estrogen and hot flashes, however, is the fact that when women who are experiencing hot flashes are given estrogen pills, their hot flashes almost always disappear.

Estrogen is not the only hormone involved in triggering a hot flash, however. Scientists have discovered that blood levels of the pituitary hormone LH rise during a hot flash. They now suspect that the chemical the hypothalamus sends to the pituitary at the beginning of the monthly menstrual cycle may play a key role in the hot flash drama. Several other hormones that interact with the temperature-regulating system of the body are also under investigation.

When to Expect Hot Flashes

The severity of hot flashes varies from woman to woman—and from day to day for individual women. A flash may last for a few seconds or a few minutes. They may occur only once a week or once or more an hour.

•　　•　　•

"I never had hot flashes the way some people describe them. I can remember perspiring occasionally, but I've had people tell me that they've drenched the sheets. I never had anything like that. I can remember feeling a little flushed sometimes, but I would just go off and fan myself and cool off. I don't remember it as being a bothersome or embarrassing thing."

•　　•　　•

For some women, hot flashes happen mostly during the day; for others, the flashes occur primarily at night, causing the women to wake up feeling hot and drenching with perspiration. These are known as *night sweats*. Like daytime hot flashes, night sweats can be relatively mild; tossing off the bedcovers may be all that is needed to provide relief. Some women, however, wake up from a night sweat in such a pool of perspiration that they must change their bedclothes or sheets—or both.

HOW SEVERE WILL YOUR FLASHES BE?

Why some women have more severe flashes than other women is not completely understood. However, studies have shown that you will be more prone to severe hot flashes if you have any of these characteristics:

- *Your menopause is the result of surgery or radiation treatment.* A sudden and dramatic drop in estrogen, such as when the ovaries are removed by surgery or are destroyed by large doses of radiation, can cause more severe hot flashes.
- *You are thin.* After menopause, the body continues to make estrogen in subcutaneous fat (the fat that lies right under the skin). Thin women, therefore, tend to experience a more dramatic drop in estrogen after menopause than heavy women—and, as a result, have more trouble with hot flashes.
- *You do not sweat easily.* An ability to sweat makes extremes of temperature easier to tolerate. Women who have trouble working up a sweat, therefore, tend to experience more problems with hot flashes than those who do not.

What You Can Do about Hot Flashes

Although hot flashes are inevitable for most women, they need not be debilitating. The sections that follow suggest some of the things you can do yourself to lessen their frequency and intensity.

Keep track of your hot flashes. By keeping a written record of your hot flashes, you may be able to see a pattern develop. You may discover, for example, that you have flashes around the same time each day or when you find yourself in a particular situation. Such knowledge can help you predict when a flash is likely to occur and thus help you manage them better.

Track your flashes on a calendar or in a day book (just use the code HF)—preferably the same calendar you are using to track your periods (see the box on page 29). Write down when the flash occurred, how long it lasted, its intensity (use a scale of 1 to 5), and what may have precipitated it. After only a few days, you may begin to see a pattern develop.

Choose your clothes carefully. Avoid synthetic clothing, such as dresses and blouses made of polyester or nylon; they tend to trap perspiration.

Cotton and other natural fabrics are better because they "breathe" more. If you have night sweats, be sure to buy cotton sheets as well. You may also want to avoid clothes with high necks and long sleeves; these can intensify the feelings of suffocation that sometimes accompany a hot flash. Instead, wear short-sleeved clothes that have V-necks or that can be unbuttoned at the neck.

Also, dress in layers. Then, when you feel a hot flash coming on, you can shed the outer layer of clothing and help yourself remain cool.

Discover ways of cooling down.   Many women find that sipping a cold drink, such as ice water or chilled fruit juice, helps relieve their hot flashes. You may want to keep a thermos of ice water handy, either on your desk at work or in your refrigerator at home. If you suffer from night sweats, keep a glass and a small pitcher of cold water on your bedside table.

•   •   •

"I think I knew with the first hot flash what it was. You just know. If you would have to compare it with something, it would be like your first orgasm—because nobody can describe it to you. It's something that seems to come from somewhere in your center and goes out through your body. It feels like it goes through your bloodstream, and it just takes this path. Unfortunately, when I describe it, it sounds like a pleasurable experience, like a rush. But it's not."

•   •   •

Taking a cold shower or splashing cool water on your face may also provide relief from a hot flash. Keep room temperatures at home at a comfortable level, perhaps 65 degrees. If you don't already have an air conditioner or an electric fan, now may be the time to invest in one, particularly if you are having trouble sleeping. You can also buy a small battery-run fan that can be carried around in your purse and pulled out whenever a hot flash hits.

Stop smoking.   Here's yet another reason to finally kick the smoking habit. Smoking constricts the blood vessels, which can intensify and prolong a hot flash.

Watch what you eat.   Several foods have been implicated as possible triggers of hot flashes. These include foods that have caffeine, such as coffees, teas, colas, and chocolate. Alcohol, which dilates the blood vessels and makes you feel warmer, has also been implicated, as have spicy foods, especially those highly seasoned with salt. Eating too much sugary food, which can cause wide swings of blood sugar, also seems to be a catalyst for hot flashes in some women. Other women have found that hot soups and drinks or very large meals can set off a hot flash.

By keeping track of when your hot flashes occur (see earlier), you will be able to determine whether any of these foods cause problems for you.

Eat more "vegetable" estrogens. Scientists have found that certain foods—most notably soybeans—contain hormone-like compounds that function like estrogen in postmenopausal women. Some researchers believe that the presence of these *phytoestrogens*, as the compounds are called, in soybeans may explain why so few Japanese women—only about 10 percent—report problems with hot flashes at menopause. The traditional Japanese diet contains a great deal of soy products, including tofu and soymilk. These foods are often used as a substitute for animal protein.

Some scientists believe phytoestrogens may also protect postmenopausal women against heart disease and breast cancer. Eating soy products also seems to help some women with the vaginal dryness that can accompany menopause. Research shows little evidence, however, that phytoestrogens protect against osteoporosis.

Interestingly, although phytoestrogens appear to have estrogenic qualities, some laboratory research indicates that they may also have *anti*-estrogenic qualities that may help protect against endometrial cancer. Population studies seem to back up this research: In Japan, women have lower rates of endometrial cancer than women in the United States and in many other developed countries.

Many studies involving phytoestrogens are currently underway. In the meantime, to relieve hot flashes you may want to increase the amount of phytoestrogen-rich foods in your diet. Don't go overboard with these foods, however. Too much of a good thing can be bad for you. (Women who are trying to become pregnant should be especially careful because a phytoestrogen-rich diet may make pregnancy more difficult.) Always strive to follow a balanced diet.

The best source of phytoestrogens is soybeans and soy-related products, such as tofu, soy sprouts, and soymilk. Try including one or two servings of these foods in your daily diet. Additional foods that contain varying amounts of phytoestrogens include:

Alfalfa	Peas
Apples	Pomegranates
Barley	Potatoes
Carrots	Red beans
Garlic	Rice
Green beans	Rye
Hops	Sesame seeds
Licorice	Wheat
Oats	Yeast
Parsley	

(For herbs that contain phytoestrogens, see herbal remedies, following.)

Try herbal remedies. For centuries, women of many cultures have used herbs to alleviate some of the discomfort of hot flashes and other menopausal complaints. You may want to follow in this ancient tradition and try a few herbal recipes yourself. Because these recipes have not been tried in standard medical tests, physicians do not recommend them routinely. Most physicians require strict statistical evidence—what they call double-blind, crossed-over, controlled trials—that a medication works and that it causes limited acceptable side effects. Although herbal remedies for hot flashes have not been put to this kind of testing, they have been used for centuries with information passed on from one generation of healers to the next, thus yielding valuable anecdotal information despite the absence of clinically controlled trials.

The following herbs are among those most frequently prescribed by herbalists for hot flashes, as well as for other menopausal complaints. Some of these herbs contain phytoestrogens, while others appear to trigger estrogen-like effects in the body. You can find these herbs at health food stores, food co-ops, herb stores, and farmers' markets. For best results, consult an experienced herbalist.

CAUTION: If you have a chronic medical condition or are taking any medications, you should talk with your health care practitioner before trying these herbs. Women who are attempting to become pregnant should avoid these herbs entirely. Remember, these herbs have a reported biological effect on the body, and they have not yet been researched fully. Therefore, you should use them only in moderation. Stay attuned to how your body reacts to them. If you experience any unwanted side effects or discomfort as a result of taking these herbs, discontinue their use immediately and see your health care practitioner.

- **Anise** (*Pimpinella anisum*). This herb contains phytoestrogens, which may explain its traditional use by women in many cultures to promote milk for nursing. Although anise's estrogen-like effects are mild, some women report that they are sufficient to relieve their hot flashes. Make a tea by pouring a cup of boiling water over 1 tsp of crushed anise seeds; steep for 10 minutes. Drink up to three times daily. Or take ½ to 1 ml of the herb in tincture form three times daily.
- **Black cohosh** (*Cimicifuga racemosa*). Used traditionally by Native American women for menstrual problems and childbirth, black cohosh is thought to produce estrogen-like effects in the body. In Germany, the herb is an ingredient in several prescription medications for menopausal complaints. To make a tea, place 1 tsp of the dried root in a cup of water and bring to a boil; simmer gently for 10 minutes. Drink up to three times daily. Or you can take 2 to 4 ml of the tincture form of the herb three times a day. Do not use this herb if you have heart disease.
- **Chasteberry** (*Vitex agnus-castus*). Used by many British women for hot flashes, chasteberry is said to help balance progesterone and estrogen levels. Make a tea by pouring 1 cup of boiling water over 1 tsp of fresh berries; steep for 10 minutes. Drink up to three times a day. Or you can take 1 ml of the tincture form of the herb three times a day. You may have to take the herb for several weeks before noticing a decrease in your hot flashes.
- **Dong quai.** Used widely by women in Asia as a tonic for the reproduction system, dong quai is said to have an estrogen-like effect on the body. To make a tea, place 1 tsp of the dried root in a cup of water and bring to a boil; simmer gently for 10 minutes. Drink up to three times daily. Or you can take 4 to 6 ml of the tincture form three times daily.
- **Fennel** (*Foeniculum vulgare*). Like anise, fennel is said to have a mild estrogen-like effect in the body and has been used traditionally to promote milk in nursing mothers. Some women have used it to help relieve their hot flashes. Make a tea by pouring a cup of boiling water over 1 to 2 tsp of crushed seeds; steep for 10 minutes. Drink up to three times a day. Or take 1 to 2 ml of the tincture three times daily.
- **Ginseng** (*Panax* spp.). Widely used for hot flashes, ginseng contains hormone-like compounds that mimic estrogen. Make a tea by placing ½ tsp of the powdered root in a cup of water; bring to a boil and gently simmer for 10 minutes. Drink up to three times a day. Do not use this herb if you have a fever, asthma, emphysema, high blood pressure, cardiac arrhythmia, or a blood clotting problem.
- **Red clover** (*Trifolium pratense*). This herb is thought to act like estrogen in the body, and women have reported that it helps relieve their hot flashes when taken regularly. To make a tea, put 1 cup of boiling water over 1 to 3 tsps of the dried flowers; steep for 10 minutes. Drink up to

37

three times daily. Or you can take ½ to 1½ ml of the tincture form of the herb three times daily.

- **Wild yam** (*Dioscorea villosa*). This herb has been used for centuries by Native Americans to relieve labor pains. It contains a substance called diosgenin, from which pharmaceutical companies have derived the processed chemicals used to manufacture contraceptive hormones and other drugs. Some women have found it helpful in relieving hot flashes. To make a tea, place 1 tsp of the herb in a cup of water and bring to a boil; simmer gently for 10 minutes. Drink up to three times daily. Or take 2 to 4 ml of the tincture form of the herb three times daily.

Try vitamin E. Although there is no scientific evidence that vitamin E can provide relief from hot flashes, personal testimonials from many women and medical professionals alike seem to indicate that vitamin E may have some possible effect on the intensity of hot flashes—at least, for some women. Vitamin E is essential to the proper functioning of blood and for the production of sex hormones, which may explain its effect on hot flashes. The best food sources of this vitamin are whole grain cereals and breads, green leafy vegetables, dried beans, and unprocessed vegetable oils, such as corn, safflower, and soybean oil. If you decide to increase your vitamin E intake through a supplement, you might try 1000 IU (international units) per day. Do not exceed 1000 IUs per day without consultation with a qualified nutritionist. If you should develop blurred vision while taking vitamin E, discontinue the supplements immediately.

To enable vitamin E to work more effectively within the body, some nutritionists suggest taking a B-complex supplement and a supplement of vitamin C (500 mg); others recommend a supplement of the trace mineral selenium (25 mcg) as well. Because vitamin E requires the presence of fats to be absorbed into the intestines, nutritionists also recommend that it be taken at the end of a meal that contains fats, especially polyunsaturated vegetable oils.

WARNING: Women with high blood pressure, diabetes, or rheumatic heart disease, as well as those who are taking digitalis, should consult their physicians before taking vitamin E supplements.

For more information about vitamin E and other important nutrients for the menopausal years, see chapter 7.

Try homeopathy. Although no reliable scientific studies have shown that homeopathic medicine can ease hot flashes, some women say they have successfully used such therapies for their hot flashes. Trying the medicines will certainly not do you any harm, as the doses are extremely small.

The theory behind homeopathic medicine, which was developed by a

German physician in the late 1700s, is that symptoms can be treated by giving a patient extremely small doses of substances that would normally produce the same symptoms—a principle similar to vaccination. Although long-vilified by conventional doctors, homeopathy received a boost of sorts when the British medical journal *Lancet* published a small study in December 1994 showing that homeopathy might actually be beneficial for people with allergic asthma—although the benefit was nowhere near that achieved by conventional medicine.

Sulphur, Lachesis, and Sepia are among the homeopathic remedies often prescribed for hot flashes. However, for best results, you may wish to consult an experienced homeopathic practitioner who will most likely prescribe a "constitutional" remedy, a combination of homeopathic medicines that will best meet your particular needs.

Give acupressure and acupuncture a try. Both acupressure and acupuncture have been reported to be successful in alleviating hot flashes. In one recent Swedish study, for example, women receiving acupuncture treatment experienced a 50-percent drop in the frequency of their hot flashes. This was a small study (involving only twenty-one women), however, and the women were treated for only three months—not really long enough to know if it was the acupuncture or the placebo effect that caused the hot flashes to decrease.

Still, the results were promising. If you decide to try either acupressure or acupuncture, be sure to seek an experienced practitioner.

Keep in shape. Regular vigorous exercise can help you cope with the discomfort of hot flashes. First, exercise improves circulation, which can make your body more tolerant of temperature extremes and better able to cool down quickly. Second, exercise strengthens the endocrine system—especially the ovaries and adrenal glands—and seems to increase the amount of estrogen and other hormones circulating in the blood. The more estrogen in your blood, the less likely it is that a hot flash will strike.

For more information about the benefits of exercise during the menopausal years—and how you can start your own exercise program—see chapter 8.

EVENING PRIMROSE OIL: STUDY SHOWS IT TO BE INEFFECTIVE

Claims have been made that evening primrose oil, an extract from the seed of the plant, can help relieve hot flashes. A 1994 English study, however, has revealed that those claims may be unfounded. The study found that women with hot flashes who took four 500-milligram capsules of evening primrose oil twice a day for six months experienced no noticeable relief from the flashes.

"A hot flash is hard to explain. You know how it is when you have the flu and you have a fever? It's this hot feeling that comes from within and then comes out. You have no control. You feel like there's a slow burn going over your body, a feverish feeling starting somewhere within. And the next thing you know, you feel your face get a little flushed."

•　　•　　•

Learn to relax.　Granted, it's not always easy to do, but relaxing during a hot flash can often diminish its intensity. If possible, find a place—preferably a cool one—where you can sit or lie quietly. Breathe deeply and slowly; feel your body relaxing and releasing all tension and anxiety. Some women find mental imagery helpful: Think of a favorite cool spot, such as the snowy mountaintop where your family goes skiing or the shaded riverbank where you used to swim as a child. Try to imagine yourself there. "I always imagined myself running naked across a large field under a full moon to help my hot flashes go away," recalls one woman.

Also, remind yourself that hot flashes are a normal part of the midlife passage, a common experience that need not make you feel embarrassed or frightened. Some women find that acknowledging their hot flashes to friends and coworkers can ease the anxiety—and thus the intensity—of the flashes. It can also help to realize that the hot flushing you are feeling all over your upper body may not even be noticeable to the people around you. Look in a mirror the next time you experience a hot flash. You may be surprised to discover that your body shows little outward evidence of the turmoil you are feeling within.

Getting Medical Help

The great majority of women have hot flashes that are mild or moderate. But 10 to 20 percent of women find them very debilitating. For these women, the flashes may occur very frequently, perhaps several times an hour, or they may continue for many minutes at a time. Or the flashes may be exhausting, continually disrupting sleep.

If you are one of these women, and the self-help tips given earlier provide no relief, you may want to consider the following medical remedies to relieve your discomfort.

Hormone replacement therapy (HRT).   Replacing the estrogen lost during menopause is almost 100 percent effective in relieving hot flashes. Progestin, a synthetic form of the naturally occurring hormone progesterone, is also sometimes effective in eliminating hot flashes when given alone. Such treatment, however, is not without its dangers. You and your physician need to discuss all the potential benefits and risks of taking hormones and your various dosage options.

For a full discussion of hormone replacement therapy, see chapter 3.

A SPECIAL NOTE FOR WOMEN
WITH BREAST CANCER

Many doctors believe that women who have had a personal history of breast cancer should not take estrogen for hot flashes because of a concern that it may stimulate cancer cells to grow. New research has shown that a progesterone, megestrol acetate, can be effective in decreasing the frequency of hot flashes, and because megestrol acetate is not an estrogen, some doctors consider it safer for women with a history of breast cancer.

Before taking megestrol acetate for hot flashes, you should consult a medical oncologist who is a breast specialist. Progesterones are known to stimulate the growth of breast tissue, so they must be used with caution, particularly in women with a history of breast cancer. Although megestrol acetate may benefit some women with advanced hormonally sensitive tumors by shrinking the tumors, it has not been studied in women with early breast cancers, so its effect on those cancers is not known. You should also be aware that this drug, which is used to stimulate appetite in cancer patients who have lost considerable weight, can cause weight gain. In addition, the long-term effect of this progesterone on the heart or bone remains unknown.

Clonidine (Catapres).   Clonidine is used primarily as a drug to prevent high blood pressure, but studies have shown that it can also be effective in partially or completely eliminating hot flashes. Side effects of the drug include low blood pressure and, in rare instances, fatigue, headaches, irritability, and dizziness.

•   •   •

"I remember the hot flashes. It was in the middle of winter when I was recovering from my hysterectomy and all of a sudden it would get so hot, it would be like I was sitting in the hottest room. You get a sense that you are perspiring and your whole face is just almost pulsating with the heat. Then, all of a sudden, it goes away and you don't know what's happening. You don't know what's wrong until after it's done and you realize, 'Oh, that was a hot flash.'"

•   •   •

DRYNESS AND OTHER CHANGES IN THE VAGINA

Although most women notice after menopause that their vaginas take longer to become lubricated during sexual arousal and may become irritated by the same stimulation that used to bring pleasure, few talk about it with their friends, or even with their sexual partners. Yet vaginal thinning and dryness is a common experience for menopausal women—and one that needs to be discussed more openly.

Your vagina is a 4- to 5-inch-long expandable muscular tube lined by moist skin. It can stretch a few inches easily for sexual activity and can expand even more for the passage of an infant during childbirth. Its skin-like walls are soft, smooth, and very resilient. The vagina produces a clear (or sometimes milky white) acidic discharge that helps protect it against infections. During sexual arousal, the vagina becomes even wetter. Droplets of liquid pass from the congested blood vessels through the vaginal walls, which lubricates the vagina and prepares it for sexual activity.

As estrogen levels fall during the menopausal years, the walls of the vagina become thinner and less elastic. The vagina itself becomes slightly smaller, both in width and length. In addition, vaginal secretions become less in volume and less acidic, thus increasing the possibility of a vaginal infection.

Many women also find that the ability of their vaginas to lubricate for sexual activity diminishes as they approach menopause. This lack of lubrication can make vaginal penetration uncomfortable or even painful.

Doctors lump all these changes in the vagina under the term *vaginal atrophy*—a term that may make it sound as if your vagina is going to dry up and wither away, along with all your sexual pleasure! But don't worry. Although some amount of vaginal dryness is an inevitable result of menopause, it needn't put an end to sexual activity. There are many things you can do to minimize or even reverse vaginal dryness (see pages 100–101).

For more detailed information about vaginal dryness and a discussion of other sexuality issues related to menopause, see chapter 5.

HEEDING THE SIGNS

As at any time of your life, during your menopausal years it's important to be aware of the physical changes going on within your body. It's also important to keep a written record of those changes—such as any new pattern to your menstrual cycle or the times at which you are most likely to experience hot flashes—so that you can take the information to your health care provider. He or she can then use the data you have collected to evaluate what is happening to your body and help you determine whether any medical care is necessary. Remember: It is quite natural for you to experience physical changes during the menopausal years. Menopause is not a medical condition, but a normal and natural part of aging. In most cases, no medical intervention is necessary.

•   •   •

"I didn't find my hot flashes uncomfortable. In fact, they were kind of exciting, like being zapped with electricity."

•   •   •

3

THE GREAT HORMONE DEBATE

These days, it isn't raging hormonal imbalance that drives a postmenopausal woman berserk. It's raging medical debate. Some 30 to 40 million American women want a definitive answer on estrogen, and instead they're getting the daily odds.

—Ellen Goodman

To take hormones or not to take them? That's the question most women face at some time during their passage through menopause.

The hormones in question here, of course, are estrogen and progesterone. You can supplement your body's declining levels of these hormones at menopause by taking manufactured versions of them. It's called *hormone replacement therapy*, or HRT for short. (In the past, this hormone supplementation was known as *estrogen replacement therapy*, or ERT, because only estrogen was prescribed. Today, progesterone is often part of the therapy; thus the change in its name.)

Few areas of women's health stir up as much debate and confusion as HRT. Trying to make an informed decision about HRT can be an exasperating experience. The studies concerning the therapy are conflicting, and almost all of them have their critics. For example, some medical studies have shown an increased rate of breast cancer in women on HRT, whereas others have shown a *decreased* rate.

This chapter takes a look at the risks and benefits attributed to HRT and the reasons why this therapy is so unsettled. By understanding what the debate is about, you should be better able to make an informed decision about whether hormone therapy is for you.

A BRIEF HISTORY OF ESTROGEN THERAPY

Drugs—particularly those prescribed for "female complaints"—tend to come in and out of vogue. Estrogen is no exception. As a "cure" for menopause, it has a long and somewhat checkered history.

The hormone estrogen (without progesterone) was first prescribed to women for menopausal "complaints" more than half a century ago, during the 1930s. By 1947, women could take their estrogen by mouth, by injection, or by putting an estrogen cream in the vagina. One company even sold it in a "pleasant-tasting cordial," which was 14 percent alcohol!

That same year, however, a New York gynecologist and cancer researcher named Saul Gusberg published an alarming report in the *American Journal of Obstetrics and Gynecology*. He cited cases of women whose endometria (lining of the uterus) had been seriously disturbed by estrogen therapy. Many of the women had hyperplasia, an overgrowth of normal uterine tissue that can sometimes be a precursor to cancer, and several had actually developed cancer. Long-term estrogen therapy, warned Gusberg, could be a dangerous health threat to women.

After Gusberg's report, the prescribing of estrogen for menopausal women slowed considerably. By 1966, however, his warnings seemed to have been forgotten. That year, another New York gynecologist, Robert Wilson, published a book called *Feminine Forever* that hailed estrogen therapy as a great elixir of youth that would protect women from the "living decay" of menopause. Making claims reminiscent of old-time traveling medicine shows, Wilson stated that a myriad of menopausal "symptoms" could be cured by estrogen therapy, including nervousness, crying spells, loss of memory, chronic indigestion, aching joints, neuroses, and even suicidal thoughts.

Considering all the cures he was offering, it's not surprising that Wilson's book quickly hit the best-seller list, selling 100,000 copies within seven months. Excerpts from the book appeared in *Look* and *Vogue*. All across the country, women began walking into their doctors' offices and asking for estrogen supplements. Sales of estrogen skyrocketed, from less than $20 million before 1966 to $83 million in 1975.

As reporter Barbara Seaman pointed out in her ground-breaking 1978 book *Women and the Crisis in Sex Hormones*, the readers of *Feminine Forever* had no way of knowing that Wilson was receiving money from drug companies for his "research." One of these companies was the Ayerst Laboratories, the makers of the top-selling estrogen product, Premarin. Nor did Wilson's readers know that many of his medical colleagues considered his research to be highly questionable. Those colleagues, however, rarely criticized Wilson in public; nor did they criticize other pro-estrogen books that were often based on Wilson's "research"—books such as Sandra Gorney and Claire Cox's *After Forty* and Dr. David Reuben's *Everything You Always Wanted to Know About Sex.*

Then, in 1975, articles in the *New England Journal of Medicine* showed that women who took estrogen were about five to fourteen times more likely to develop cancer of the endometrial lining of the uterus than women who never used the drug. Furthermore, the longer a woman remained on estrogen therapy, the greater the cancer risk. This was, of course, the same danger Saul Gusberg had warned about some 25 years earlier.

The enthusiasm for estrogen suddenly sagged.

In 1976, the FDA passed a regulation requiring any drug containing estrogen to have a package insert for patients that clearly described the health risks associated with the hormone. The Pharmaceutical Manufacturers Association (PMA) fought this regulation, claiming it would reduce sales. They were joined by the American College of Obstetricians and Gynecologists and the American Society of Internal Medicine, who argued that the patient warning insert would interfere with the physician-patient relationship and lead to more self-diagnosis and self-medication on the part of women.

Some physicians seemed concerned that the information in the inserts would prove too emotionally upsetting to women. "It is hard to imagine a class of patients more susceptible to adverse psychological reaction from the patient package insert than the menopausal female," one doctor told the FDA.

Despite the efforts of the drug manufacturers and the medical establishment, many physicians and women did hear—and heed—the warning about estrogen and endometrial cancer. Between 1975 and 1978, sales of estrogen plummeted by 40 percent. In addition, the incidence of endometrial cancer also fell—by about 27 percent nationwide.

HORMONE THERAPY TODAY

Since the mid-1970s, pharmaceutical companies have been spending large sums of money to persuade women—and their doctors—that taking hormones during the menopausal years is a good and safe thing to do. They have organized pro-HRT medical conferences and seminars, sponsored speeches by pro-HRT physicians, and put together massive public education campaigns to get their message into the media.

In addition, the drug companies have sent fleets of salespeople—known as detail men and women—to make calls on physicians, praising the benefits of hormone therapy and playing down its risks.

These efforts to counter negative publicity about HRT have been remarkably successful. In 1989, more than 3.5 million women were taking hormones for menopause-related reasons.

• • •

"During a regular check-up my doctor asked me if I was menstruating anymore. I said no, and he said, 'How about taking some estrogen?' I decided that if he thought I should have it, okay. He gave me a low dose. I didn't really feel that different, though. So I stopped taking it. I just didn't like the idea of taking hormones."

• • •

It's important to keep all of these high-powered sales efforts in mind when you sit down to discuss the possibility of hormone therapy with your physician. Make sure that any decision about the use of hormones is based on clear medical facts, not optimistic promises from drug company literature.

The drug companies have been able to rehabilitate estrogen and reestablish their market with a sales campaign that stresses the differences between current and past methods of hormone therapy. Their campaign consists of three main tenets:

- The new hormone therapy combines estrogen with progestins, synthetic forms of progesterone. This new therapy, say its advocates, is safer than the previous estrogen-only therapy because it more closely imitates the natural menstrual cycle.
- The dosage of estrogen used in HRT is typically lower than it was in the past. This, according to estrogen advocates, significantly reduces the adverse effects reported with high doses of estrogen.
- Hormone therapy is essential to protect older women from the debilitating effects of cardiovascular disease and osteoporosis. Some physicians are now recommending HRT to all postmenopausal women as a preventive measure.

The underlying message from estrogen proponents is clear: Put aside your fears. Not only is today's combination hormone therapy safe, but it's also essential to your health.

But is it really safe? And is it for every woman?

THE HORMONES IN HRT VERSUS THOSE IN BIRTH CONTROL PILLS

The amount of estrogen and progesterone prescribed for hormone replacement therapy is much lower than that found in birth control pills. Typically, the Pill contains seven times more estrogen and ten times more progesterone than HRT tablets. The reason is that stopping the development and fertilization of an egg requires higher doses of hormones than relieving hot flashes and vaginal dryness.

The Pill has been associated with several health risks, particularly an increased risk of circulatory disorders, such as abnormal blood clotting, heart attacks, and stroke. A few studies have also linked the Pill to an increased risk of breast cancer in some women. The fact that hormone doses in HRT are lower than those in the Pill may reduce these risks, but it doesn't eliminate them altogether.

It is important to know that there are many physicians who strongly disagree with the position that we no longer have to worry about the risks of giving hormones to all women during their menopausal years. Unfortunately, the enthusiastic sales pitches of the drug companies and other pro-HRT advocates often drown out these voices of moderation.

As a woman facing the decision about whether to use hormones, you will need to educate yourself about the pros and cons of hormone therapy. Discuss the conflicting information and talk to knowledgeable people before choosing the course for you.

WHAT HORMONE THERAPY WILL NOT DO

Hormone Therapy Will Not Cure Depression

You should not use hormone therapy as a treatment for feelings of depression. Using HRT for this purpose may even backfire on you: Some women report feeling *more* depressed after going on HRT. This may be particularly true if you are taking a progestin along with estrogen. Studies suggest that progestin may induce depression or other emotional problems in some women.

Almost all studies that have looked at using estrogen to prevent or treat depression have a significant flaw: They include women who are suffering from significant physical problems associated with menopause—

most notably, hot flashes throughout the night. Night sweats, as nightly hot flashes are often called, can severely disrupt sleep, even if a woman does not wake up entirely when she has them. Disrupted sleep can lead to fatigue, irritability—and depression. Women who are losing sleep because of night sweats are understandably going to feel better after going on estrogen therapy, because it eliminates night sweats and thus restores unbroken sleep.

This doesn't prove, however, that estrogen cures depression. Yet there has been at least one small, well-designed study that suggests estrogen therapy may help some women's psychological well-being. This study, which was reported in the December 1991 issue of *Obstetrics and Gynecology*, involved thirty-six women who had experienced a natural menopause and who were not depressed before going on estrogen. The study found that the women scored better on a depression test after three months of estrogen therapy. More research is needed.

Psychological counseling, stress-reducing techniques, and perhaps antidepressant drugs are better ways of dealing with depression (see chapter 4 for more details). Some women who take estrogen report that it not only lifts depression, but helps them think more clearly. Although some studies have shown that estrogen can improve cognition, short-term memory, and abstract reasoning, it is not clear whether these effects were the direct result of estrogen's interaction with brain cells or whether they were simply due, once again, to the fact that women were sleeping better at night.

Several factors may help explain why some women report a better mental outlook after going on HRT:

- A few HRT products contain either an antidepressant or a tranquilizer. It is these drugs, not the estrogen, that are relieving the depression and anxiety. When such drugs are necessary, it would be wiser to take them without the estrogen and under the supervision of a psychiatrist, not your gynecologist.
- Depression is often a self-limiting illness—in other words, it tends to go away by itself in time. Women whose depression lifts after going on hormone therapy may mistakenly attribute their spontaneous recovery to the estrogen rather than to the passage of time.
- The mind is a strong healer. If you believe that a particular pill will cure your anxiety or moodiness, it may very well do just that—even if the pill contains no medication at all. Studies have consistently shown that up to 40 percent of people suffering from a variety of disorders—from high blood pressure to arthritis—improve after taking placebos. Some of the minor psychological complaints often attributed to menopause—

including mild depression, anxiety, and irritability—also have been shown to have a strong placebo response.
- Estrogen therapy *does* provide relief from hot flashes and night sweats. Thus it can also help ease any anxiety or insomnia caused by flashes and sweats. You may also be successful in eliminating hot flashes with other, less risky methods (see chapter 2).

In the absence of more conclusive evidence, you should be wary of efforts to treat your depression or perceived moodiness with HRT. Taking hormones may just delay your getting the help you need. Explore other treatment options first; they may be less risky—and more effective.

Hormone Therapy Does Not Prevent Wrinkles

One of the strongest myths about hormone replacement therapy is that it will prevent wrinkling of the skin. No well-designed studies have been done to support this belief. A few recent studies have indicated that estrogen—usually when delivered into the body by means of an implant or skin patch—increases the skin's collagen content. (Collagen is the body protein that gives skin its strength.) But these studies have design flaws: None has been double-blind, placebo-controlled, or randomized. In fact, the Food and Drug Administration (FDA) requires manufacturers of estrogen to state specifically in their labeling that estrogens should not be prescribed to maintain supple skin.

Estrogen can make skin retain more water, causing a "puffiness" that can make fine skin lines less visible. However, it does not prevent wrinkles. Skin experts say the benefits of hormonal effects are minimal compared to avoidance of risk factors, such as exposure to sunlight, cigarette smoking, alcohol consumption, and poor diet. Heredity also plays a role in the development of wrinkles.

Taking estrogen to keep your skin "youthful" is just not a good idea. Your skin may even become worse in some ways. Some of the reported side effects of HRT include dryness of the skin, rashes, and brown blotches on the skin that may remain even after HRT is discontinued.

For more information about skin care during the menopausal years, see chapter 9.

Hormone Therapy Does Not Prevent Weight Gain

Falling levels of estrogen have nothing to do with the weight gain that many women experience during their menopausal years. You gain weight at midlife because your body's metabolism slows down as you age—not because of a drop in estrogen. Going on hormone replacement therapy will not keep you from putting on pounds.

Hormone Therapy and Breast Fullness

Some women find that taking estrogen and progesterone keeps their breasts firm and full. Both of these hormones promote the growth of cells in the breast. They also promote a greater retention of body fluid. These factors can make the breasts swell and look fuller.

Most women who take hormones do not experience a change in their breast shape, however; and for those who do, the swelling of the breasts can be accompanied by pain and tenderness. This may be an indication that the estrogen dose is too high.

Hormones should not be taken to maintain breast size. As you will see later in this chapter, the health risks associated with hormones are just too great to justify their use for this purpose.

WHAT HORMONE THERAPY CAN DO

According to the general medical consensus, hormone replacement therapy can relieve two common menopausal complaints: hot flashes and vaginal dryness. In addition, estrogen has an impact on cholesterol levels in the blood and on the body's ability to absorb calcium, which may offer protection against heart disease and osteoporosis for women at high risk of getting these diseases.

Hormone Therapy Can Relieve Hot Flashes

No doubt about it. Hormone replacement therapy does provide relief from hot flashes, usually within days of starting on the therapy.

You should know, however, that once you go off HRT, your hot flashes are likely to return—and perhaps with a vengeance. So by taking hormones you may only be putting off the day of reckoning with hot flashes, not preventing or curing them.

Hormone Therapy Can Relieve
Vaginal Dryness

Taking estrogen will help keep the walls of your vagina from thinning and drying out as you pass through menopause. For women who find intercourse painful because of severe vaginal dryness, taking estrogen can provide welcome relief—usually within a couple of weeks. (Nonestrogen lubricants can also help with this problem—see chapter 5.)

Estrogen also helps the vagina retain its acidity, which makes it more resistant to infections.

Hormone Therapy Affects Cholesterol
Levels in the Blood

Estrogen has been shown to have an effect on lipoproteins, the cholesterol compounds that carry fat through the blood. There are both "good" and "bad" lipoproteins. The good ones are known as high-density lipoproteins (HDLs). They help prevent fatty substances from accumulating on the walls of the arteries. The bad ones are called low-density lipoproteins (LDLs). They encourage fatty substances to gather in the arteries. When the arteries become too thick with deposits of fat (a condition known as arteriosclerosis), blood flow becomes restricted and a heart attack or stroke can occur.

Estrogen raises the "good" lipoproteins (HDLs) and lowers the "bad" ones (LDLs). And because low levels of HDL are a strong predictor of heart disease risk in women, many physicians believe taking estrogen after menopause will therefore help protect older women against heart disease and possibly stroke. Others believe better studies are needed before it can be stated with certainty that using estrogen to change lipoprotein concentrations in women will impact their risk of heart disease.

For a fuller discussion of HRT and heart disease, see the section called "The Risk of Heart Disease" later in this chapter.

Hormone Therapy Can Reduce
Bone Loss

Most medical researchers agree that taking estrogen can prevent or greatly reduce bone loss after menopause. By keeping bones from thinning and weakening, estrogen therapy also appears to reduce the risk of bone fractures. Studies have shown that women who begin estrogen therapy within a few years of their last menstrual period have fewer hip and wrist fractures and possibly fewer spinal fractures than women who do not take estrogen.

Some people theorize that progesterone may have its own beneficial effect on preventing bone loss. Studies have not shown, however, that taking progesterone along with estrogen slows bone loss any more significantly than taking estrogen alone.

Physicians disagree about who should be treated with hormones for the prevention of osteoporosis. Some argue that all postmenopausal women should go on hormones, others advocate it only for women who are at high risk for osteoporosis, and still others believe that the long-term risks of HRT are just too great to recommend its widespread use for the prevention of osteoporosis.

For it to be most effective in stopping bone loss, HRT must be started within three years of menopause, and preferably earlier. If you begin HRT later, you will be less protected against fractures because significant bone loss may have already occurred. In fact, according to the American College of Obstetricians and Gynecologists, of the total amount of bone lost after menopause, half is gone within seven years of the last menstrual cycle.

It's important to remember that *no amount of hormones can restore your bones to their premenopausal density*. All HRT can do is help prevent the accelerated loss of bone that occurs after menopause.

Also, once you stop HRT, you will lose bone in the same quantities and at the same speed as if you had never started on the therapy. Taking hormones to prevent osteoporosis is therefore a long-time commitment— possibly 30 or more years.

This long-term use of these hormones is precisely what worries many researchers and physicians. They argue that not enough research has been conducted on the long-term effects of these drugs for us to know what their risks really are.

For more information about osteoporosis and its prevention, see chapter 6.

A TREATMENT FOR ALZHEIMER'S?

Women are at greater risk of developing Alzheimer's disease than men. Of the approximately 4 million Americans who have Alzheimer's, about three-quarters are women. Of course, one reason more women have the illness is simply that they live longer and thus are more likely to develop the symptoms, which usually begin during the patient's mid-60s. Still, a longer lifespan does not explain all of the discrepancy in risk between women and men, which is why some researchers suspect that declining estrogen levels after menopause may play some part in the disease.

Scientists have proposed two basic theories about how estrogen may help protect against Alzheimer's. One theory proposes that estrogen helps promote the formation of synapses—the junction between two nerve cells through which information is transferred—in the hippocampus, a part of the brain where new memories are formed. The other theory suggests that estrogen may help prevent the degeneration of acetylcholine-producing nerve cells. Acetylcholine is a chemical that enables nerve signals to cross synapses and may help regulate memory. People with Alzheimer's are known to be deficient in both acetylcholine and synapses.

Experiments on laboratory rats have supported both theories. But, of course, rats are not humans. And so far, studies that have looked at estrogen therapy and Alzheimer's in humans have been contradictory. In 1994, for example, two simultaneously published studies reported conflicting results. One, in which researchers compared the death certificates of women who had been living in a retirement community with the women's earlier medical records, found that women who had taken estrogen were 40 percent less likely to have developed Alzheimer's than women who hadn't used the hormone. The second study, however, reported that women who took estrogen therapy were neither more likely nor less likely to have gotten the disease. A 1996 retrospective study of more than 1,100 elderly New York women reported that women who took estrogen for menopause had a lower risk of developing Alzheimer's. However, this study had several important design limitations.

So what does this mean for women trying to weigh the risks and benefits of postmenopausal estrogen? Most scientists agree that it's way too early to know whether or not estrogen therapy can relieve some of the effects of Alzheimer's. Furthermore, no one is suggesting that falling levels of estrogen in older women is a cause of Alzheimer's—if so, all women would develop the illness. At most, declining estrogen may be one of several risk factors in the disease. Much more research is needed.

HORMONE THERAPY AND THE RISK OF
ENDOMETRIAL CANCER

Straight estrogen replacement therapy (in other words, taking estrogen without a progestin) greatly increases your risk of getting cancer of the endometrial lining of the uterus. Of that there is little serious dispute. For this reason, physicians usually prescribe estrogen alone only to women who have had a hysterectomy. Other women are often prescribed a combination of estrogen and progesterone.

Most studies seem to indicate that the risk of getting uterine cancer becomes significant after two to four years of estrogen-only therapy. At that point, the risk of uterine cancer increases four- to eightfold.

Here's another way of understanding the risk: Overall, about 4 percent of postmenopausal women who are not on any hormonal therapy will develop an endometrial cancer. Among postmenopausal women who take estrogen alone, 28 to 40 percent will eventually develop the disease.

The risk appears to fall once a woman stops taking estrogen—perhaps eventually as low as for women who never took the hormone. But at least one study, which was conducted at the Boston University School of Medicine and involved 1,217 women, shows that women may be at a higher risk of developing endometrial cancer for as long as ten years after going off estrogen.

Fortunately, endometrial cancer—if caught in time—is highly curable. If the cancer is found and treated before it has spread beyond the uterus, the survival rate can be as high as 90 percent. But the cure for endometrial cancer almost always involves a hysterectomy and sometimes radiation treatment as well—treatments that can have a profound and long-lasting effect on a woman's life. This is why estrogen-alone HRT is recommended only for those women who have undergone a hysterectomy.

What Causes the Cancer

Scientists believe that estrogen therapy leads to endometrial cancer by stimulating the cells of the uterine lining to grow constantly without a corresponding amount of progesterone to provide a monthly check on the growth. Estrogen, remember, is the hormone that stimulates the endometrium to grow and thicken each month so that it will be able to nourish a fertilized egg (see chapter 1). Progesterone, on the other hand, is the hormone that causes the endometrium to stop growing and, if an egg is not fertilized, to shed—the process we recognize as menstruation.

If a woman's body becomes exposed to amounts of estrogen that are "unopposed" by corresponding amounts of progesterone, the endometrium may become too thick—a condition known as *hyperplasia*, which means "overgrowth." Usually, endometrial hyperplasia, which is diagnosed by a uterine biopsy, is not a serious condition; but it requires treatment with a progestin, followed by another biopsy to confirm that the condition has been successfully reversed. Sometimes this overstimulation of the endometrial lining cannot be reversed, in which case a hysterectomy is required. If untreated for many years, endometrial hyperplasia can lead to cancer.

When a Progestin Is Added

Several studies have shown that taking a progestin drug in addition to estrogen prevents endometrial hyperplasia. This regimen most closely mimics the natural menstrual cycle. As a result, taking a progestin reduces the risk for estrogen-associated endometrial cancer as well. Several studies back up this position. In one study, for example, women who received both estrogen and a progestin were at less risk of developing endometrial cancer than women who were taking estrogen alone. In fact, the study indicates that they were at less risk of developing the cancer than women who were taking no hormones at all. The study also indicates that the progestin must be taken for a minimum of ten days each month for it to be effective in protecting against hyperplasia. Other studies indicate that for maximum protection from hyperplasia, women should take the progestin even longer each month—for twelve to fourteen days.

The idea that giving a progestin along with estrogen can reduce the risk of endometrial cancer was also supported by findings reported in 1995 from the Postmenopausal Estrogen Progestin Intervention Study (also known as the PEPI Trial). Funded by the National Institutes of Health and conducted at various medical centers around the country, this highly regarded four-year prospective study of 875 women found that while one-fourth of the women in the study assigned to an estrogen-only therapy developed hyperplasia, none of the women assigned to a progestin-estrogen regimen developed either hyperplasia or endometrial cancer.

Another prospective study has indicated that progestin can be taken by many women only every third month without increasing their risk of hyperplasia and cancer. The progestin must be taken in full dose for fourteen days, however. This regimen results in a heavier flow, but the flow occurs less often—an outcome some women prefer.

Weighing the Evidence

The evidence is strong that estrogen-only hormone replacement therapy will increase your risk of developing endometrial cancer. Based on the evidence to date, most members of the medical community strongly recommend that women who are on HRT (and who still have a uterus) take a progestin to protect themselves against endometrial cancer.

HORMONE THERAPY AND THE
RISK OF BREAST CANCER

Much of the concern about hormone replacement therapy and cancer has centered on endometrial cancer. Yet breast cancer is a much more common—and more dangerous—disease for women.

WOMEN WHO ARE AT GREATEST RISK FOR DEVELOPING ENDOMETRIAL CANCER

Some women are more likely to get endometrial cancer than others. Taking an estrogen supplement, therefore, may increase their risk of getting the disease even more. When evaluating whether to take estrogen supplements, you should consider the following risk factors:

- *History of menstrual irregularities.* Women who have irregular periods ovulate infrequently. Because ovulation is needed for the hormone progesterone to be released, the uteri of these women receive almost constant estrogen-only stimulation. About 80 percent of young women with endometrial cancer have a history of menstrual irregularities. You should request a uterine biopsy from your physician before considering HRT if you have a long history of irregular vaginal bleeding.
- *Being overweight.* The risk of uterine cancer is three times higher than normal for women 25 to 50 pounds overweight, and nine times higher for women who have more than 50 pounds of excess weight. The excess layers of fat tissue convert inactive hormones into active estrogens. Heavy women who cannot lose weight through eating less and exercising may, in fact, need cycles of progesterone to keep their uterine lining safe from hyperplasia. Again, a biopsy will reveal this information.
- *Body shape.* A study published in 1991 indicated that *where* you have fat on your body may be even more important that how much of it you have. The study found that women who carry weight at and above the waist (or who are "apple" shaped) have up to fifteen

---

times as great a risk of endometrial cancer than women who carry their weight in the thighs and hips (or who are "pear" shaped). Fortunately, the researchers also found that "apples" who lose weight can reduce their risk of endometrial cancer significantly.

- *Late menopause.* The longer you are menstruating, the longer your uterus is exposed to estrogen. Because these later ovulations do not produce as much progesterone as earlier cycles, and may, in fact, be anovulatory (bleeding caused by fluctuating estrogen levels without progesterone secretion or the release of an egg), women who experience menopause after the age of 50 are twice as likely to develop endometrial cancer as those who go through menopause at a younger age. Short-term progesterone therapy may be necessary to regulate bleeding and reduce the cancer risk when menopause is protracted.
- *Childlessness.* If you have never borne children, you are twice as likely to develop endometrial cancer as those women who have had children. This may be related to menstrual irregularities, however, for women with irregular periods often have difficulty conceiving.
- *Diabetes.* Women with diabetes also appear to have double the risk of developing this form of cancer. This risk factor may relate to being overweight. Many women with diabetes are overweight.

In the United States, about 182,000 new cases of breast cancer are diagnosed in women each year, compared with 33,000 new cases of endometrial cancer. Of all types of cancers, only lung cancer kills more women than breast cancer; about 74,000 women in the United States are diagnosed with lung cancer each year.

Breast cancer is much more difficult to treat than endometrial cancer. Despite modern drugs and technology, the death rate for breast cancer is about the same now as it was in the 1930s, whereas the death rate for all forms of uterine cancer—including endometrial cancer—has been steadily declining.

Because so many more women die of breast cancer (about 46,000 annually in the United States) compared to endometrial cancer (about 6,000 women), even a small increase in the risk of breast cancer has more serious implications for women.

So how does going on HRT affect your risk of getting breast cancer? If you were just to look at the thirty or so retrospective studies that have examined whether taking menopausal estrogens increases the risk of breast cancer, you would see a confusing picture. (A *retrospective* study is one that gathers data by going back through medical records. A *prospective* study is one that gathers data as the study progresses. The findings from prospective studies are generally considered more reliable than those from retrospective studies.) While a very few retrospective studies have indeed shown a statistically higher incidence of breast cancer among estrogen users, a few others have actually shown a *protective* effect. Most retrospective studies, however, have produced risk increases that are considered statistically nonsignificant. In other words, the elevated risk found among hormone users in the studies might be due to the hormones, but it might also be due to chance alone.

As a result of these ambiguous results, most physicians have remained unconcerned during the past two decades about prescribing estrogen to their menopausal patients. They simply did not believe it would increase the women's risk of breast cancer. Their belief that estrogens were safe was reinforced when researchers analyzed the data from all the retrospective studies together—a research technique known as a meta-analysis—and found no significant increase in breast cancer risk.

But not all studies are equal. Some are much better designed and controlled than others. Studies involving menopausal hormones are no exception. And as higher-quality studies were published, a less ambiguous pattern began to emerge: Long-term use of estrogen *does* raise the risk of breast cancer. Furthermore, the studies began to show that adding progesterone may not reduce the risk (as it does with endometrial cancer)— and may even increase it slightly.

The evidence of the increased breast cancer risk for menopausal women taking estrogen began to accumulate twenty years ago. In 1976, Robert Hoover, a scientist at the National Cancer Institute (NCI), studied the medical records of 1,891 menopausal women in Kentucky who had taken estrogen for six months to 15 years. He found a 30-percent increase in the risk of breast cancer among those women who had used the hormone for 10 to 14 years and a 50-percent increase among those who had taken it for 15 years or longer. In 1981, Hoover and an NCI colleague, Louise Brinton, published another study that revealed that postmenopausal women whose ovaries were intact and who had taken estrogen replacement therapy for *any length of time* had a 20-percent increase in breast cancer risk. The increase in risk climbed to 54 percent for estrogen users whose ovaries had been surgically removed and to a whopping 700 percent for women in this last category who also had a family history of breast cancer.

More studies showing a link between breast cancer and estrogen soon followed. In 1989, for example, the *New England Journal of Medicine* published a study involving more than 23,000 Swedish women. It showed a 10-percent increased risk of breast cancer among women taking estrogen, with the risk rising the longer the women used the hormones. After nine years of use, the increased risk was 70 percent. Furthermore, women who took both estrogen and a progestin ran an even greater, fourfold risk of getting the disease—and after only four years on the hormones. This study was dismissed, however, by estrogen replacement therapy defenders in the United States, who pointed out that Swedish women use forms of estrogen and progesterone that are stronger than those most commonly used in the United States.

Harder to dismiss were the findings of a 1991 meta-analysis, which summarized sixteen of the best-designed breast cancer studies. Conducted by researchers from the Centers for Disease Control and Prevention (CDC), the analysis found that women who used estrogen for ten or more years increased their risk of breast cancer by about 30 percent. The CDC researchers concluded that for every three million women taking estrogen for 15 years or longer, "there would be 4,708 new cases of breast cancer and 1,468 breast cancer deaths each year."

Shortly before the meta-analysis was published, another group of researchers had analyzed data from the Harvard-sponsored Nurses Health Study, a large, well-designed prospective study that has followed the health of about 122,000 women since 1976. They found that postmenopausal women taking estrogen were 36 percent more likely to develop breast cancer than those who did not. Some people challenged these findings, noting that the women in the study who took HRT were more likely to have mammograms—and thus were more likely to have their cancer detected—than women not using HRT. The authors of the study answered that they had carefully examined the data for just such a bias and had concluded that "it cannot explain the association between estrogen use and breast cancer incidence."

In 1995, a team of Harvard researchers looked again at data from the Nurses Health Study. Of the 70,000 women in the study who had reached menopause by 1992, roughly a third had taken estrogen, and about a third of those had taken a progestin along with the estrogen. Once again, researchers found that women who used HRT were 30 to 40 percent more likely to develop breast cancer than those who did not. To put it another way: Women who took hormones continuously from age 55 onward had a 3-percent risk of getting breast cancer between the ages of 60 and 65 compared to a 1.8-percent risk for women not taking the hormones. Taking progestin along with estrogen neither increased nor decreased the risk of taking estrogen alone.

The study was reassuring in one respect: The increased risk of getting breast cancer was found to decrease after women stopped taking the hormones, dropping back to normal within two years.

Despite the mounting evidence connecting HRT to an increased risk of breast cancer, many doctors continue to defend HRT to women who express concern about taking hormones because of a fear of developing breast cancer. The doctors point to all the retrospective studies and have found no link between the estrogen and breast cancer. As one doctor told the Associated Press after the 1995 Harvard study was published, "If you look at the entire literature on breast cancer and estrogen therapy, there is no consistent conclusion. This means to me that if there is an effect, it is not a big one."

Indeed, only one month after the 1995 Harvard study was published, researchers at Fred Hutchinson Cancer Research Center in Seattle, Washington, reported in *The Journal of the American Medical Association* that women taking estrogen and progestin did not face an increased risk of breast cancer. The retrospective study compared hormone use among 537 postmenopausal women with breast cancer and 492 postmenopausal women without breast cancer (the control group). It found that HRT was used by 57.6 percent of the women with breast cancer compared to 61 percent of the control group, indicating that HRT did not increase the risk of breast cancer.

Critics point out several problems with the study, the most notable being that it included few long-term HRT users. In fact, the failure to include a large number of long-term users is the major criticism of most studies that have failed to find a connection between breast cancer and HRT. Yet many in the medical community continue to give equal weight to all the studies—no matter how the studies were designed or how many long-term users of HRT were included. This is in large part due to the fact that few physicians read the individual studies themselves, relying instead on the media's or various drug companies' interpretations of the studies. Relatively few physicians have the necessary skills to critically analyze the quality of research reported in medical journals.

So what is the current bottom line on all these studies? Perhaps the Women's Health Network puts it best in their 1995 guide to hormone replacement therapy: "[R]eassuring statements [about the safety of hormone replacement therapy] hide information from women that is well-known to cancer researchers, epidemiologists, and federal officials. Well-done studies of the most rigorous design consistently find an increase in breast cancer in women who use estrogen for ten or more years."

The Link with Cancer

Breast tissue, like the tissue that lines the inside of the uterus, is sensitive to fluctuations in estrogen and progesterone. Each month, breast tissue undergoes changes similar to the kind of changes that occur in the uterus. During the second half of the menstrual cycle, there is an increase in blood flow, a build-up of body fluid, and a proliferation of cells in the glandular tissue (the part of the breasts designed to make milk). These changes, triggered by hormones, are geared to preparing the breasts for a possible pregnancy. When menstruation happens instead of a pregnancy, the build-up of breast fluids reverses itself and most of the extra glandular cells are reabsorbed. Some aren't, however, which is why a woman's breasts tend to become more cystic, or "lumpier," as she grows older.

Because breast tissue is influenced by changing levels of hormones, many medical experts are concerned that hormones, particularly estrogen, may play a role in the development of breast cancer. Researchers have been able to link estrogen and breast cancer in a variety of female laboratory animals.

The problem with identifying what role, if any, estrogen plays in breast cancer lies in the nature of the disease itself. Breast cancer is a complicated disease—or, more accurately, group of diseases. Some types of breast cancer are fast-growing and quickly fatal; some develop so slowly that a woman may die of old age before succumbing to the cancer. Breast cancer appears to have a variety of causes and associated factors, including heredity, diet, and hormones. Researchers doubt that estrogen causes the cancer directly but suspect instead that the estrogen affects breast tissue in a way that makes it more susceptible to abnormal changes.

Most of the studies that link breast cancer and estrogen-only therapy indicate that the higher the dose of estrogen and the longer it is taken, the greater the risk. Indeed, one study has shown that *any* exposure to estrogen supplements increases a woman's risk of breast cancer. According to that study, women who used any dose of estrogen for any length of time were twice as likely to develop breast cancer fifteen years after first going on the drug than women who never took the hormone.

It's important to remember that breast cancer often takes a long time to develop—anywhere from ten to twenty years or longer. The increased risk of breast cancer in women who took the estrogen diethylstilbestrol (DES) to prevent miscarriages did not become apparent until more than twenty years after exposure to the drug. Some experts worry that, as more years pass from when menopausal estrogen first became popular in the mid-1960s, we will see an increase in studies showing a link between the hormone and breast cancer. The fact that many of the women now taking estrogen for menopause took estrogen in birth control pills at a younger age also concerns some experts.

Already, the statistics concerning breast cancer reveal a disturbing trend. After many years of being relatively stable, the incidence of breast cancer is on the rise in women 50 years old or older. According to statistics compiled by the National Cancer Institute, there was a 35-percent increase in the incidence of breast cancer between 1973 and 1991. Most of that increase—30 percent—has occurred since 1980. Although the increased use of mammography during the 1980s and the fact that women are living longer explains some of that sharp rise, it does not explain all of it.

When a Progestin Is Added

Until 1989 and the publication of the Swedish study, which suggested that adding a progestin to hormone therapy may actually increase the risk of breast cancer, the general consensus was that progestins helped protect breasts from cancer. Researchers no longer believe that this is true, particularly given the results from the 1995 Harvard study which indicated that taking a progestin along with estrogen had neither a negative nor positive effect on breast cancer risk.

Weighing the Evidence

Ongoing research seems to be pointing more and more to a link between estrogen and breast cancer. As Robert Hoover, chief of the Environmental Epidemiology Branch of the National Cancer Institute, has commented, "The fact that ovarian hormones might relate to increased risk of breast cancer is not on the bizarre fringe of biological reasoning. The biological plausibility was established 100 years ago, so new data which shows that women on replacement therapy have an increased risk is exactly what you would predict. You can argue about what level of risk there is, but the reasonableness of the observation is firmly steeped in biology."

The medical community is currently debating the level of that risk. To be on the safe side, most physicians do not recommend estrogen therapy for women who have had breast cancer. A few believe that women who have a history of breast cancer in their families should also avoid taking the hormone. But even if you do not fall into one of these two categories, you should be aware that taking HRT may increase your risk of breast cancer. And the longer you take the hormones, the greater the risk. Short-term—less than five years—use of the hormones is the safest. Unfortunately, however, estrogen must be taken for much longer periods— perhaps the rest of your life—for protection against heart disease and osteoporosis. That's why only women who have a solidly documented risk for heart disease or osteoporosis—and who have not responded to other preventive measures—should consider HRT.

HORMONE THERAPY AND
THE RISK OF HEART DISEASE

Heart and blood vessel disease is a much greater threat to the health of menopausal women than breast cancer. In fact, heart disease and stroke rank together as the number one killer of women over the age of 40. More than 325,000 American women die of heart disease each year.

Women appear to be relatively protected from heart disease until menopause. At that point, women gradually begin to lose their advantage over men. Ten to fifteen years after menopause, women run the same risk of heart disease as men.

Because this advantage is lost after menopause, when estrogen levels drop, it has generally been assumed that estrogen helps protect women against heart disease. In fact, this is often cited as the reason women live longer than men.

Of course, if estrogen protects women from heart disease before menopause, the big question is can estrogen supplements provide the same protection *after* menopause? The answer to this question is not universally agreed upon by the experts. However, to date most research seems to indicate that estrogen supplements do offer some protection against heart disease. Of nineteen major retrospective studies conducted before 1991 on the subject, eleven found that women who took estrogen for menopausal reasons experienced a reduction in the risk of heart disease of 50 percent or greater, four studies showed a risk reduction of 30 to 50 percent, and two reported no difference. Only two studies found an increased risk—and in one of those, the heart disease occurred mostly in women over the age of 60 who smoked.

Interestingly, when *men* take estrogen supplements, the risk of heart disease increases dramatically. No one knows why.

In 1991, three studies came out that made the spotlight shine even more favorably on the idea of giving estrogen supplements to women as protection against heart disease. One, a fourteen-year study from the Johns Hopkins Medical Institutions, found that women who used postmenopausal hormones were 63 percent less likely to die of a heart attack. The other, a National Health and Nutrition Examination Survey, revealed that women who did not use hormones doubled their risk of dying of stroke.

The third study—the largest and most publicized one to date involving estrogen and heart disease in women—was published in the *New England Journal of Medicine*. Researchers led by epidemiologist Dr. Meir Stampfer of Boston's Brigham and Women's Hospital reported results from the ongoing Nurses Health Study that indicated that estrogen supplements did protect against heart disease. The study monitored 48,470 postmenopausal women for ten years. About half of the women took or had taken estrogen (but not progesterone). The researchers found that women who took estrogen had only half the risk of heart attacks and death from coronary heart disease as women who did not take the hormone. Even women with a low risk of having a heart attack—nonsmokers who weren't obese and who didn't have high blood pressure or diabetes—had a significant reduction in their risk of heart disease when they took estrogen, reported the researchers.

The greatest criticism lobbied against this and other studies that show estrogen supplements lowering the risk of heart disease in women involves something called "selection bias." Critics point out that there is an inherent bias in the way women are chosen to be on hormone replacement therapy—and thus a hidden bias in the studies. They note that women who take estrogen tend to be upper middle class and relatively well educated, two factors that provide significant protection from heart disease. Women who take estrogen also tend to be healthier, often in subtle ways, than women who do not take the hormone. They tend to be less likely to smoke, for example, or to have diabetes. They are more physically active and leaner. Their blood pressure is lower, and their HDL levels (the "good" lipoproteins) are higher, on average, than that of other women even before they take the hormones. In addition, women who take estrogen, by very definition, are more likely to follow their physician's instructions, including, perhaps, advice about making healthful lifestyle changes that would reduce their risk of heart disease. Indeed, good drug adherence—*even when the prescribed drug is a placebo*—has been shown in studies to lower the risk of cardiovascular disease significantly. Finally, because the women who take estrogen supplements see their physicians regularly, they may be receiving preventive treatment for cardiovascular disease, treatment that women who are not taking hormones may not be receiving, such as monitoring of their blood pressure or cholesterol levels.

One study even found that women who used estrogen had lower mortality rates not only from heart disease, but also from accidents, suicide, and homicide! As Cindy Pearson of the Women's Health Network has wryly noted, "Does this mean we can conclude that estrogen use protects one from being murdered?"

In May 1994, a team of Dutch epidemiologists published a report in the *British Medical Journal* entitled "Cardioprotective Effect of Hormone Replacement Therapy in Postmenopausal Women: Is the Evidence Biased?" After analyzing eighteen large HRT studies the researchers concluded that yes, the evidence was biased, although unintentionally. Women in the eighteen studies who took postmenopausal hormones, the Dutch researchers noted, not only experienced a lower incidence of heart disease, but also of cancer—all kinds of cancer. Since HRT has never been shown to protect against cancer and, in fact, may actually increase the risk of breast cancer, the researchers concluded that the women who used hormones in the various studies were healthier than nonusers and probably had a lower risk of heart disease even before they went on the drugs. If taking hormones did lower a woman's risk of heart disease, the researchers added, it was more likely to be by about 20 percent, rather than by the 30 to 40 percent cited in the various studies. All of this confusion makes the need for prospective, controlled studies even more obvious.

"Even within a socio-economically homogeneous [group of women] with ready access to medical care, women taking estrogen are quite different from nonusers with regard to health promotion and disease prevention measures," wrote Dr. Elizabeth Barrett-Connor in a September 1991 issue of the *Annals of Internal Medicine*. "Despite considerable current enthusiasm for estrogen replacement therapy as a panacea, only a randomized clinical trial can adequately address these biases and resolve this question."

That study has yet to be done, although the National Institutes of Health is now sponsoring such a study, known as the Women's Health Initiative. Begun in September 1993, it is the first large, long-term study to look at the safety and effectiveness of giving hormones to women at menopause. Some 25,000 women will take either estrogen, estrogen and a progesterone, or a placebo for nine years. During that time their health will be closely monitored. The study promises to help resolve questions about the effect of estrogen and progesterone supplements on many aspects of women's health, including heart disease, diabetes, stroke, and bone density.

The Link with Estrogen

Just how does estrogen protect women against heart disease? Researchers believe that it has to do with lipoproteins—those tiny particles that carry fat through the blood. After menopause, a significant change occurs in the levels of both LDLs (the "bad" lipoproteins) and HDLs (the "good" lipoproteins). LDL levels rise dramatically; HDL levels, on the other hand, tend to fall.

Your cholesterol profile is an important predictor of your risk of heart disease. In fact, it's actually a more precise predictor than other risk factors, such as obesity, lack of exercise, smoking, high blood pressure, and diabetes. Although your total cholesterol level can give some idea of your heart disease risk, the ratio of your total cholesterol to your HDL (TC/HDL) is an even better indicator.

If you know your cholesterol levels, the following chart can help you determine your heart disease risk.

	Low risk	Medium risk	High risk
HDL	>60	41–59	<40
LDL	<130	130–159	>160
TC/HDL	<3.3	4.4	>5.5

Improving your diet, exercising, and losing weight can dramatically improve your cholesterol profile. But so can taking estrogen. According to one study, a daily dose of .625 milligrams (mg) of estrogen (the dose most often recommended for menopausal women) increases HDL levels by 10 percent and lowers LDL levels by 4 percent. When the dose is doubled to 1.25 mg, even greater changes are seen: a 14-percent increase in HDL levels and an 8-percent decrease in LDL levels. Those changes should mean less clogging of the arteries.

Improving your cholesterol profile may not be the only way that estrogen works to lower your risk of having a heart attack. In the PEPI Trial, estrogen was shown to lower levels of fibrinogen, a clotting protein in the blood, significantly. High levels of fibrinogen have been associated with higher rates of heart attacks and strokes. Other studies have shown that estrogen helps to dilate, or keep open, arteries throughout the body, including the aorta, the great artery that delivers oxygenated blood from the heart to all parts of the body. Estrogen also appears to prevent cholesterol from accumulating in the walls of the arteries. All these findings may explain why postmenopausal women who have had heart attacks and who are taking estrogen are less likely to have a repeat heart attack than women who have a similar medical history and are not taking estrogen.

When a Progestin Is Added

Progestins may blunt the beneficial effects of estrogens on high-density lipoprotein levels in the blood. Animal research indicates that progestins may block some of the benefits of estrogen by reducing the rise in HDL levels and the drop in LDL levels. In addition, use of high doses of progestins—higher than those commonly prescribed for menopause—may increase the risk of blood clots, strokes, and heart disease.

So if your hormone therapy includes both hormones, you should be aware that any benefit your cardiovascular system may be receiving from the estrogen may possibly be reduced, if not eliminated, by the progestin. The PEPI Trial found that medroxyprogesterone acetate, a synthetic progesterone (which under the brand name Provera or Cycrin is the most commonly prescribed progestin) significantly interfered with estrogen's beneficial effect on HDL levels, but that micronized progesterone, a natural progestin derived from plants, interfered significantly less. Specifically, the researchers found that women in the study who took estrogen alone experienced an 11-percent increase in HDLs, while those who took estrogen in combination with a natural progesterone had an 8-percent increase and those who took estrogen with medroxyprogesterone acetate had only a 3-percent increase. Those women in the study who took a placebo experienced a slight decrease in their HDLs.

The PEPI Trial also found that both the natural and synthetic progestin increased triglyceride levels, which are believed to be a risk factor for heart disease in women. It's not yet clear, however, if this hormonally induced elevation in triglycerides is significant enough to increase the heart disease risk in women.

To date, very little evidence is available on whether women taking a progesterone along with estrogen experience fewer heart attacks. Most of the research has been done on women taking estrogen alone. This lack of information about HRT's effect on heart disease is due to the fact that not enough women have taken combination hormones for a long enough time. More long-term research is needed. The Women's Health Initiative, when completed, should help provide some answers.

If you go on HRT primarily to protect your cardiovascular health, be sure to have your cholesterol levels checked at the time that you start the treatment and again six months later. That way you and your physician will be able to tell if the HRT is providing you with this specific benefit. If your cholesterol levels show no significant improvement, then you should stop the treatment.

Also, should you decide to go on HRT to lower your risk of heart disease, you should consider using natural progesterone rather than a synthetic progestin. Besides interfering the least with the beneficial effects of estrogen, natural progesterone also appears to produce less intense side effects; women report fewer problems with mood swings and depression when taking a natural progesterone than they do when taking a synthetic progestin.

When Using Vaginal Cream or a Skin Patch

It used to be thought that to get any cardiovascular benefit from estrogen supplements women had to take their estrogen in pill form. Research has now shown, however, that women who wear an estrogen patch experience the same improvement in their cholesterol profiles as women who take their estrogen orally. It just takes longer for the benefits to show up—three months for patch wearers versus about one month for pill users. Vaginal estrogen creams, if used in high enough doses, can also improve cholesterol profiles; however, using the creams consistently at the doses required for this benefit would be unwieldy for most women. Ordinary use of vaginal estrogen creams does not result in any change in cholesterol profile and thus is unlikely to offer any cardiovascular benefits.

•　　•　　•

"My doctor put me on the patch. I really thought I actually felt better for the first month or so. I felt lighter, freer. Then I noticed that my breasts were becoming really engorged. They were huge and kind of uncomfortable. I also noticed a lot of swelling. My wedding ring became very, very tight. And then I began breaking out in a small rash from the adhesive on the patch. It itched a lot. I finally decided that something was real wrong with this patch. I just didn't like it. I went back to my doctor and told her I wanted to try something else."

•　　•　　•

Weighing the Evidence

In general, the current medical thinking is that estrogen does provide some postmenopausal women protection against heart disease. Whether all women would benefit from its use is not clear, however.

If you are considering using estrogen supplements as protection against heart disease, you should first determine whether you are indeed at risk for this disease. The risk factors for heart disease are well established. They include high blood pressure that fails to respond to treatment, diabetes, a poor cholesterol profile, an addiction to smoking, a sedentary lifestyle, and obesity. Often, women who have none of these risk factors are offered estrogens by their gynecologists to "prevent heart disease." You should be aware, however, that no prospective studies have shown any benefit regarding heart disease from estrogen supplements to women who have none of the risk factors for the illness. A woman not at risk of developing heart disease who is prescribed HRT to "prevent heart disease" may only be taking on an increased risk of breast cancer without the benefit of a decreased risk in heart disease. Even the best improvement in HDL levels that estrogen can offer—11 percent—would change a low-risk level of 60 to 66, an improvement that has not been shown to save lives. The benefit of raising a high-risk HDL level of 40 by 11 percent to a medium-risk level of 44 may be questionable as well, although estrogen's reported effect on the arteries—keeping them open and free from an accumulation of cholesterol—may prove to tip the scale in favor of estrogen for such high-risk women.

Before going on hormones, it would be far more prudent for you to explore other, natural ways of improving your heart disease risk profile. Start exercising, quit smoking, lower the amount of fat in your diet to 20 to 30 percent, control your blood pressure and blood sugar levels carefully, and reduce stress. After you have improved your lifestyle as much as possible, have your cholesterol profile checked again and reassess your risk for heart disease. If you are still at significant risk of developing the disease, you may want to consider taking estrogen with a natural progesterone (omit the progesterone if your uterus has been removed). HRT may offer you a longer life by reducing your heart attack risk. Scientists theorize that this is due to estrogen's ability to dilate blood vessels and to reduce fibrinogen levels.

Some studies have also indicated that once a woman has had a heart attack, the use of estrogen can reduce her chance of having another. Be aware, however, that taking estrogen as a protection against heart disease is a lifelong commitment. Because long-term use of the hormone raises your risk of breast cancer, you will need to stay up-to-date on all important breast cancer screening recommendations.

You should also be aware that the claim that estrogen supplements will lower a woman's risk of heart disease is not universally accepted. Dr. Sidney Wolfe, director of the Public Citizen Health Research Group, outlined his concerns and those of others in his book *Women's Health Alert*: "There is no direct data from properly conducted studies which shows that modifying lipid and lipoprotein concentrations in women will impact their risk of coronary heart disease, or cut down on the number of women who die each year from heart attacks. In fact, for reasons that are still unclear, women with comparable levels of cholesterol to men have much lower rates of coronary heart disease. . . . Since there is little data to show that reducing lipid levels in women will reduce the incidence of death from heart disease, there is no evidence that long-term use of estrogens will ultimately provide this much-acclaimed protection." More research, he argues, is needed.

Once again, it's important to remember that falling estrogen levels are not the only cause of heart disease in older women. Diet, smoking, alcohol, and stress all contribute importantly to this life-threatening illness. Heredity also plays a role. No amount of estrogen will protect you from heart disease if you have unhealthful lifestyle habits.

OTHER RISKS FROM HRT

In addition to the risks of cancer and heart disease, the following health concerns have been linked to hormone therapy:

- Women on estrogen therapy are two to three times more likely to have gallbladder disease than women who do not take the hormone. They are also twice as likely to require surgery to remove the diseased gallbladder.
- Taking estrogen may cause existing fibroid tumors of the uterus to become larger. Such fibroids often go away by themselves after menopause because of falling levels of estrogen. Taking estrogen supplements, however, may make the fibroids continue to grow to such a size that a hysterectomy or other treatment to remove the tumor may become necessary.
- Women who take estrogen alone are eight times more likely to experience abnormal vaginal bleeding than women who go through menopause naturally, without taking any hormones. The estrogen users are also six times more likely to have a hysterectomy, which is sometimes prescribed to control abnormal vaginal bleeding. Women who take a progestin along with estrogen, however, have no increased risk of hysterectomy.

WILL HORMONE THERAPY
HELP YOU LIVE LONGER?

Several retrospective studies have reportedly "proven" that women who take estrogen live longer. But a close look at those studies reveals a hidden selection bias that calls the studies' findings into serious question.

In a 1993 report in the medical journal *Obstetrics and Gynecology*, the official journal of the American College of Obstetricians and Gynecologists, researchers examined the advice given to physicians regarding postmenopausal hormone replacement therapy over the past four decades. They also looked at whether that advice might have biased the results of retrospective studies involving hormone replacement therapy users. Retrospective studies rely on information gathered after the fact, often through interviews or by reviewing old medical records. Prospective studies, on the other hand, are designed to gather information in real time, as the studies progress.

The researchers found that since 1950 physicians have been advised not to prescribe menopausal estrogens to women with a personal history of either breast or genital cancer. After 1970, physicians were being told that the list of noncandidates for estrogen therapy also included overweight women or those with cardiac dysfunction, diabetes, swelling, kidney problems, or liver, gall bladder, or bone disease. After 1975, most major medical books also viewed heart disease as a contraindication to prescribing estrogens.

In other words, estrogen was not being recommended for women in poor general health. If physicians were following this advice—and all evidence indicates they were—it would certainly explain why women receiving estrogen were living longer. They were simply in better health to begin with. Furthermore, noted the researchers in *Obstetrics and Gynecology*, the selection bias inherent in retrospective studies of estrogen replacement therapy might be significantly underestimating the therapy's risk of breast cancer and overestimating its bone-sparing and cardioprotective effects.

All the more reason why more prospective, randomized, controlled studies of hormone replacement therapy are needed.

HOW HORMONES ARE PRESCRIBED

If you decide to take hormone replacement therapy, you will then need to consult with your physician about which type, form, and dosage of hormones to use. Be sure to discuss all the options with your physician. And be sure all your questions are answered to your satisfaction. What works for one woman may not work for another. One reason it is often difficult to get good information about hormone replacement therapy from physicians is that residency programs for obstetrician-gynecologists (the four years of specialty training after medical school in which physicians become certified in the field of obstetrics and gynecology) do not include formal medical training about how to advise menopausal women about hormones and related issues. So, while most physicians learn the basics about hormone regimens and their common side effects, few obtain the kind of in-depth experience or knowledge required to successfully tailor regimens to the needs of individual women. If your physician is unable or unwilling to explore various options with you, switch to another physician who will. Remember who is paying whom for advice.

Types of Hormones

Estrogen is available in several different chemical forms. In the United States, the most commonly prescribed form is known as *conjugated estrogens* and is sold under several brand names. Premarin (manufactured by Ayerst Laboratories) is the brand most widely prescribed by physicians. Conjugated estrogens are considered "naturally occurring" because they are usually extracted from the urine of pregnant horses. In fact, that's how Premarin got its name: Pre (pregnant), mar (mare's), in (urine).

Most of the horse estrogen in Premarin is estrone, an estrogen that humans as well as horses make naturally in their ovaries. But two of the other horse estrogens in Premarin—equilin and equilinen—are not found naturally in humans. Their effects on the body are different than those of estrone. Equilin, for example, has been found to be more effective than human estrogen in lowering LDLs (the "bad" cholesterol) and raising HDLs (the "good" cholesterol) in human blood. Equilins are also better at suppressing the oxidation of fatty acids in human cells, a process involved in aging. Both equilin and estrone, when given alone, have a similar ability to preserve bone, but neither is as potent at keeping bones strong as conjugated estrogens, which suggests that some other form of estrogen in the conjugated estrogens is responsible for this effect. So far, however, all of the commonly available conjugated estrogens preparations have been found to have similar effects on cholesterol profiles and bone maintenance.

Other common estrogen preparations that are sometimes prescribed for menopausal complaints include micronized estradiol (Estrace), ethinyl estradiol (Estinyl), esterified estrogen (Estratab), and quinestrol (Estrovis). These preparations are usually made synthetically. Although the body reacts slightly differently to each type of estrogen preparation, no one preparation has been found to be more effective than the others for all women. However, the synthetic preparations—particularly ethinyl estradiol—appear to carry a slightly greater risk of blood clots. Also, according to the Swedish study that looked at the link between breast cancer and HRT, estradiol may carry a greater risk of breast cancer.

Progestins are also available in several different forms. Those used in hormone replacement therapy either are made synthetically, such as norethindrone (Norlutin) and norethindrone acetate (Norlutate), or are derivatives of natural progesterones, such as medroxyprogesterone (Provera, Curetab, Amen), or natural progesterone itself. As noted earlier in this chapter, some studies indicate that the naturally occurring progestins may be a better choice for women because they appear to reduce the beneficial effects of estrogens on blood lipoproteins less than synthetically made progestins. Progesterone intrauterine devices (IUDs) are also available. Some physicians prescribe them to women for whom oral projestins cause debilitating PMS-like symptoms. Blood levels of progesterone do not appear to rise when the hormone is delivered through an IUD, thus resulting in a lessening of some of the hormone's unwanted side effects.

Pills, Patches, and Other Ways of Taking Hormones

Estrogen and progestin are usually taken by mouth in the form of small, coated pills. Estrogen can also be delivered to the body through a paper-thin plastic skin patch. The patch, which is about the size of a silver dollar, is usually worn on the abdomen, thighs, or buttocks and is changed twice weekly. Brand name examples include Estraderm, Vivelle, and Climera. Estrogen can also be prescribed in the form of a vaginal cream. This form of the hormone is usually used by women who are specifically concerned with vaginal dryness or bladder irritation.

When taken orally, estrogen must pass through the liver before it is circulated into the bloodstream. Estrogen delivered from a skin patch or from vaginal cream, on the other hand, goes directly into the bloodstream, where it has the same effect as oral preparations. Some women find they are allergic to the skin patch or develop a painful rash at the site where it is worn. Sometimes switching to a different brand of patch eliminates this problem.

Estrogen may also be taken by injection. Each shot of the hormone lasts from three to six weeks. However, this method is inconvenient and expensive, for patients have to make frequent trips to their doctors for the shots. It also offers less dosage flexibility.

Determining the Right Dosage

How much supplemental estrogen do you need to control hot flashes or vaginal dryness? That depends on how much of the hormone your body is already making. Some women find relief from relatively small doses of supplemental estrogen; others need larger amounts to relieve their discomfort. Use the lowest effective dose.

Some women report that they can tell when they are taking the right dose by an overall sense of wellness. They know that their dosage is too high when they start getting headaches, feeling bloated, experiencing breast tenderness, or sensing that physically they are just "not themselves."

Remember: the lower the dosage, the lower the risk of cancer and other health complications. So it's always best to begin hormone replacement therapy with the lowest possible dose of estrogen. The same goes for progestin. You can increase the doses of these hormones gradually later if they prove to be ineffective.

Estrogen tablets. These come in various dosages. Conjugated estrogen tablets, the most commonly prescribed estrogen in the United States, are available in dosages of .3, .625, and 1.25 mg. Estradiol tablets, the most commonly prescribed estrogen in Europe, are available in dosages of .5, 1.0, and 2.0 mg, which are considered roughly equivalent to the strengths of the dosages in conjugated estrogens. For women who are still menstruating, but experiencing hot flashes, the lowest dose of either tablet is usually strong enough to provide relief from the flashes. Women whose periods have stopped sometimes require a dose of .625 mg of conjugated equine estrogens or 1.0 mg of estradiol to alleviate their hot flashes. The higher doses of either estrogen are usually given only to younger women who have had their ovaries surgically removed in an attempt to match the amount of estrogen their ovaries would have been producing naturally. Once a woman who has had her ovaries removed nears the age of 50, however—the age when she would normally be experiencing menopause—she should switch to the lower doses.

Many doctors start women with the .625 mg dose, largely because it has been shown to be the lowest daily amount required to maintain bone density and protect against osteoporosis. If you are not concerned with osteoporosis but are taking estrogen solely to relieve hot flashes, you may wish to begin with the lower dose of .3 mg.

Estrogen is usually prescribed to be taken once daily. One frequently used regimen employs estrogen tablets from the first through the twenty-fifth day of each month. No estrogen is taken during the remainder of the month in order to give the body—particularly the uterus—a break from estrogen stimulation. Subsequent studies have shown that this end-of-the-month hiatus, often associated with severe hot flashes and insomnia, offers no real benefit in terms of cancer risk reduction. Most regimens now deliver the estrogen on a daily basis without a break.

Progestin tablets.   Medroxyprogesterone tablets are available in daily dosages of 2.5, 5.0, and 10 mg. Natural progesterone is available in dosages of 100, 200, and 300 mg. At one point, women were told to take the tablets for seven days each month. Now, however, researchers believe progestin must be taken for a minimum of twelve to fourteen days, starting on day one of each calendar month, to provide meaningful protection against the risk of endometrial cancer.

Currently, you can choose among three different progesterone regimens. All seem to be equally effective in protecting the endometrium from cancer.

Monthly.   To most clearly mimic the natural ovarian cycle and cause a "period" to occur, most women need only 5 mg of a synthetic progestin or 200 mg of a natural progesterone daily for twelve to fourteen days each month. The natural progesterone should be taken with food for best absorption into the body. If you develop bleeding before the progesterone cycle is completed, you should speak to your physician, who will likely recommend increasing the dose to either 10 mg of the synthetic progestin or 300 mg of the natural progesterone. Heavier women usually require these higher doses in order to counteract the higher levels of estrogens naturally made in the fatty tissue of their bodies.

For most women, the monthly withdrawal bleeding (withdrawal from the progesterone) that accompanies this regimen is usually slight, and may even disappear over time. If the bleeding does cease, you may want to consider taking progesterone every two or three months (see the following). If you have persistently heavy bleeding every month, you may need a lower dose of estrogen.

Quarterly. Studies have recently shown that women whose withdrawal bleeding is slight or moderate on the monthly cycle described above can switch to taking a progesterone only every three months and still be protected from developing endometrial hyperplasia. In this regimen, you take a 10 mg dose of a synthetic progestin or 300 mg of natural progesterone for fourteen days every three months. As a result, you experience a "period" only four times a year.

One drawback to this regimen is that for some women those four periods produce heavy bleeding and cramps. This is because the endometrium has had three uninterrupted months of estrogen stimulation. Some women also experience spot bleeding during the months when they are taking only the estrogen. All of these symptoms usually can be eliminated by taking the progesterone at shorter intervals—every two rather than three months. A few women, however, may have to return to taking progesterone monthly.

Continuous. Another widely used HRT regimen involves taking a continuous low daily dose of progesterone along with the daily dose of estrogen. Like the monthly and quarterly regimens, this continuous regimen has been shown to be effective in keeping the uterine lining thin and thus protecting against endometrial cancer. A dose of 2.5 mg of synthetic progestin or 100 mg of natural progesterone is usually prescribed, although larger women may require larger doses—5.0 mg of synthetic progestin or 200 mg of natural progesterone. Unfortunately, this regimen often results in unscheduled bleeding. Many women find this side effect so troublesome that they switch to the more predictable monthly or quarterly regimens.

IUDs. Progesterone intrauterine devices (IUDs) are currently being studied to determine if they provide enough protection of the endometrium to be used in postmenopausal women. These IUDS release progesterone for about one year, at which time they need to be taken out and replaced. Some women report that taking progesterone via an IUD reduces or eliminates the premenstrual syndrome (PMS)-like side effects associated with oral progestins. Further research is needed to determine the cost-effectiveness and safety of these devices.

Estrogen creams. Vaginal creams containing conjugated estrogens or estradiol are available. Manufacturers of these creams provide applicator tubes that are marked at 1- and 2-gram filling levels, the dosages most commonly recommended for relieving vaginal dryness. Estrogen creams are rarely prescribed for other purposes, such as the prevention of heart disease or osteoporosis, because it takes 4 grams of the cream to have the same effects on blood cholesterol or bone density as .625 mg of conjugated estrogen. That's a lot of cream! And it would have to be applied daily.

For relieving vaginal dryness, the cream should be inserted daily for about a month, and then the dose can be tapered to whatever minimum use is effective in keeping your vagina moist and comfortable for sex. About 85 percent of women using vaginal creams find that using the lowest dose—1 gram—is sufficient to relieve vaginal dryness. The other 15 percent find they need the higher dose. Vaginal estrogen creams are not lubricants for sexual activity and should not be used during sex. It is okay to have sex if you inserted the cream earlier, but it is best to try and anticipate when you will be having sex and insert the cream at a later time after sex.

Vaginal estrogens can also sometimes relieve mild urinary incontinence, urinary urgency, and frequent urinary tract infections in postmenopausal women. If you are using an estrogen cream for one of these purposes, you should insert it daily for three months before trying to taper the dose to its minimum effective use.

Estrogen skin patches. Patches are designed to release either .5 mg or 1.0 mg of estradiol into the body each day. Those doses are the equivalent of .625 mg and 1.25 mg of the conjugated estrogens found in many estrogen tablets. To maintain the correct dosage, you will need to change the patch either once or twice a week, depending on the brand. Estrogen patches have the same effect on the body as estrogen tablets, so if you still have your uterus you will need to take an oral progestin as prevention against endometrial cancer.

WHEN OTHER DRUGS ARE ADDED
TO THE TABLETS

Tranquilizers. Some estrogen tablets contain tranquilizers. Doctors occasionally prescribe these tablets to menopausal women who appear depressed or anxious. Make sure you know whether your estrogen prescription includes a tranquilizer. Tranquilizers can cause dizziness, mental confusion, and drowsiness, thus making it difficult for you to go about your everyday tasks. Driving under the influence of a tranquilizer can be particularly dangerous. Some tranquilizers can also become addictive if used over a long period of time. If you should need medication for depression, ask your doctor to recommend a therapist who is skilled in treating women with depression.

Testosterone. Estrogen is also sometimes prescribed in combination with testosterone, which is an androgen, or male hormone. Doctors usually add testosterone to the estrogen in order to improve a woman's libido or sense of well-being. Be wary, however. Not all women experience a lift in libido after taking testosterone. Furthermore, the hormone can exact a high cost. Even low doses of supplemental androgens can cause oily skin and acne, and higher doses can lead to such virilizing side effects as a deepening of the voice, excess hair growth, or shrinking of the breasts. These changes do not always go away after the drug has been discontinued. High doses of testosterone may also have a bad effect on blood cholesterol, which may, in turn, increase the risk of heart disease. Research is needed. For more information about testosterone and menopause, see chapter 5.

MEDICAL TESTS YOU WILL NEED TO TAKE

Before you go on hormone therapy, you should undergo a complete general physical examination by your physician. This physical should include the following:

- A breast and a pelvic examination.
- A blood pressure check.
- A Pap smear to screen for cervical cancer. Because the Pap smear is not reliable in detecting uterine cancer, some experts recommend that women going on hormone therapy—particularly those who will be taking estrogen without a progestin or those who have had irregular bleeding patterns—also undergo an endometrial biopsy before any hormones are prescribed.
- A mammogram if you have not had one in the past year.
- Blood tests, including a cardiac lipid profile.
- An assessment of bone density, using dual-photon absorptiometry.
- A check of your stool for occult (hidden) blood, which may be a symptom of early gastrointestinal cancers.

Your doctor should also get a complete personal and family medical history from you during this examination. The two of you should then analyze this information together to determine the risks and benefits of hormone therapy for you.

ONGOING CARE

While you are taking hormones, you will need to make regular visits to your physician. Your doctor will probably schedule your first follow-up visit for a few weeks after the therapy begins. After that, you should see your doctor every six months or yearly.

These visits should be similar to your initial physical examination with your physician: They should include both a breast and a pelvic exam, as well as a check of your blood pressure. You should also have a yearly mammogram if you are over the age of 50, or every other year if you are between the ages of 40 and 50. Because of the increased risk of breast cancer associated with HRT, this yearly test is especially important for women taking hormones.

Between check-ups, you should be monitoring your health carefully. Be sure to examine your breasts for lumps at home each month. Also, be alert for unusual symptoms, such as vaginal bleeding, coughing, headaches, dizziness, unusual lumps or swellings, leg pain, yellowing of the skin or eyes, vision changes, or difficulty breathing. Report these to your physician immediately.

Finally, be sure you follow your physician's instructions carefully. Never take more than the prescribed dose of hormones. If you feel your current prescription is not strong enough to relieve your hot flashes or vaginal dryness, talk to your physician before you increase the dosage. Self-prescribing can lead to serious problems.

SIDE EFFECTS

This section describes some of the side effects you may experience once you begin hormone therapy. It also suggests how to manage them.

Vaginal Bleeding

If your hormone therapy includes both estrogen and a monthly twelve- to fourteen-day cycle of a progestin (see page 77), you will probably experience vaginal bleeding each month during the week following the progestin. This withdrawal bleeding is shorter and scantier than a normal menstrual period, usually lasting only two or three days each month. Although it can be a nuisance, withdrawal bleeding is quite normal and not a cause for concern. It usually becomes lighter over the years and gradually most women will have no period at all, even if they stay on the hormones. Be sure to alert your physician immediately, however, if the bleeding is much heavier or more prolonged than usual, for it may be an early warning sign of uterine cancer.

As noted earlier (see page 78), if you are on a continuous HRT regimen—one in which you are taking a low daily dose of progestin along with your daily dose of estrogen—you may experience some unscheduled bleeding, especially during the first twelve to eighteen months of taking the hormones. You should inform your physician about each episode of bleeding, no matter how scant, because cancer must be ruled out. To help determine whether or not cancer is present, your physician may recommend that you undergo an endometrial biopsy, particularly if you have not had one during the previous twelve months. If the biopsy reveals no cancer, your physician may suggest that you alleviate the bleeding by switching instead to a cyclic regimen, during which you would take progestin for two weeks every month or every few months. Spot bleeding that begins after a year of continuous HRT regimen might be due to excessive thinning of the lining of the uterus, in which case your physician may recommend that you take only estrogen for a month to thicken the lining.

Although an endometrial biopsy can often be done right in a doctor's office, it can be a painful procedure. To reduce unnecessary biopsies, many physicians now use a procedure called *transvaginal sonography*. It involves inserting a long, thin wand with an ultrasound transducer inside its tip into the vagina—a usually painless, but sometimes uncomfortable, technique. The transducer measures the thickness of the endometrium. When the measurement is less than 4 mm (about ⅙ of an inch), no cancer is present. If the measurement is larger, the presence of cancer is still unlikely, but possible. In such cases, therefore, a biopsy should be performed. If your physician recommends a biopsy, ask if you can undergo a transvaginal sonography first.

Fluid Retention and Weight Gain

For some women, estrogen supplements can cause a decrease in the amount of salt and water excreted by the kidneys, which means that more fluid is retained in the body. Your legs, breasts, and feet may become swollen, and you may experience a general bloated feeling. Your weight may also reflect this excess amount of fluid. This is usually a sign of a too-high dose of estrogen.

Some women gain a pound or two of weight after starting on HRT. This is perfectly normal, and may be due to fluid retention. If you find yourself gaining more than a couple of pounds while on HRT, however, the added weight is most likely due to excessive eating, which may or may not have been triggered by the hormones. Although progestins are sometimes prescribed to help cancer patients and others who are unhealthily thin gain weight, the dose prescribed for this purpose is about ten times greater than that prescribed to postmenopausal women. For most women, therefore, the progestins in HRT are not going to lead to overeating. Still, if you tended to overeat during the premenstrual phase of your natural monthly cycle, you may find your appetite similarly increasing during the progestin phase of your HRT cycle. Be aware of this and watch what you eat!

B6 Deficiency

Taking synthetic estrogen supplements for menopause can sometimes lead to a vitamin B6 deficiency, just as it sometimes does for women who use birth control pills. Be alert for the symptoms: fatigue, depression, inability to concentrate, loss of libido, and insomnia. The problem can be corrected easily by taking a B6 supplement (for dosage amount, see chapter 7).

Nausea

This is a common complaint among high-dose estrogen users, particularly if their bodies were not introduced to the high dose gradually. Decreasing the dosage of estrogen may help. The problem can often be prevented by starting with a very low dose of estrogen and then, very gradually, increasing it to the planned daily dose.

Other Side Effects

In addition to the major side effects listed above, you may also experience the following while on hormone therapy:

* Headaches.
* A skin discoloration known as melasma—it usually occurs on the face and may not return to normal after you stop the therapy.

- An increase in cervical mucous secretion.
- A secretion of liquid from the nipples of the breasts.
- A change in the curvature of the cornea (which may make it impossible to wear contact lenses).
- Jaundice.
- Loss of scalp hair.
- Itching.
- Lowering of the voice.

As you can see, hormones are potent drugs that can have a considerable effect on your body. It is important that you be aware of how your body is reacting to the drugs—and that you keep your doctor aware of any changes.

A VERY INDIVIDUALIZED DECISION

Should you go on hormone replacement therapy? Only you can really answer that question. How you answer it will depend on several, very personal factors: why you want to take the hormones, your health history, and how comfortable you feel after weighing the benefits and the risks involved.

• • •

"I used to experiment. I'd take the estrogen for a while and then think, 'Okay, now you can deal with this. You're now going to go off these pills and your mind is going to tell you that you're not going to have these hot flashes.' So I would go off the estrogen, but sure enough, the flashes would come back. It would take maybe two to three weeks, but they'd come back. They'd start slowly, maybe once a day. Then they'd start elevating in quantity and quality to the point where I was back to the same old place again. I've tried that several times over the last few years, but it never works. I don't know how long I'll have to wait to finally go off the stuff—maybe until I'm in my fifties."

• • •

For some women, the decision may be fairly clear-cut. If, for example, you are experiencing severe menopausal discomfort—say, night sweats that keep you from sleeping night after night—you may need HRT to keep from losing your sanity to exhaustion. Or if you had your ovaries removed and are at high risk for getting bone fractures, you may benefit greatly from the therapy.

A NOTE TO WOMEN WITH BREAST CANCER

Hormone replacement therapy has not been recommended in the past to women who have had breast cancer, primarily because both estrogen and progesterone are known to stimulate some forms of breast cancer, but also because HRT can cause breast tissue to thicken, making recurring tumors more difficult to detect. Recently, however, some doctors have begun to prescribe HRT to some breast cancer survivors who are struggling with hot flashes. You may wish to discuss this option with your oncologist. Be aware, however, that the long-term safety of HRT for breast cancer survivors is not yet known.

If you have had your ovaries removed as part of your therapy for breast cancer and are under the age of 50, you should not use HRT, as you most likely have a type of breast cancer that is easily stimulated by the hormone. Be sure, however, to have your physician monitor your cholesterol profile and bone density. Do as much as you can naturally to protect your heart and bones, but if those efforts fail, ask your physician about non-HRT medications for preventing heart disease and osteoporosis.

Some doctors recommend tamoxifen to their postmenopausal patients who have had breast cancer and who are at high risk of developing heart disease or osteoporosis. Tamoxifen is a nonsteroid hormone that is often used to treat certain kinds of breast cancer. It has antiestrogenic properties, which means it reduces the overall effects of the estrogen that naturally circulates in the body, including estrogen's ability to stimulate some kinds of cancerous breast tumors. Surprisingly, however, tamoxifen also creates weak estrogenic effects in the body, and, as a result, has been found to improve cholesterol profiles, maintain bone density, and stimulate the uterine lining to thicken. This last effect has led to serious concerns about prescribing the drug for purposes other than breast cancer treatment. Studies have shown that tamoxifen increases the risk of endometrial cancer up to sixfold, which is why annual endometrial assessment by biopsy or sonography is strongly recommended for any woman taking tamoxifen.

On the other hand, if you are experiencing a natural menopause with only mild discomfort, and if you know that you are at low risk for osteoporosis and heart disease, the risks of HRT most likely outweigh the benefits.

Of course, many women find themselves somewhere in the middle of these two situations, which is why the decision about whether to take HRT is usually so complicated. Again, it comes back to personal choice: You will need to decide which risks and benefits are most important to you.

WHEN NOT TO TAKE HRT

You definitely should not take HRT if you have a personal medical history of any of the following:

- Endometrial cancer, most types.
- Breast cancer, most types.
- Undiagnosed abnormal vaginal bleeding.
- Liver dysfunction.

Many doctors also consider the following to be moderate contra-indicators to HRT—or reasons not to take the hormones:

- Sickle cell disease.
- Migraine headaches.
- Uterine fibroids.
- Gallbladder disease.

You will also need to decide for yourself which diseases you most want to avoid. As one woman who decided not to take HRT put it, "I decided I felt more comfortable taking the risk of dying of osteoporosis at eighty than dying of breast cancer at sixty or seventy."

Of course, the situation is somewhat different if you are under the age of 50 and have entered menopause as the result of surgery or radiation treatment. You have become suddenly deficient in the hormone. In addition, your body may not be proficient at converting androgens into estrogen—a process that occurs naturally in older women. HRT may therefore be very appropriate for you—at least until the age when you would have naturally gone through menopause—but must be specifically tailored to your personal medical history. One woman who had a hysterectomy at age 39 and who has a family history of stroke and heart disease, opted to take estrogen supplements as a protective measure against those two diseases. "I'm more worried about heart disease than I am about cancer," she says.

Taking hormones is not something you should do casually. It's a decision that should be arrived at slowly and carefully, after considerable thought and study. A simplified decision flowchart which might help to guide you through the process is available in Appendix A. In general, it is a good idea to lean toward the conservative side when it comes to HRT. Many serious questions about the health risks of these drugs remain unanswered. Also, be sure to keep informed about new developments in HRT research. Some good resources for this kind of information are listed in the Resources section at the end of this book.

4

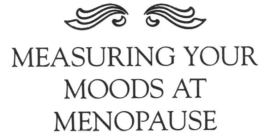

MEASURING YOUR
MOODS AT
MENOPAUSE

The most profound gift of life after menopause is the awareness of my own self-worth.

—Charlotte Markman Stein

One of the oldest and most stubborn myths about menopause is that it can turn an otherwise sane woman into an irritable nag, a nervous neurotic, or a screaming lunatic. As far back as 1857, an author of a book on menopause wrote that "a large class of women are thoroughly unhinged by the change of life. . . . Eccentricity embitters their existence and the lives of those around them." Some seventy years later, attitudes had not changed. "The majority of women have psychic symptoms," noted a gynecology text of the 1920s. "They are peevish, irritable, morose, and depressed. . . . Many have full-blown insanity with melancholia, paranoia, and maniacal conditions."

Another seventy years have passed, and the idea that a woman can become "unhinged" or "eccentric" as a result of menopause persists. Menopause continues to be blamed for a variety of emotional disturbances, everything from nervousness and anxiety to insomnia and depression. One doctor even cites "antisocial behavior" and "aggressiveness" as two of the "commonest emotional symptoms" of menopause, although he does not bother to explain what he means by those terms.

The message, however, remains clear: Menopause is an especially emotionally stressful time in a woman's life.

But is it? In this chapter we'll take a look at the research that has examined the role that menopause does or doesn't play in the mental health of midlife women. We'll also look at some of the steps you can take to ease any stress or depression you may be feeling at this time in your life.

• • •

"I don't have any investment in still being able to have children, so that whole part of menopause, that part that so many women I know are still hung up on—the end of your childbearing years stuff—isn't important to me. I suppose the message implied by society is that the end of your periods means the end of your value as a human being. I won't have any of that. I don't need to be menstruating to feel vital."

• • •

THE MYTH OF INVOLUTIONAL MELANCHOLIA

Psychiatrists used to believe that a particular kind of depressive illness was directly related to menopause. They called the depression *involutional melancholia* and described it as "a disorder occurring in the involutional [menopausal] period and characterized by worry, anxiety, agitation, and severe insomnia. Feelings of guilt and somatic preoccupations are frequently present and may be of delusional proportions."

Today, the concept of involutional melancholia has been largely discredited. In fact, in 1980 the term was dropped from the American Psychiatric Association's *Diagnostic and Statistical Manual of Mental Disorders*. Several studies have failed to show any increase in depression among women during their menopausal years. Furthermore, women who do become depressed at this time of their life do not exhibit a depressive pattern distinct from that of younger or older women.

That's not to say women at midlife don't become depressed. They do. But it's not menopause that's making them depressed.

The best evidence of this can be found in the Massachusetts Women's Health Study, the largest and most comprehensive study of its kind to date. Conducted by Sonja and John B. McKinlay of the New England Research Institute in Watertown, Massachusetts, the study followed more than 2,300 women for five years. All of the women were between the ages of 45 and 55 at the start of the study; they lived in both rural and urban areas of Massachusetts.

Most important, the women in the study were chosen at random from the community, not from a clinic or hospital setting. Most past information about menopause has been drawn from studies that used women who had already sought medical help for one reason or another, a group that is not representative of women as a whole.

The McKinlays found that the biological event of menopause has almost no impact on how a woman perceives her health, including her mental health. "The overwhelming majority of women reported positive or neutral feelings about the cessation of menses," the McKinlays noted in their study's conclusions. Many women, in fact, expressed relief that they would no longer have to worry about pregnancy, contraception, or menstruation. Interestingly, as the women passed through menopause, their attitudes toward it became even more positive.

The McKinlays also found that the onset of natural menopause had no effect on the rate of depression. About 10 percent of the women in the study reported occasional depression—a figure similar to the rate of depression in women of all ages. The remaining 85 percent said they were never depressed.

Although the study did not find that menopause causes depression, it did find that an already existing depression increases the likelihood of a woman reporting problems with menopause to her physician. Women in the study who were already depressed were twice as likely to see a doctor about hot flashes, cold sweats, and irregular menstrual periods. No wonder, therefore, that so many physicians are inclined to link depression with menopause! Chances are that the patients coming to them with menopausal complaints are depressed, although the depression most likely existed long before the onset of menopause.

•   •   •

"My husband died while I was going through menopause. I think maybe my emotional turmoil took my mind off some of the physical changes I was going through. But I kept very busy and tried to put all that behind me. Also, I was taught that menopause was all very natural. My mother never talked about her experiences with menopause and she didn't seem to have any physical indications that she was going through it either. I think you should try to treat it as intelligently as possible. Actually, I was very relieved. I mean, if I'm going to be that age, I'm very glad to have my periods behind me."

•   •   •

MENOPAUSE AND INSOMNIA

Many women report sleeping problems as they approach and pass through menopause. Women who have previously had no trouble sleeping and who are not depressed or leading a lifestyle that might interfere with their sleep suddenly find themselves struggling with insomnia night after night. Whether this is due to the hormonal changes that occur around menopause is not known, for very little research has been conducted on menopause and sleep. Scientists do know, however, that night sweats can cause menopausal women to wake up during the night—sometimes even without them being aware that they are doing so. This can lead to restless nights—even insomnia—and daytime fatigue. Preventive measures to eliminate the night sweats, whether an herbal remedy or estrogen replacement therapy, is sometimes all that is needed to help some women get a good night's sleep.

Estrogen therapy does not cure all menopausal women of their insomnia, however, which is why some sleep researchers believe other factors may be at work. Until more is learned about menopause and insomnia, you may want to try the following standard recommendation from sleep experts:

- Don't worry about an occasional sleepless night. You do not have to get a good night's sleep every night.
- When you can't sleep, get out of your bed and your bedroom. Find something quiet and relaxing to do. Take a warm bath. Make a list of the things on your mind. Or read a book. Or watch a quiet, even boring, television show. When you begin to feel sleepy, return to bed. Do *not* get up and start cleaning the house or attacking a project from work. Those kinds of activities are too stimulating and will just make it more difficult to fall asleep.

If your insomnia continues over a long period of time, you will need to take more stringent measures at breaking the sleepless habit:

- Follow a regular sleep schedule: Go to bed at the same time every night and get up at the same time every morning.
- Avoid going to bed until you are tired. If you fail to fall asleep within 15 minutes, get out of bed and do something relaxing until you feel tired again.
- Avoid caffeine, chocolate, and alcohol in the evening.
- Avoid daytime napping.

DEPRESSION AND HYSTERECTOMIES

In their overall findings about depression and menopause, the McKinlays did not include in their study those women who had had hysterectomies. They looked at these women separately and found that their experiences with depression were much different than those who underwent a natural menopause. The women who had a surgical menopause were twice as likely to be depressed. They were also more likely to consider their health "worse than that of others" and to seek professional medical help. Not surprisingly, therefore, they were also twice as likely to be using prescribed drugs, such as sleeping pills and tranquilizers. In addition, they were more likely to be using hormone replacement therapy, which is also not surprising because some of the surgeries included removal of the ovaries, inducing a sudden menopause.

•   •   •

"After the hysterectomy, Robert and I had some counseling just to deal with the grief part of this. The culminating episode, the one that really pushed me over the edge, was when a good friend had a baby. I went to the hospital and held the baby and coo-cooed it. That night when I came home I was very angry and I didn't know why. I was picking on Robert; I shouted at the dog. Then I finally burst into horrible, horrible, deep grieving sobs. I recognized and came to a deep understanding with myself that it would never be possible for me to have a child. Since then I've realized that my nurturing is for the world at large. I don't need to focus on one small individual. That's how I dealt with the grief. I have learned to take the grief outside of myself and put it into a much more joyous way of being. I know that sounds a little like a fairy tale, but it's true."

•   •   •

Although the evidence is by no means conclusive, some other studies have also shown a link between hysterectomies and depression. Researchers have found that women are more likely to have psychological problems after a hysterectomy (whether or not the ovaries are removed) than after other kinds of surgery. They are also more likely to have problems than if they had had no surgery at all.

The research also seems to indicate that depression does not always show up immediately after a hysterectomy. Often a woman will not report feeling depressed until the end of the first year or during the second year after her operation. These depressions may or may not be directly related to the surgery.

Just why women become depressed after hysterectomies is not entirely clear. Some experts point to the emotional trauma caused by the removal of a uterus: Many women view it as a symbolic loss and report feeling less "whole" or "feminine." This cause for depression after hysterectomy varies across cultures; it occurs more often when women's roles as mothers are emphasized culturally. Other experts believe, however, that there are strong physiological reasons, perhaps having to do with sudden hormonal changes, for the depression. More research is needed.

Most women, however, do *not* experience any major depression after a hysterectomy. Still, you should be aware of the possibility and seek professional help should the need arise. As Susanne Morgan points out in her book, *Coping with a Hysterectomy*, "We need to know that there is a chance we will become depressed, so if we do have those feelings we can seek out appropriate support. It is easy for many of us to convince ourselves that any problems are due to our own inability to cope and that we do not deserve help."

• • •

"My hysterectomy was the beginning of the beginning for me. No more cramps, no more PMS, no more bleeding on my white panties. I've been on estrogen for the last four years and it's been smooth sailing. Sometimes I forget to take them and I notice difficulty falling asleep, then later I get a few flashes to remind me to take my pills. A couple of times, I got sad that I will never have the choice to have a baby, but I'd sum it up with 'No regrets.' "

• • •

No one should suffer through depression alone. So get help, perhaps through a woman's support group or through individual therapy. You do deserve to be happy.

MENOPAUSAL "MOODINESS" OR PMS?

If you are a woman who suffers from premenstrual syndrome, or PMS, you may have experienced intensified symptoms as you approach menopause. Studies have shown that a woman in her thirties or forties is much more likely to have symptoms of PMS than a younger woman and that her PMS symptoms may become more intense and prolonged as she ages.

Included among PMS's psychological symptoms are fatigue, anxiety, irritability, crying spells, emotional outbursts, and insomnia. For some women, the irritability, fatigue, and other minor emotional troubles they experience around menopause may be due simply to the fact that their sleep is being disrupted by hot flashes. People who are tired are often irritable and anxious. If you are experiencing this problem, you may wish to try the self-help tips for relieving hot flashes listed in chapter 2. Those tips may relieve your moodiness as well.

If you suspect that your mood swings are PMS-related (and you can find out by charting your menstrual cycles for three months and recording your symptoms daily), you can try the following to minimize your discomfort:

- *Watch what you eat during the two weeks before your period.* Specifically, avoid refined carbohydrates (otherwise known as sugary junk foods). The hormone changes that occur before your period are associated with a more rapid than usual drop in blood sugar after you eat refined carbohydrates. This can cause temporary bouts of fatigue, irritability, and agitation, often accompanied by headaches.

  Of course, avoiding sugary junk foods right before your period is not always easy, because a craving for sweets is, for many women, one of the symptoms of PMS. Your best bet is to clear your house of any candy bars or cookies when you know your period is approaching. Then, stock up on fresh fruit and other wholesome snacks. Also, try eating several small meals during the day to lessen sugar cravings and to keep your blood sugar at a steadier level.

- *Eat less salt.* Salt tends to make the body retain more fluid. Cutting back on salt, therefore, may help ease PMS symptoms, such as water retention and bloatedness.

- *Avoid alcohol and caffeine.* These two substances can aggravate many of the emotional symptoms of PMS.

- *Avoid tranquilizers.* These drugs can make many of the psychological symptoms of PMS more intense.

- *Try taking selected vitamins.* Good evidence exists to support vitamin therapy for reducing the emotional symptoms of PMS. Experts recommend daily dosages of calcium (500 mg), magnesium (250 mg), vitamin B6 (50 mg), and vitamin E (600–1,000 IU).

- *Get plenty of exercise.* Exercise is a great mood lifter and can help you work off tension and anxiety. Several studies have shown that women who exercise are less likely to suffer from severe symptoms of PMS.

- *See a psychologist or psychiatrist.* Some types of PMS respond well to supportive therapy alone. If your PMS is severe, however, and significantly impedes your ability to function normally, you may want to consider some of the newer antidepressants, such as Zoloft, Paxil, and Prozac. When prescribed and used correctly, some women have found great relief with them. These medications do not help all women with severe PMS, however, and there has been significant controversy over their possible side effects. Be sure to discuss all the risks and benefits of these medications with your therapist before taking them.

MENOPAUSE IN OTHER CULTURES

In many non-Western cultures, which do not place so much emphasis on youth and glamour, menopause is viewed not as "the beginning of the end," but as a marker of increased social status. Thus, it's not surprising that women in these cultures report few problems with menopause, including no problem with depression.

Here are just a few examples of cultures in which menopause enhances a woman's social status:

- In Rajasthan, India, women who have gone through menopause may leave the women's quarters to talk and drink with men. They need no longer stay in *purdah* (veiled and secluded) with the other women.
- Among the Qemant people of Ethiopia, a woman who has achieved menopause is permitted to walk on sacred ground and participate in other rituals for which she was considered too unclean during her menstruating years.
- In Ulithi, Micronesia, a woman may become a healer after menopause and may practice sorcery and magic.
- According to the traditional culture of the Cree in Canada, a woman who has achieved menopause may exercise shamanistic powers and play a direct role in religious ceremonies.
- After menopause, the Thonga women of Mozambique can eat monkeys and porcupines if they wish—a taboo for menstruating women.

•   •   •

"I didn't go to my gynecologist about menopause. I think the reason I didn't is that I don't like doctors that much, even though I go to a really good one. Anyway, I just assumed that the feelings I was experiencing were stress-related. There were some major things going on in my life at the time. Both my parents were dying, and I had been fired from a job because I wouldn't sleep with somebody. Then I was engaged to somebody who, it turned out, was engaged to somebody else at the same time. He married her. It was like all of these things were going on at this time, and I just assumed that during all of this that it was just a major hormonal screw-up because of stress. I didn't really mind that I wasn't getting my periods because they had always been bad my whole life. I didn't see where not having them was a problem."

•   •   •

THE STRESSORS AT MIDLIFE

The shifts in emotions some women experience around menopause are more likely to be caused by external factors—worries about a career, child, or spouse, for example—than by the internal churnings of hormones.

As the McKinlays point out in their study, several negative events can occur to women as they pass through their menopausal years: A spouse or close relative (particularly a parent) may die or become chronically ill or disabled; children may leave home—or return home to live, sometimes bringing grandchildren with them; employment may become less secure, leading to financial stresses; friends and family members, once relied upon for emotional support, may die or move away; a marriage may end in divorce. These dramatic changes impact heavily on a woman's sense of self-worth and her emotional outlook on life.

•   •   •

"I don't miss my periods, but I miss the fact that I can't have children. That really hit home the last couple of years. It's been hard."

•   •   •

Given all that can happen to women during their midlife years, it seems a miracle that any woman survives that period of her life without sinking into a severe depression! Any one of the experiences listed above can lead to stress and depression. And sometimes they do. But not for all women, and not because of anything to do with falling levels of estrogen.

Often, the stress experienced by midlife women comes from another person. According to the women in the McKinlay study, children account for 39 percent of their stress, parents or in-laws for 24 percent, other relatives for 22 percent, husbands or partners for 11 percent, and friends and coworkers for 4 percent.

Work was found to be a positive factor in most of the women's lives, actually relieving some of the stress caused by family members. In addition, as the McKinlays point out, not all the significant events that occur at midlife are necessarily negative. Many good things happen as well! The birth of grandchildren, freedom from the fear of pregnancy, the opportunity (now that the children have grown) to pursue new activities and interests—these and other experiences provide positive counterbalances to the negative stresses that often afflict middle-aged women.

THE EMPTY NEST IS NOT
ALWAYS AN UNHAPPY ONE

It has long been believed that women whose children have grown up and left home are at greater risk for depression—the "empty-nest syndrome." New research has shown, however, that this is not true. In fact, many women find that emptying the nest is a liberating experience, enabling them to take on new, more independent roles.

In a 1988 study conducted at Northwestern University Medical School, researchers gave psychological tests to 50 working women between the ages of 43 and 51. Half had teen-aged children still at home, half had "empty nests." The women with children at home tended to see themselves as cautious, dependent, submissive, and nurturing. Those whose children had left home described themselves as self-confident, independent, goal-oriented, and assertive.

The study seems to indicate that empty nests are not always unhappy ones. For many mothers (and fathers, too) having children finally "fly the coop" is a welcomed and positive experience.

HOW TO RELIEVE THE STRESS
IN YOUR LIFE

You can take several steps to help minimize the impact of negative stress on your emotional health during your menopausal years:

- *Identify the source of your stress.* Then evaluate ways in which you can distance yourself from the stressor—if only temporarily. If your teenaged children are causing you stress, plan a vacation away from them. If you are taking care of a chronically ill parent, be sure you allow yourself some respite from the caregiving. Insist that other family members help from time to time, or, if you can afford it, hire professionals to give you an evening or a weekend off. Remember, nurturing others is only possible if you nurture yourself first.
- *Pace yourself.* At midlife, our lives are often so full of activities and responsibilities that we forget we are human and not work machines. Try to avoid overscheduling your life, particularly with events you know will be stressful. And remember, you can't be everything to everybody. Learn how to say no.
- *Listen to your body.* Stress sends out early warning signs: indigestion, fatigue, eating disorders, sleeping problems, and daydreaming, for example. Take note of these signs; they're telling you to slow down.
- *Spend time with people you like.* Talking about the stress in your life with

someone who cares about you can go a long way toward easing tension and anxiety. Also, joining a group of people who have a common purpose, whether it is pursuing a favorite hobby or providing a service to others, can be a great stress-reducer.

- *Exercise regularly.* Exercise is a great tension-reliever and mood uplifter. It will also give you more energy. You must exercise regularly, however, to experience these benefits. Sporadic exercise, such as an occasional game of tennis or a long hike, can be a harmful stressor for your body.
- *Try some relaxation techniques.* Yoga, deep-breathing exercises, Transcendental Meditation, progressive muscle relaxation, biofeedback, and other relaxation techniques have been shown to be extremely useful in relieving the ill effects of stress. You can teach yourself many of these techniques by reading a book on the topic, or you can seek out the guidance of an instructor. Call your local mental health association for a listing of classes or individual professionals in your community who can help you get started with the relaxation technique of your choice.
- *Seek professional help if the stress in your life gets out of control.* Don't be a martyr. Everyone could benefit from professional counselling from time to time. Growing to be a better person through therapy is the smart way to combat the effects of stress in your life.

•   •   •

"I think the low times of menopause are very similar to PMS. Did you see the movie Broadcast News? *A woman producer in it starts crying at her desk, just out of the blue. I had never really experienced crying spells like that until the last few years. It just feels like something is really building up and you need to cry. It's hard to put into words, but the crying is a kind of release. Afterwards, it feels great."*

•   •   •

IF A MAJOR DEPRESSION HITS

Although menopause does not cause it, major depression can descend upon you during your menopausal years, just as it can at any other time in your life. Major depression is not the same as a bout with the blues. It's a debilitating illness that can last for weeks, months, or even years if left untreated. It affects all of you, your body, your mood, your thoughts; and it severely interferes with normal life. As a woman, you are twice as likely as a man to experience a major depression at some time in your life.

Psychiatrists and others who treat people with depression have come up with the following common symptoms for major depression. A person who has experienced at least four of these symptoms for at least two weeks is generally considered to be suffering from depression.

- Eating too much or too little.
- Sleeping too much or too little.
- Feeling exceptionally lethargic or restless.
- Feeling an inability to enjoy once pleasurable activities, including a loss in sex drive.
- Debilitating fatigue or loss of energy.
- Feelings of worthlessness and self-reproach.
- Difficulty concentrating, remembering, and making decisions.
- Thoughts of death or suicide, or suicide attempts.

Some types of depression seem to run in families, leading experts to believe a vulnerability to depression can be inherited. But major depression can also occur in people who have no family history of the illness. Background and personality seem to play a role; people who have low self-esteem or who had troubled childhoods, for example, are prone to becoming seriously depressed.

•   •   •

"I tend to think changes are in some ways unpredictable. You can't control all the stress in your life. There can be joy, there can be kids growing up, there can be family deaths, there can be family crises. There can be vocational changes. But I think the best thing is to enjoy life one day at a time. You also have to have some support, like a good physician and wonderful women friends. That's really important."

•   •   •

Depression also takes on different forms in different people. Some people experience episodic depressions that occur only once or twice in a lifetime. Other people suffer from chronic depression, which persists for long stretches of time and requires ongoing treatment.

If you think you are suffering from a serious depression, it's important that you seek professional help. You may benefit from some kind of psychotherapy or treatment with antidepressant medications, or both. Don't think you can simply pull yourself together without help or that you can will or wish the depression away. And don't berate yourself for being depressed. It is not a character flaw or weakness. Every year, about ten million people in the United States experience a depressive episode. You are not alone. Nor should you suffer alone. Get help.

5

HOW MENOPAUSE
WILL AFFECT YOUR
SEXUALITY

Menopause has brought with it a new freedom in sex with my spouse—as well as a feeling of control of my life and a new spurt of energy, never having those "tired days." I love it!

— Woman responding to a *Consumer Reports* survey about love, sex, and aging

One of the great myths about menopause is that it marks the end of a woman's sexuality. Nothing could be further from the truth. As sex researchers from Kinsey to Masters and Johnson have shown, women can continue to enjoy sex well into old age—indeed, as long as their health remains good. Many women, in fact, report that their sexual pleasure increases greatly after menopause because they are no longer worried about becoming pregnant.

Still, as you pass through the menopausal years you will notice some changes in the way your body responds to sexual arousal. Some of these changes are just the normal and inevitable consequences of aging; others are a direct result of changing hormone levels.

This chapter takes a look at menopause and sexuality, specifically at the physical changes that may take place during the menopausal years and how those changes may affect your sexuality. It also examines what actions you can take to keep your sex life exciting and fulfilling. And it looks at birth control options for the woman over 40 who has not yet experienced her final period.

YOUR CHANGING BODY

As noted in chapter 2, falling estrogen levels cause the walls of the vagina to become thinner, smoother, drier, and less elastic. The shape of the vagina can also change, becoming shorter and narrower after menopause—although it still remains sufficiently big for sexual activity.

As estrogen levels decline, the clitoris may become slightly smaller and the labia (lip of the vagina) thinner and flatter. The covering of the clitoris may also thin and pull back, leaving the clitoris more exposed. This can make the clitoris extremely sensitive to touch. You may find that you will need a great deal of lubrication to tolerate having it touched or rubbed during lovemaking.

●   ●   ●

"One of the positive things that came out of my early menopause is that it made my vagina more dry. I have always had a problem with being over-lubricated, so this is probably kind of like a benefit. It's cut down on the lubrication enough to make sex more comfortable."

●   ●   ●

KEEPING THE VAGINA MOIST

As the vaginal lining becomes thinner and drier, sexual activity can become uncomfortable, even painful. In severe cases, the lining may actually crack and bleed. Needless to say, this can quickly diminish a woman's interest in sex and may even cause her to question whether her days of enjoying sex are gone forever.

Vaginal dryness, and the discomfort that it can cause during inter-course, is one of the least talked about aspects of menopause. Yet it is very real for many—but not all—postmenopausal women. Fortunately, there are several things you can do to help keep your vagina lubricated:

*   Before sexual activity, smear a teaspoon or two of a sterile, water-soluble jelly, such as K-Y or Astroglide, on the outside of your vagina. You may want to put a small amount inside your vagina as well—or on your partner's penis or fingers. Water-based lubricants are recommended over oil-based ones because they are less likely to promote bacterial growth and cause infection. Use a jelly specifically made for sexual activity.

    You may also want to try one of the several vaginal moisturizers available today; these products claim to replenish vaginal moisture when used regularly. The lubricant is inserted tamponlike into the vagina two or three times a week, where it coats the surface of the vagina and moisturizes the vaginal tissue. For more information about vaginal moisturizers talk with your physician or pharmacist.

- Avoid douches, perfumed toilet paper, and bath soaps and oils. These can dry and irritate your vagina.
- Avoid antihistamines and other medications that can cause dryness.
- Have a longer period of foreplay before intercourse. The longer the foreplay, the longer your body will have to release its own natural lubricants. According to research conducted by Masters and Johnson, a woman in her mid-fifties usually needs a longer period of sexual stimulation for her vagina to become fully lubricated than a woman in her mid-twenties.
- Try a vitamin E vaginal suppository. Naturopath Judyth Reichenberg-Ullman recommends that postmenopausal women use the suppository nightly for six weeks, then weekly or as needed.
- Drink plenty of water. Water is a great lubricant for your entire body.

You should also know that some research seems to indicate that regular sexual activity may help keep the vagina lubricated. Women who remain sexually active after menopause—whether with a partner or through masturbation—appear to have less of a problem with dryness and the ability to achieve orgasms than women who are not sexually active. Scientists are not sure why this is so, but some believe sexual activity may stimulate estrogen production in the adrenal glands which, in turn, helps keep the vagina lubricated. In addition, the muscle contractions and increased blood flow that occur right before and during orgasm seem to "exercise" the vagina, helping it retain its premenopausal condition.

HORMONE THERAPY FOR VAGINAL DRYNESS

If vaginal dryness becomes a serious problem for you and using an artificial lubricant does not seem to help, you may wish to consider hormone replacement therapy. Taking estrogen, either in pill or cream form, can help relieve any dryness or soreness in the vagina, usually within a week or two. Estrogen cream is a better choice than the pill or patch form of the drug if your only concern is relieving vaginal dryness, primarily because the estrogen is delivered directly to the vagina, where the effect is wanted, while lesser amounts of the hormone reach the rest of the body. It thus poses fewer health risks. Yet there is another reason to use estrogen cream rather than pills or patches for vaginal dryness: It is often more effective at resolving the problem. Although not widely known, estrogen pills and patches do not always provide enough stimulation to the lining of the vagina to sufficiently lubricate it for comfortable sexual activity. As a result, women using pills or patches are sometimes surprised to find that, despite their hormone therapy, they continue to develop postmenopausal vaginal dryness or vaginitis. Some doctors respond to these complaints by increasing the dose of estrogen in the pill or patch. Unfortunately, this unnecessarily increases your body's exposure to estrogen—and thus your risk of breast or endometrial cancer. A better solution would be to use an estrogen cream. The creams can effectively improve vaginal health and moisturizing ability after use at very low doses—so low, in fact, that studies have shown that the estrogen does not show up in a user's bloodstream even after six months of daily low-dose use.

So, if your sole reason for taking hormones is to relieve vaginal dryness, then you should strongly consider using only an estrogen cream. Creams are especially beneficial for this purpose for women with breast cancer, who are often advised by their physicians not to take systemic forms of hormone therapy because it might stimulate their cancer. Estrogen creams should be applied daily for about a month, or until the vaginal dryness and soreness is gone. Then apply the cream only occasionally as "maintenance." Do not use estrogen cream right before or during love-making; it is a powerful drug and can be absorbed into your partner's body as well as into your own.

• • •

"I don't recall having any problem with vaginal drying. I had an active sex life well into my late fifties. I have noticed a decrease in my sex drive during the past few years, though. I just don't seem to have any urges anymore."

• • •

An androgen cream (a small amount of testosterone in a water-soluble solution) is sometimes prescribed for vaginal dryness. Be aware that too-high doses of testosterone can have "masculinizing" effects on women, such as increased clitoral size, new body hair, and a lowering of the voice. These effects may not go away even after the drug is discontinued. Nor is it known what effect testosterone has on the risk of heart disease.

For more information about testosterone, see pages 105–107. For more information about hormone replacement therapy in general, see chapter 3.

OTHER CAUSES OF PAINFUL SEXUAL ACTIVITY

If you experience any pain during sex, be sure to report it to your doctor. The cause of the pain may be something other than a dry vagina, such as adhesions to the ovary, endometriosis, or water in the Fallopian tube (hydrosalpinx). All of these conditions require medical diagnoses.

MENOPAUSE AND YOUR LIBIDO

Your sex drive need not decline after menopause! The research clearly shows that women can enjoy sex throughout and beyond their menopausal years. In fact, many women develop an increased sex drive during their late forties and early fifties. Women who report an increased interest in sex at this age often say it's the result of the simple fact that their children have finally grown up, leaving the women more time and energy to devote to their own needs, including their sexual needs. Other women say that freedom from the fear of an unwanted pregnancy is the reason for the unleashing of their sexual desires.

There may even be a biological reason why some women's libido increases around the time of menopause. Researchers have found a higher testosterone-to-estrogen ratio in postmenopausal women, due to the fact that estrogen levels fall while testosterone levels stay the same or sometimes even increase after menopause. This can cause an increase in sexual desire, because it is the hormone testosterone that is responsible for libido in women as well as in men.

Kinsey's research has shown that women who have a happy sex life before menopause are highly likely to continue to enjoy sex after it. But women who have not enjoyed sex throughout their lives, for whatever reasons, may use advancing age—or menopause—as an excuse to stop having any sex at all. If you find yourself in this latter group you may want to get professional counseling from a trained and accredited therapist. It is never too late to begin to enjoy the physical and emotional pleasures of sex.

• • •

"During this whole crisis year I have had a very high off-and-on libido, which surprised the heck out of me. I mean, I thought what could be better? But I also wonder, is this the last stop before the desert?"

• • •

CHANGES IN SEXUAL AROUSAL

Although your sex drive can remain unchanged after menopause, your body will respond somewhat differently during the act of lovemaking than it did when you were younger. It's already been noted in this chapter that the vagina requires more sexual stimulation after menopause to become fully lubricated. Here are some of the other changes in sexual response that occur after menopause:

- During sexual arousal, lubrication and swelling occur because blood flow out of the genitals is slowed by constriction of the blood vessels, a process known as *vasocongestion*. After menopause, less blood flows to the genitals. As a result, there may be less engorgement of the clitoris, vagina, and other tissues associated with sexual stimulation. This can contribute to a more subdued feeling of arousal. Some women notice it; others don't.
- After menopause, the breast does not increase as much in size during sexual arousal. In younger women, the breast can increase in size by one-fifth to one-fourth during sexual arousal. This is caused by a rush of blood to the tiny veins of the breast. After menopause, there is little or no increase in breast size during lovemaking. This should cause you no concern, however, for it will not affect your breasts' sensitivity to being stroked and touched. Also, it should be noted that after a woman of *any* age has breastfed a child, her breasts rarely show any significant increase in size during lovemaking.
- The sex flush—the measleslike rash that sometimes spreads over a woman's breasts and other body surfaces just before orgasm—is not as frequent or as long-lasting after menopause. Again, you needn't be concerned about this change. The lack of such a flush during sexual arousal will not affect your sexual enjoyment.
- The vagina does not expand as much during sexual arousal. But, as noted earlier, it still remains large enough to accommodate lovemaking.

SEX AFTER HYSTERECTOMY

Some women who enter menopause as a result of a hysterectomy report that their sexual pleasure decreases after the operation. For a long time, doctors believed that such reports were all psychological. Recent research, however, has revealed that there may be sound physiological reasons why hysterectomies adversely affect sexual pleasure for some women. With the uterus gone, for example, less tissue gets engorged with blood during sexual arousal. For some women, this means a reduced sensation of sexual stimulation. Many women also receive sexual pleasure from pressure strokes on the cervix by their partner's penis or fingers. After a hysterectomy, with the cervix removed, some women may find this aspect notably absent, although orgasm is still achievable.

If a woman's ovaries are removed as well as her uterus, she may also experience a loss of libido. The ovaries, along with the adrenal glands, produce small amounts of androgens—the "male" hormones responsible for libido in women as well as in men. When the ovaries are gone, androgen levels may drop to a point where libido is affected. For this reason, many doctors are now beginning to question the once-prevalent practice of routinely removing ovaries during a hysterectomy. And when the ovaries are removed, many doctors prescribe a regimen of combined conjugated estrogens with small amounts of testosterone to help a woman's libido return to normal. Women who note that their libido has not returned to normal may ask for this prescription.

For many women, however, having a hysterectomy actually enhances their sexual pleasure. The severe bleeding or pain that these women experienced before their hysterectomies—and that kept them from enjoying sex—is, of course, gone after the operation. With the pain gone, sex can become a pleasurable experience once again.

*   *   *

"Sex for me after hysterectomy was scary. My doctor said we could do it a week after surgery, but to expect some spotting. Well, I sure did bleed that first time, but except for that, it's been fine."

*   *   *

Should You Take Testosterone?   In recent years, more and more women are taking supplemental testosterone as they pass through their menopausal years. They have heard, either from friends or from their doctors, many positive testimonials about testosterone—most notably that it increases the libido and makes sex more enjoyable. Some people claim that testosterone supplements can also relieve depression and insomnia and increase self-confidence, among other things.

You should know that all of these claims are controversial. Furthermore, taking testosterone supplements, like any other hormone therapy, is not without its side effects and health risks.

Testosterone is generally known as the "male" sex hormone. It is found in much higher levels in men than in women. Even at their peak production of the hormone, women generally have about one-tenth the testosterone level found in men. In men, testosterone is responsible for sexual maturation and the "side effects" of that maturation, including deepening of the voice and development of a beard. Testosterone also builds muscles, which is partly why men generally have greater muscle development than women. Until recently, the role of testosterone in women's health was largely ignored. But the hormone appears to build muscles and burn fat cells in women just as it does in men, only at a lower intensity. In both sexes, testosterone appears to influence the limbic system, a group of brain structures that help regulate emotion. Research has also shown that high levels of testosterone in both men and women can instigate sexual desire.

Testosterone is manufactured mainly in men's testes and women's ovaries, although the adrenal glands of both sexes also produce the hormone. At menopause, the amount of testosterone produced in the ovaries declines, although most women's adrenal glands continue to produce the hormone well into old age. During the past decade or so, several studies have attempted to examine what effect testosterone supplements would have on the physical, emotional, and sexual lives of women whose ovaries were no longer producing the hormone and women who have had their ovaries surgically removed. Most of these studies found that women who take testosterone along with estrogen have higher levels of sexual desire and arousal. Some have also found that women taking the testosterone-estrogen combination score better on tests that measure overall psychological well-being.

These studies have their critics, however. The critics point out that the best of these studies were conducted on women whose ovaries were surgically removed. To date, no well-controlled testosterone study has been done using women who experienced menopause naturally, without surgery. Also, the dose of testosterone used in some of these studies was very high—high enough, in fact, to cause virilizing side effects, such as deepening of the voice and the growth of facial hair. Even at lower doses, testosterone can cause oily skin and acne.

Furthermore, other studies on the female libido have tended to contradict the idea that giving postmenopausal women testosterone would have that big an impact on their sex lives. New research has shown that women's libido does not increase at mid-cycle of the menstrual cycle, when testosterone levels are at their peak, but rather right before or after menstruation, when the levels are at their lowest. Still other studies indicate that testosterone may increase sexual arousal, but not sexual pleasure, among postmenopausal women who take it in supplementary form.

The Food and Drug Administration has not approved testosterone therapy for treating low libido in women. One of the agency's concerns about using the hormone for this purpose is the possibility that it may raise the risk of heart disease. Testosterone has been shown to lower HDL cholesterol levels in men. (HDL is the "good" cholesterol that appears to help protect against heart disease.) However, in studies of women taking low doses of testosterone along with estrogen, HDL levels did not decrease, but actually increased. It appears from these studies that estrogen's positive HDL is not overrun by low doses of testosterone.

Experts on human sexuality point out that a decrease in libido is a frequent side effect of depression. If you find that your desire for sex drops after menopause, you should thoroughly explore getting psychological counseling before taking testosterone. If you do decide to take a testosterone supplement, you and your physicians should monitor your use of the hormone carefully for side effects. Have your cholesterol checked regularly. Also, be aware that the hormone's masculinizing effects—facial hair growth, lowering of voice—can be permanent. That means that these effects can stay with you even after you discontinue the drug.

• • •

"I think our culture tells us that once you're of menopausal age you're of no value because somehow you're not going to be able to have sex. You get the message that somehow the end of having periods is the end of having sex. Where does that come from? Who ever said that?"

• • •

MEN CHANGE, TOO

Men also experience changes in their sexual response as they age. These changes, like those experienced by women, need not decrease a couple's enjoyment of sex, although they may require the couple to make some minor adjustments during lovemaking.

Sometime during their middle years, men begin to need more time to obtain an erection—several minutes instead of several seconds. Their ejaculation becomes less forceful and shorter in duration, and they tend to lose an erection more quickly following orgasm. Older men also have a longer refractory period, the length of time after an erection before the next erection is possible. This "waiting" period can increase from several minutes in youth to several hours in middle age to several days in old age.

It's not surprising, therefore, that many men begin to worry in middle age that they are becoming impotent. In most cases, however, these worries are unnecessary. Enjoyment from sex need not decrease—for either partner—as age increases. In fact, the physical changes that accompany age can sometimes make sex more pleasurable. Older men, for example, are less likely to ejaculate prematurely, which can extend lovemaking for both partners.

POSTMENOPAUSAL VAGINITIS

As estrogen levels fall, the acid/alkaline balance in the vagina changes. Before menopause, the pH of most women's vagina is usually about 4.5 to 5, which is a fairly acid environment. After menopause, the vagina typically has a more alkaline pH of about 7. The more alkaline the environment of the vagina, the more vulnerable it is to infection—which is why postmenopausal women are prone to vaginitis.

The term *vaginitis* really refers to several different diseases, all of which cause an inflammation of the vagina. Trichomonas, yeast, and hemophilus bacterial infections are the most common forms of vaginitis. Their main symptoms are burning, itching, and an excessive vaginal discharge, which may have a bad odor.

Although a bout with vaginitis will not seriously threaten your general health, it can cause considerable pain and discomfort. Vaginitis is also a stubborn disease; recurrences are common. Be sure to take all of the medication prescribed by your physician. If you don't, some of the diseases' stronger organisms may survive treatment and eventually reproduce in sufficient quantities to cause a recurrence of symptoms.

Of course, the best treatment is prevention. Here are some self-care suggestions that may help you prevent vaginitis:

- Limit the amount of sugar in your diet. Sugar can make the environment in your vagina more alkaline and thus more susceptible to an infection. If you have diabetes, try to keep closer control of your blood glucose levels.
- Avoid commercial douches. Douching can alter the pH balance in your vagina; it also removes the normal secretions that coat and protect the vagina. Some women do report success in treating mild infections with yogurt douches, however. The yogurt must contain the active live bacteria Lactobacillus acidophilus. Most commercial yogurts do not contain a live strain of this bacteria. You can buy acidophilus in a drugstore or

health food store and add it to commercial yogurt (about two table-spoons of powder to ½ cup of plain yogurt). Insert the yogurt into the vagina using a vaginal applicator. To help keep the yogurt in the vagina for at least an hour or two, use a tampon or wear a sanitary napkin to catch any of the yogurt that may leak out. Or you can douche with the yogurt at night, right before you go to bed; then rinse it out the next morning.

If you prefer to douche frequently, after lovemaking or periods of bleeding, use a dilute vinegar solution consisting of one tablespoon of white vinegar to whatever size of douche kit water container you have. This restores the normal vaginal pH and rinses out discharge, creams, jellies, and old blood.

- At the first sign of a mild infection—perhaps some itching in the vagina or a change in the thickness or color of your vaginal discharge—take nightly sitz baths in either a saltwater solution (½ cup table salt in a bathtub of water) or a vinegar solution (½ cup of white vinegar in a few inches of warm water). The salt water will help kill the invading organisms; the vinegar solution will help restore the pH balance of your vagina and discourage further bacteria growth.
- To avoid spreading bacteria from the rectum into the vagina, always wipe from the front to the back after urinating. Avoid contamination of the vulva with stool by wiping the anus last and in a backward direction.
- Wear cotton underpants and pantyhose with cotton sewn into the crotch. By permitting air to circulate, cotton clothing helps keep the vaginal area dry and thus makes it a less inviting breeding site for bacteria.
- Avoid using feminine hygiene sprays and bath soaps and oils; they can irritate the vulva and vaginal opening and can also mask the telltale odor of vaginitis, which may keep you from seeking prompt treatment.
- If you develop a new or recurrent odor, or have spotting or staining not related to sexual activity, consult your doctor. One of the warning signs of an early cancer in a postmenopausal woman is a new malodorous or bloody discharge.
- Get enough rest! If you let your body get run down, you will be more susceptible to any kind of infection, including vaginitis.

POSTMENOPAUSAL CYSTITIS

The thinning of the vaginal walls that occurs after menopause can leave the bladder and urethra (the tube lying next to the vagina that lets urine out from the bladder) more vulnerable to being bruised and irritated when the penis or fingers are thrust repeatedly into the vagina during sexual activity. A bruised urethra and bladder can become inflamed, causing pain and frequent urination—a condition known as interstitial cystitis. Although this can occur after sexual activity at any age, it occurs more easily and frequently during the menopausal years.

• • •

"I don't know if there's any connection to menopause, but I feel like it takes longer to climax. I'm assuming there's some kind of connection, but I don't know."

• • •

Bacterial cystitis—the kind caused by a bacterial infection—may also become more frequent after menopause. The bladder and urethra lose some of their tone, making it easier for bacteria to enter. Also, the urethra produces less fluid after menopause, which diminishes its ability to cleanse itself of bacteria.

If you are experiencing any symptoms of cystitis—burning on urination, an almost continual urge to urinate, low abdominal pain and backache, or pain with sexual activity—be sure to seek medical care. You can also take the following preventive steps to avoid a recurrence of the infection:

• Get yourself to a bathroom as soon as you feel the urge to urinate. Retaining small volumes of urine in the bladder appears to be a key factor in urinary infections. One study conducted by researchers at the State University of New York at Stony Brook found that the single most important difference between women who had frequent urinary tract infections and those who had never had such an infection was when they urinated. Women who experienced frequent infections were often noted to have waited an hour or more to urinate after initially feeling the urge, while those women who remained infection-free urinated as soon as they felt the urge.

• Be sure to empty your bladder before and after making love. A full bladder is more easily irritated during intercourse. Also, by urinating soon after making love you can "flush out" any bacteria that may have entered the urethra during sexual activity.

• Avoid sexual activity that irritates the urethra or that puts pressure on the bladder.

• Drink plenty of water every day—an 8-ounce glass every two or three hours. Also, drink cranberry juice; it contains hippuric acid, which inhibits the growth of bacteria.

• Follow the tips for avoiding vaginitis (see pages 108–109). They will also help prevent cystitis.

- Finally, if none of the above seems to work and your cystitis keeps returning, you may want to try a low-dose vaginal estrogen cream. Use it nightly for the first month, then every other night, then twice weekly or as often as needed.

PROBLEMS WITH INCONTINENCE

As you pass through your menopausal years, you may find yourself going to the bathroom more often than when you were younger. Or, you may find your body leaking small amounts of urine when you sneeze, cough, laugh, or exercise. As one woman good-humoredly told her doctor: "I was laughing so hard that tears ran down my legs!" This problem—known as urinary incontinence—is quite common, but, unfortunately, many women feel too ashamed to talk about it.

Urinary incontinence has a variety of causes. The muscles of the pelvic floor and abdomen sometimes weaken with age, particularly in women who have borne several children or who smoke. In fact, using cigarettes increases your risk of urinary incontinence sixfold. This loss of muscle tone can lead to "stress incontinence," leakage that occurs when a sudden movement (such as a sneeze or cough) puts increased pressure on the bladder. Repeated bladder infections can also produce incontinence, as can several illnesses and physical disorders, such as diabetes, Parkinson's disease, and bladder cancer. If you are experiencing a problem with incontinence you should bring it to your physician's attention so that it can be properly diagnosed and treated.

Women who have had a hysterectomy sometimes experience incontinence either because their urinary structures have begun to drop down after bearing many children or because the removal of the uterus has left the bladder and urethra without support. In rare cases, the urinary tissues may become damaged during the surgery itself. In addition, the drop in estrogen levels that occurs within the body after a total hysterectomy or around the time of natural menopause can lead to changes in the urethra similar to those in the vagina, exacerbating incontinence problems or sometimes causing them to occur for the first time. For this reason, physicians sometimes prescribe estrogen pills or creams to menopausal-aged women for bladder-control problems. Low-dose estrogen creams have been shown to be effective in relieving incontinence in half of all women treated. Because of the health risks associated with estrogen drugs, however, you may wish to try some of the following self-help actions first:

- If you are overweight (see the chart on page 152), try losing some weight. Women who are overweight are more likely to have problems with incontinence. It may be that having extra fat in the abdomen puts too much stress on the bladder and urethra and causes them to sag down and leak.
- Review with your physician or pharmacist any prescription or over-the-counter drugs you may be taking. Some drugs, such as antihistamines and tranquilizers, can cause or aggravate bladder-control problems.
- Watch your diet. Some foods—such as citrus fruit juices and spicy foods—can irritate the bladder and worsen the problem of leakage. Also, cut back on your consumption of caffeine or alcohol; better yet, eliminate those two substances from your diet altogether.
- Follow the suggestions for avoiding cystitis on pages 110–111. Bladder infections can cause incontinence.
- Finally, add exercises that specifically strengthen your abdomen and pelvic muscles to your regular exercise program—especially Kegel exercises, which will help you strengthen the pubococcygeal muscle that supports the bladder and uterus. (See the box on page 113.) And if you haven't started a daily exercise regimen, now's the time to begin!

BIRTH CONTROL—WHAT TO USE
UNTIL YOU'RE SURE
YOU'VE HAD YOUR LAST PERIOD

As you approach menopause, your menstrual periods may become quite irregular—sometimes heavy, sometimes very light, and sometimes even nonexistent for a month or two. Such a confusing pattern can be misleading and can make you mistakenly believe that you are pregnant.

•   •   •

"It's kind of difficult to say whether I've noticed any change sexually because my sexual encounters are fewer and farther between than they were before the surgery. The times I have had sex I haven't noticed any change at all, but I've been on estrogen so that might help it."

•   •   •

Of course, it can also be quite possible that you *are* pregnant—if you truly haven't experienced menopause yet. Although fertility rates decline rapidly for women after the age of 40, many women in their forties do become pregnant, some for the first time. Non-artificially inseminated pregnancy after the age of 50 is very rare; although in 1956, a 57-year-old woman gave birth to a girl in Glendale, California, making her the oldest naturally pregnant woman on record. New *in vitro* fertilization techniques, however, appear to have made it possible for more older women—*even those who have gone through menopause*—to bear children. In 1990, researchers at the University of Southern California reported in the *New England Journal of Medicine* that they had successfully implanted fertilized eggs from three donors in seven postmenopausal women 40 to 44 years old. Six pregnancies resulted. One ended in miscarriage, another in a stillborn birth, and five healthy babies were born, including a pair of twins. Since then, dozens of postmenopausal women around the world—many in their fifties—have used the new *in vitro* techniques to successfully bear children, often for the first time in their lives. As one doctor noted, "The limits on childbearing years are now anyone's guess; perhaps they will have more to do with the stamina required for labor and 2 A.M. feedings than with reproductive function."

If you are over 40 and feel you might be pregnant, you should see your physician as soon as possible. Women at the earliest and latest years of the reproductive span (ages 13 to 25 and 40 to 50) are at increased risk of

---

DO YOUR DAILY KEGELS

During the late 1940s, Dr. Arnold Kegel, a University of California surgeon, designed a special exercise to help women who complained of leaking urine. This exercise—known now as the Kegel—helps strengthen the pubococcygeal (PC) muscle, which supports the bladder and urethra. This is the muscle you use to stop the flow of urine in midstream, or to "hold back" on a bowel movement. It also may be important to keep your PC muscle strong during your menopausal years to avoid potential bladder-control problems.

A well-toned PC muscle can also contribute to increased sexual satisfaction, as this is the muscle that rhythmically contracts during orgasm. In fact, this muscle is sometimes called the "love muscle."

To do your Kegels, think of your pelvic floor as an elevator in a five-story building. As you slowly tighten the PC muscle, imagine that the elevator is moving up floor by floor. At each "floor," count to five before tightening the muscle further. When you reach the top, go down floor by floor again, relaxing the PC muscle gradually.

Try to do at least five Kegels in a row, several times a day. Fortunately, this is an exercise that can be done anytime, anywhere—at your desk at work, while waiting in line at the supermarket, while watching television, or even while making love.

---

developing a type of tumor of the placental tissue that mimics many of the signs of pregnancy.

Experts recommend that women who wish not to get pregnant continue using a birth control method for one full year after they have experienced what they believe is their final period. This will ensure that ovulation has completely ceased. You can also have your FSH blood levels checked. If your FSH is more than 50 units, your chance of conceiving is almost nil.

The birth control method you choose for your forties may not be the same one you used in your twenties or thirties. As you age, you must take different factors into consideration when selecting contraception. For example, if you are having heavy or long periods, as some women do as they approach menopause, you will not want a method, such as an IUD, that might make the bleeding even heavier.

What method, then, is the right one for you? Here are your current options, with their pros and cons for women at midlife.

The Pill

Most experts used to discourage women over age 40 from using birth control pills for contraception. The risks for older women on high-dose oral contraceptives was just too great. Studies showed that for every 100,000 women over the age of 40 who used the Pill, about 32 died from related complications, usually a heart attack or a stroke. That compared with only two deaths per 100,000 Pill users in the 30 to 34 age range.

If you smoked, the danger was even greater. Of every 100,000 women over the age of 40 who smoked, about 117 could be expected to die as a direct result of taking the Pill. That was simply too great a risk to take for effective contraception.

Today, however, you can receive birth control pills that are at doses as low as one-sixth that of the earlier prescriptions. In addition, the synthetic formulations of the hormones used in the Pill today are considered more cardiac-friendly. These low-dose pills can be used by nonsmoking women right up to the menopause.

By the way, taking birth control pills will not speed up or postpone your menopause. The estrogen in the pills, however, can mask some of the signs of menopause, especially hot flashes. So if you go through menopause while on the Pill, you may not be aware of that fact until you go off it and you begin experiencing hot flashes, which may happen within days of taking your last tablet.

IUDs (Intrauterine Devices)

Because it has been linked with a greater risk of pelvic inflammatory disease (PID) and, thus, infertility, the IUD is now being marketed to older women for whom infertility, presumably, is less of a concern. Still, a bout with PID is not a minor matter for a woman of any age, particularly since it frequently ends in hospitalization. So if you decide to use an IUD, be sure to report signs of problems—lower abdominal pain, fever, chills, cramping, and unusual vaginal discharge—to your physician immediately.

The most common problem reported by women who use IUDs is increased bleeding. Some 15 to 20 percent of women who are fitted with an IUD discontinue using the device for this reason alone. For midlife women, whose periods may already be heavy or prolonged, the thought of even more bleeding is enough to rule out the IUD as a contraceptive option. If you should use an IUD, be sure to report any change in your bleeding pattern to your physician. The bleeding may have nothing to do with the IUD but may instead be a warning sign of an underlying health problem, most notably cancer of the uterus. Also, be aware that an IUD is recommended only for women who are in a monogamous relationship (and thus less likely to be exposed to sexually transmitted diseases) and who have no prior history of PID.

Barrier Methods
(Diaphragm, Cervical Cap, Contraceptive
Sponge, and Condom)

These are the methods of birth control most often recommended for women at midlife. Studies have shown that these methods become more effective as women age. Some of this increased effectiveness is no doubt due to the fact that older women are less fertile—and thus run less risk of becoming pregnant, whether or not they use contraception. Older women also tend to be more knowledgeable about their bodies and thus more confident about using these methods. And they are more motivated— which is really the key to the effectiveness of the various barrier methods. Several studies have shown, for example, that when a diaphragm is fitted and used properly, it can be up to 98 percent effective in preventing pregnancy—essentially as effective as an IUD or the Pill. The condom can be up to 97 percent effective when used exactly as directed; and when used together with contraceptive foam its effectiveness rate climbs even higher—to almost 100 percent.

For women who are experiencing dryness in the vagina as they approach menopause, the contraceptive cream, jelly, and foam used with the barrier methods offer an extra benefit—increased lubrication. They also provide some protection against sexually transmitted diseases.

• • •

"My sexual drive has certainly changed since my hysterectomy. I don't have any problem with actual dryness, but I miss the days during the month when my whole system seemed geared toward desire. I feel I have lost that core, animalistic desire. Making love now comes from the emotion of love, deeply from love, which is very, very different from when I was younger. I just don't have that va-va-va-voom any more. But I have it in a different way. I've established a new, very soft, sensual relationship with my husband. It's just different."

• • •

The diaphragm does have its disadvantages for women at midlife. As women grow older, they are more likely to develop certain medical conditions—a prolapsed uterus, a large uterine fibroid, or a bladder that protrudes through the vaginal wall (called a cystocele)—that may make it difficult, if not impossible, to use a diaphragm, cervical cap, or contraceptive sponge. The diaphragm has also been found to make women more susceptible to urinary tract infections, which, as noted earlier in this chapter, midlife women are already more prone to get. The diaphragm contributes to urinary infections by pressing its front rim on the urethra, making it difficult to empty the bladder completely after intercourse. If you suspect your diaphragm may be playing a role in your urinary infections, you may wish to discuss with your doctor the possibility of being fitted with a smaller diaphragm. Also, be sure you urinate immediately after sexual activity.

Sterilization

This is now the leading method of contraception for couples in the United States. Close to 100 percent effective, sterilization has become safer, less expensive, and easier in recent years. Male sterilization, or vasectomy, is particularly easy; it takes about half an hour and can be performed in a doctor's office under local anesthetic. Female sterilization, which requires general anesthesia, is a more involved procedure, although it is now often done in a hospital on an outpatient basis. During the procedure, the fallopian tubes are cut, tied, or sealed to prevent passage of eggs between the ovaries and the uterus. Besides being a highly effective form of birth control, female sterilization has been shown to reduce the risk of ovarian cancer by half.

Sterilization should be considered permanent. This, of course, is usually not a concern for women in their forties. Female sterilization is a surgical procedure, however, which means complications, such as severe bleeding or infection, occasionally occur. If you are close to menopause, using barrier methods for a short time longer may be preferable to the risk and expense of a sterilization operation.

Natural Family Planning

None of the natural family planning methods of birth control—the calendar method, the temperature method, or the cervical mucus method—are recommended for midlife women. This is because the closer you get to menopause, the more difficulty you will have recognizing when you are ovulating. Ovulation will occur erratically, and you will have less secretion of cervical mucus and thus are more likely to miscalculate and conceive an unintended pregnancy.

6

UNDERSTANDING OSTEOPOROSIS

I had lunch with a 98-year-old woman. . . . Sparkly, vivacious, alive, with a lightness of step, she didn't fit my stereotype of geriatric at 98. I sensed that the words of the American writer Gertrude Stein applied to her: "We are always the same age inside." And that age is not defined by a calendar.

—Judy Mahle Lutter

Most of us associate osteoporosis with old age. When we hear the word, we tend to picture in our minds a thin, frail woman in her eighties with a rounded, "dowager's hump" of a back. Or perhaps we envision an elderly relative or friend who broke a wrist or, more seriously, a hip as a result of a minor fall.

Most of us don't associate osteoporosis with midlife. Yet it is during our late thirties and forties that our bones begin to become less dense. By our fifties, this thinning of the bones may lead to a loss of teeth or wrist fractures. And as early as our mid-fifties, the bones in our spine may be so weak that they begin to fracture and compress, causing gradual curvature of the upper back (the infamous dowager's hump) and a loss in height.

Osteoporosis afflicts more women than men, partly because of the estrogen loss that occurs after menopause. Fortunately, however, osteoporosis is not an inevitable part of aging—or of menopause. Recent studies have shown that it may be preventable and even treatable. In this chapter, we'll take a look at this "silent disorder" and the steps you can take both before and after menopause to help keep your bones strong and fracture-free.

WHAT IS OSTEOPOROSIS?

Osteoporosis literally means "porous bones." It has also come to mean a disease that causes once sturdy bones to thin and weaken, leaving them susceptible to fracture. Yet how to use this definition to actually identify people with the disease is a matter of some controversy. Some osteoporosis researchers have defined osteoporosis as having a bone density that is significantly less than that found in the average young adult. But, as the Women's Health Network points out, that would mean that almost half of all white women over the age of 50 have a disease—osteoporosis. The Network argues—rather persuasively—that it would be more accurate to describe low bone mass as just one of several risk factors for osteoporosis, not as the disease itself. The Network also contends that it would be more appropriate to determine who has "low" bone density by comparing older women to each other, much like we do when determining "high" cholesterol levels. "High" cholesterol in an older adult is ascertained by comparing that person's cholesterol level with the average levels of other older adults, not with those of young adults. Fortunately, many bone density reports now give results in both formats: They will compare your current bone density with an age- and ethnicity-matched group of women as well as with the "average" 35-year-old woman. Make sure you receive your report in both formats.

For women who truly do have osteoporosis and who suffer fractures as a result, the condition can be debilitating. In the United States, osteoporosis is associated with an estimated 1.3 million bone fractures in women each year, including about 500,000 fractures of the vertebrae or spine, 200,000 of the hip, and 170,000 of the wrist. Hip fractures, which usually occur after age 75, are more dangerous—and expensive—than all other osteoporotic fractures combined. The risk of hip fracture is about 16 percent for white women and about 6 percent for African-American women. A woman's chance of dying increases by 12 to 20 percent in the year following a hip fracture, mostly due to the development of blood clots or pneumonia.

The medical costs associated with osteoporosis are staggering: an estimated $7 billion to $10 billion a year. These costs are expected to rise dramatically as the Baby Boom generation ages.

WHAT CAUSES BONE LOSS?

Our bones, like many other tissues of the body, are constantly regenerating themselves. Old bone is torn down, or "resorbed," and replaced with new bone. This continuous process is called remodeling, and it enables bones to remain strong. It also helps the body keep a constant level of calcium in the blood, which is needed for such essential biological tasks as the beating of the heart and the clotting of blood. Calcium is the stuff that makes bones hard. Ninety-nine percent of the body's calcium is found in the bones and teeth. When blood calcium drops below a certain level, the body takes calcium from the bones.

When we are young, new bone is formed faster than old bone is resorbed. Although our bones stop growing around age 18, they keep increasing in density until about age 35, when bone mass reaches its peak. This is when our bones are most dense and strong. During our late thirties—especially if we smoke, do not exercise, or ingest inadequate calcium—our bones begin to lose calcium faster than they can replace it. The bones become less dense. Both men and women experience this gradual change in bone mass as they age. For women, the loss speeds up for the first three to seven years after menopause and then proceeds more slowly.

Our bones become less dense as we age for another reason as well: The older we get, the less efficient our bodies become at absorbing calcium from food. For women, this problem begins around age 45; for men, around age 60.

• • •

"My sister, who is a few years older than I, has begun breaking bones and has been told she has nearly a 50 percent bone loss. They said that if she hadn't been on hormones she would be in a wheelchair. But she always believed she could never be too thin and has subjected herself to very strict dieting throughout her life. Eating any dairy products was an anathema to her."

• • •

Estrogen's Role in Osteoporosis

Estrogen appears to influence bone loss in women. When present in sufficient quantities in the body, estrogen seems to slow or halt the loss of bone. The hormone appears to improve the absorption of calcium from the intestinal tract and to help keep higher levels of estrogen in the blood.

Estrogen's role in protecting against bone loss makes sense biologically. During the years when she is capable of bearing a child, a woman needs a good store of calcium to draw upon in case she becomes pregnant and must provide extra calcium for a developing fetus. After menopause, this need no longer exists.

Other Factors

Although the drop in estrogen that accompanies menopause is a factor in osteoporosis, it is not the only one—otherwise the condition would affect women equally in all cultures around the world and would not affect men. Medical anthropologists have found otherwise. Osteoporosis is twenty-four times higher in the United States than in some other countries. People living in Singapore, for example, have very low rates of osteoporotic fractures, as do the Maori of New Zealand. And anthropologist Susan Brown has described some Africans living traditional lifestyles as being "almost immune" to the disease.

Evidence also indicates that osteoporosis is a relatively recent condition of Western women. In 1993, scientists examined the femurs, or thighbones, of 87 female skeletons who had been buried in a London graveyard between 1729 and 1852. The women had ranged in age from 15 to 89 years old at the time of their deaths. After dividing the skeletons into premenopausal (under 45) and postmenopausal (over 45) groups, the scientists looked for signs of bone loss. They then compared their findings to the bone profiles of 300 living British women. The scientists found that, unlike the bones of modern women, the 18th and 19th century premenopausal skeletons showed no sign of bone loss at all. Furthermore, the postmenopausal skeletons had lost bone density after menopause, but at a somewhat lower rate than their late 20th century counterparts. "Because there was no premenopausal loss," noted one of the scientists, "these women reached menopause much better off than do modern women and were therefore much less likely to drop to bone-density levels low enough for fractures to occur."

The idea that osteoporosis is *only* a female disease also crumbles under the weight of the anthropological evidence. Although men in the United States suffer one-sixth as many spinal fractures and approximately one-half as many hip fractures as women, in other parts of the world—for example, in Hong Kong, some areas of the former Yugoslavia, and South African Bantu communities—men have the same *or higher* rate of osteoporosis and fractures as women.

So what could explain the excessive high rate of osteoporosis in women in the United States, Britain, and other Western industrialized countries? The typical Western diet, to begin with. The amount of calcium in a person's diet can affect bone mass. Adults lose calcium daily in their urine and feces and, in smaller amounts, through their skin. This calcium must be replaced in the diet or the body will break down bone to get the mineral. Sadly, Western diets tend to be low in calcium and high in

---

DISEASES AND DRUGS THAT
CAN WEAKEN BONES

The following diseases and drugs can accelerate bone loss and lead to osteoporosis:

- Certain prescription and over-the-counter drugs, including aluminum-containing antacids, corticosteroids, and blood pressure medications, such as hydrochlorothiazides.
- Diseases of the small intestine, liver, or pancreas that impair the body's ability to absorb calcium from the intestine.
- Certain kinds of cancer, such as lymphoma, leukemia, and multiple myeloma.
- Chronic diarrhea caused by ulcerative colitis or Crohn's disease.
- Surgical removal of part of the stomach or small intestine.
- A condition known as idiopathic hypercalciuria in which excessive amounts of calcium are excreted in the urine.
- Nicotine, from smoking.

---

calcium-depleting ingredients, particularly alcohol, caffeine, and protein. Women in Western societies also tend to have less exposure to sunlight, which helps the body make vitamin D, an essential nutrient for calcium absorption.

Western culture also does not encourage women to be physically active, and physical activity—or the lack of it—can directly affect bone density. People bedridden with paralysis or illness, for example, experience a rapid and severe calcium loss from their bones. The tendency of people to become less active as they age may, therefore, contribute to the thinning of their bones. Conversely, recent studies have shown that exercise—specifically, weight-bearing exercise—can help keep bones stronger longer.

Your peak bone mass—the amount of bone you had before it began to lose its density—will influence the quality and quantity of your bones later in life. The more bone mass you start with when your bones reach their peak density—which is around age 35 for European-American women and around age 42 for African-American women—the less likely it is that you will develop osteoporosis later.

WHO'S AT RISK?

Experts have identified a variety of factors that can increase your risk of osteoporosis. These factors are discussed in the following sections.

Being a Woman

In many Western cultures, osteoporosis is six to eight times more common in women than in men. This is partly because women have 30 percent less bone mass at age 35 than men. Also, as noted earlier in this chapter, the drop in estrogen that follows menopause seems to speed up bone loss in women.

Early Menopause (Before Age 45)

The earlier a woman goes through menopause, whether naturally or as a result of surgery, the greater her chance of developing osteoporosis. This is because she will spend more years deprived of estrogen's protective effect on bone.

Light Skin Color

The lighter your complexion, the greater your risk. Some experts estimate that one-fourth of all white women experience at least one osteoporosis-related fracture by age 65. Red- or blond-haired women of northern European ancestry are especially susceptible to developing the condition. Women of Asian descent are also believed to be at greater risk for osteoporosis, although not enough data have been collected yet to confirm this. Osteoporosis is rare in black women, who have 10 percent more bone mass than white women and whose bodies may produce more calcitonin, the hormone that strengthens bones.

Small Bone Structure

Women who are short and small-boned are more at risk for osteoporosis than those with larger frames, because they have less bone to lose.

Low Weight

Women with low body fat (less than 15 percent of their weight) put less stress on their bones; thus their bones do not become as dense. In addition, thin women have fewer fat cells in which to convert the hormone androstenedione into estrogen after menopause (see chapter 1). Thus they have less estrogen circulating in their bodies—and protecting against bone loss—than heavier women.

Women who are overweight should not use this as an excuse to stay overweight, however. Carrying around excess weight puts the menopausal woman at greater risk for a variety of ailments, including heart disease, cancer, and painful arthritis. In some cases, it may actually increase the risk of fractures in old age by putting too much stress on bones.

Both underweight and overweight women should strive to attain their desirable weight. (To find out how much you should weigh for your height and age, see the chart on page 152.)

Low-Calcium Diet

A diet that has been chronically low in calcium appears to increase the risk of osteoporosis. Studies have found that women who consume large amounts of calcium-rich foods throughout their lives have more bone at midlife than women whose calcium intakes were low.

Still, the link between a low-calcium diet and osteoporosis is not clear. More research is needed. In the meantime, scientists believe other risk factors—particularly skin color, body build, and early menopause—play a greater role in the development of this disease.

Lack of Exercise

Women who avoid weight-bearing activities—the kind of activities that put stress on the bones—increase their risk of developing osteoporosis. Our bones need good, regular workouts to stay strong.

Family History of Osteoporosis

Some research seems to indicate that osteoporosis is hereditary. One study found that women whose mothers had a hip fracture are twice as likely to suffer a similar fracture as other women. Some researchers believe, however, that it may be lifestyle factors—a low-calcium diet, an aversion to physical exercise—rather than a genetic predisposition to weak bones that women with osteoporosis inherit from their mothers.

AN OSTEOPOROSIS GENE?

Scientists believe they may have found a gene that plays a role in the risk of developing osteoporosis. The newly identified gene appears to make it easier for bone cells to absorb calcium by slightly altering the receptors—or docking sites—for vitamin D on the cells' walls. Australian researchers have found that women with genes that produce the most calcium-absorbing vitamin D receptors have denser bones than other women. These women tended to avoid fractures until age 71 compared to age 63 for women whose genes produce more passive receptors.

If the existence of an "osteoporosis gene" is confirmed, you may one day be able to take a simple genetic test to predict your chances of developing weak bones. All women, however, will still need to make sure they follow a lifestyle that keeps their bones as strong as possible into old age.

Too Much Caffeine or Alcohol

Although the research is not conclusive, heavy use of alcohol or caffeine appears to contribute to bone loss. Both of these substances act as diuretics, increasing the amount of calcium lost in the urine.

How much is too much? No one knows for sure, but it appears that a glass of wine or beer, or 1½ ounces of hard liquor daily probably do no damage to the bone. As for coffee, if you enjoy it, you may want to consider switching entirely to decaffeinated. Researchers in one study found that one cup of caffeinated coffee a day appears to increase the risk of hip fractures by 69 percent.

Yet you can have your coffee and drink it, too—as long as you also drink milk regularly. A recent study indicated that women who drank one 8-ounce glass of milk each day along with their two cups of coffee had bones that were 6.5 percent denser than those of women who downed the coffee, but not the milk. Still, your best bet for strong bones may be to cut out the caffeine altogether.

Smoking Cigarettes

Women who smoke experience menopause earlier than nonsmokers and thus are without estrogen's protective effect against bone loss for a longer period of time. By the time they reach old age, smokers have 20 to 30 percent less bone mass than nonsmokers. This means weaker bones and a greater risk of fractures.

Too Much Protein

Research suggests that a diet high in protein causes the body to excrete too much calcium in urine. Osteoporosis is more common in areas of the world where people eat a great deal of protein, especially animal protein. Even in the United States, low bone density has been shown to be more common among meat eaters than vegetarians. One study involving vegetarian and nonvegetarian women in southwestern Michigan found that although both groups had comparable bone mass at age 50, by age 80, the vegetarians had lost 18 percent of their bone mass while the nonvegetarians had lost 35 percent. Another study, this time in Florida, involving 150 vegetarian and nonvegetarian women aged 45 to 65, revealed that vegetarians have greater bone density and excrete less calcium in their urine than their meat-eating peers. Most Americans consume more protein than they need. Try to reduce your protein intake to no more than 15 percent of your total diet. (See chapter 7 for more information.)

No Pregnancies

When a woman is pregnant, she gets an extra surge of estrogen, which appears to enhance the body's absorption of calcium and build stronger bones. Because childless women do not experience this hormonal surge, they are believed to be at a somewhat higher risk for osteoporosis later in life.

Certain Medications

Some drugs, such as antiseizure medications, the high-blood pressure medication hydrochlorothiazide (HCTZ), and corticosteroids, which are commonly used to treat arthritis and asthma, can promote bone loss if taken in high doses or over a long period of time.

Excess Thyroid Hormone

Overproduction of this hormone, whether because of an overactive thyroid gland or excess treatment for an underactive gland, can speed bone loss.

HOW TO LOWER YOUR RISK

All women should take at least some steps to slow down the process of bone loss after menopause. Taking action is especially important if you have several of the risk factors listed earlier.

Preventing bone loss—or osteoporosis—falls into two general categories: exercising and getting enough of the right nutrients (and not too much of the wrong ones) in your diet. The earlier you begin these preventive measures, the more successful you will be in slowing or halting the disorder.

Yet it's important to remember that almost everyone who lives long enough gradually loses some bone mass. The fact that your bone density is lower than it was when you were younger does not mean you have a disease. Furthermore, not every women who has been identified as having osteoporosis suffers a bone fracture. Studies have shown that many factors other than bone density play a role in whether or not a postmenopausal woman—or an older man, for that matter—breaks a bone. These factors include the use of certain medications, a loss of muscle strength, impaired vision, and neurological conditions. All of these factors increase an older person's risk of falling—and falling is far and away the most common cause of hip fractures.

In other words, life-threatening fractures are not synonymous with osteoporosis. Not all women with low bone density have fractures, and not all women with fractures have low bone density. In fact, studies have shown only a modest relationship between bone density and the rate of hip fracture. One recent study found that *how* a woman falls is at least as important as her bone density in determining whether or not she breaks a hip. Falling to the side directly on the hip presents the greatest risk of hip fracture.

So although you want to keep your bones as strong as possible, your primary goal should be preventing falls, not just changing your bone density.

EXERCISING FOR STRONGER BONES

A growing number of studies indicates that exercise can increase bone mass. It's long been known that inactivity can lead to bone loss. People who become paralyzed as a result of a spinal-cord injury lose one-third of the trabecular part of their bones (the spongy inner part) within six months of the injury. Also, people who wear casts experience a decrease in bone density in the limb rendered immobile by the cast.

But can exercising rebuild weakened bones? Yes, according to some recent studies. For example, at the Washington University School of Medicine in St. Louis, Missouri, a group of 35 women between the ages of 55 and 70 were followed for twenty-two months. Some were placed in a sedentary control group; the others underwent exercise training, lasting from nine to twenty-two months. All the women took 1,500 milligrams of calcium daily.

At the end of nine months, the women in the exercising group had increased their bone mass by an average of 5.2 percent. At twenty-two months, this percentage had increased to an average of 6.1 percent.

By comparison, those women in the nonexercising group showed a *decrease* in bone mass of 1 percent.

Nor is it ever too late to begin exercising to build bones. One study compared a group of nursing-home patients who participated in exercise classes with another group who simply engaged in normal, everyday activities. The average age of both groups was 82. After three years, the exercise group experienced an average bone-mass increase of 4.2 percent, whereas the control group lost 2.5 percent.

Regular exercise, therefore, seems to increase bone mass. In addition, it appears that exercising is more effective at this task than taking calcium supplements. Indeed, many researchers believe that for calcium supplements to do any good, they must be accompanied by a regular exercise program.

What Type of Exercise Is Best?

The best exercises for building strong bones are "weight-bearing" ones— those that put stress on the bones. Walking, running, biking, aerobic dance, and cross-country skiing are good weight-bearing exercises for the spine and legs. Recent research has also shown that swimming, although not traditionally classified as a weight-bearing exercise, can also be effective in building strong bones.

The more strenuous the activity, the greater its effect on bone mass. Running, therefore, strengthens bones more than walking. But even light-to-moderate exercise can build stronger bones, according to recent studies. Researchers at Tufts University found that postmenopausal women who walked briskly an average of just one mile a day had a

7 percent higher bone density in their legs and a 4 percent higher bone density overall than women who didn't exercise. (Walking "briskly" was defined as walking a mile in about fifteen minutes.) This meant the walkers were losing bone mass much more slowly than they would have if they had chosen not to exercise.

Your fitness program should also include exercises that strengthen the bones of your shoulders, chest, and arms. Try carrying weights while walking or running; or, better yet, incorporate two or three weight-training sessions into your weekly exercise routine. In one recent study, postmenopausal women who worked out for a year on weight machines twice a week for 45 minutes each session improved the bone density in their legs and spine by 1 percent. This compared with a 2.5 percent *loss* in bone density in a "control" group of women who did not train. The women who worked out also improved their balance by 14 percent—a significant finding, because the better your balance, the less likely you are to fall and fracture a bone. In addition, weight training improved muscle strength in the exercising women's hips and spines by 36 to 76 percent and lowered their overall body fat.

For more information about getting started on a weight-bearing exercise program, see chapter 8.

TAKE STEPS TO PREVENT FALLING

Preventing a fall is an important—and often overlooked—strategy in reducing the risk of a life-threatening fracture. More than 90 percent of hip fractures among the elderly, for example, are the result of a fall.

So what can you do to protect yourself from falling as you grow older? First, if you are taking any medications, check to see if any of them cause impaired vision, confusion, or low blood pressure upon rising. Many falls can be avoided simply by stopping or changing a medication. Look up your medication in a drug resource book and talk to your doctor.

Also, check your home for hazards. Researchers have found that half of all falls are due to common obstacles in the home. Here are some steps you can take to make your home safer:

- Make sure the lighting in your home is neither too bright nor too dim, especially on stairways, where most falls occur.
- Use nonskid backing for rugs and nonskid strips or mats in the bathtub and shower and on uncarpeted steps.

- Make sure your stairways have handrails and install grab bars around the shower and toilet.
- If you have any unstable furniture, remove it from heavily trafficked areas of your home.
- Put brightly colored adhesive strips at door thresholds, the edges of steps, places where the floor changes height, and other sites where you might easily trip or lose your balance.
- Wear shoes that have low heels and nonslip soles.

Finally, exercise regularly to improve your leg strength and balance. A recent study involving 2,328 people over the age of 60 showed that regular, concentrated exercise helped reduce the risk of falling by about 13 percent. Interestingly, the study also revealed that one of the best forms of exercise for the elderly is the ancient Chinese martial art of Tai Chi, which involves slow, controlled movements that emphasize maintaining good balance. One group of elderly people in Atlanta who practiced Tai Chi on a regular basis experienced 25 percent fewer falls than a control group that did not exercise.

MAKE SURE YOU GET ENOUGH CALCIUM

The general consensus among scientists today is that a diet low in calcium increases a woman's risk of developing osteoporosis later in life. As a result, most doctors recommend that their female patients, no matter what their age, either increase the amount of calcium-rich foods in their diets or take calcium supplements.

Yet, surprisingly, the idea that increasing calcium intake, either through food or supplementation, helps prevent osteoporosis is not universally accepted. Although some studies have shown a modest increase in bone density when calcium intake is increased, many others have failed to find that connection. As the journal *Science* has stated: [A] "large body of evidence indicates no relationship between calcium intake and bone density." Some researchers believe that calcium *depletion*—how quickly and in what quantities calcium leaves your body—may be even more important in keeping your bones strong than the amount of calcium you take in. But much more research is needed.

So, in the meantime, what should you do? Well, all scientists agree that calcium is needed to build healthy bones. So until more is learned about the balance between the body's intake and outtake of calcium, you would be wise to make sure that you get enough calcium in your diet—and that you take steps to retain it in your body for as long as possible.

What exactly is "enough" calcium? Here's the latest recommendation of a panel of scientists from the National Institutes of Health:

- 1,200 to 1,500 mg of calcium daily for young women aged 11 to 24.
- 1,000 mg of calcium daily for premenopausal women aged 25 to 50.
- 1,000 mg of calcium daily for postmenopausal women who are taking estrogen.
- 1,500 mg of calcium daily for postmenopausal women who are not taking estrogen.

Some physicians believe that women who already have osteoporosis should take even higher amounts of calcium—up to 2,000 mg daily. This amount is still within the safe range established by the Food and Drug Administration. Experts caution women not to exceed 2,000 mg per day, which could cause kidney stones.

Food: The Best Source of Calcium

When you get your calcium from food, you can be sure of its "bio-availability," or its ability to be absorbed by the body. Milk and other dairy products are often cited as the richest and most convenient sources of calcium. An 8-ounce glass of skim milk contains about 300 mg of calcium; an ounce of mozzarella cheese, about 200 mg.

You should be aware, however, that some doctors are concerned about the emphasis on taking dairy products for calcium. One concern is the high fat content in these foods. Nutritionists recommend that low-fat dairy products should be selected whenever possible. Too much fat can be hazardous to your health (see chapter 7).

Another, lesser-known problem with relying on dairy products as a primary source of calcium involves their protein content. Dairy foods are high in animal protein, which some scientists blame for the high rate of osteoporosis in Western countries. The theory is that the amino acids in protein, when digested, increase the blood's acidity. To neutralize the acid, the body releases several substances into the blood. One of these sub-stances is calcium. After neutralizing the acid, the calcium is excreted from the body in urine. Thus, although eating dairy products will help bring calcium into your body, it will also cause some calcium to be pulled out of your bones.

GOOD FOOD SOURCES OF CALCIUM

Food	Serving Size	Calories	Calcium
Skim milk	1 cup	85	302
Low-fat milk (1%)	1 cup	100	300
Low-fat milk (2%)	1 cup	120	297
Whole milk	1 cup	150	291
Buttermilk	1 cup	100	285
Dry, nonfat, instant milk	¼ cup	61	209
Plain, whole milk yogurt	8 ounces	140	274
Plain, lowfat yogurt with added milk solids	8 ounces	145	415
Fruit-flavored, lowfat yogurt with added milk solids	8 ounces	230	345
Cheddar cheese	1 ounce	115	204
Mozzarella (whole milk)	1 ounce	80	147
Mozzarella (part skim milk)	1 ounce	80	207
Muenster cheese	1 ounce	105	203
Swiss cheese	1 ounce	105	272
Lowfat cottage cheese (2%)	1 cup	205	155
Ice cream, vanilla	1 cup	270	186
Ice milk, vanilla	1 cup	185	176
Sardines (with bones)	3 ounces	175	371
Oysters	1 cup	160	226
Salmon (canned)	3 ounces	120	167
Broccoli, cooked, drained, from raw, ½" pieces	1 cup	45	172
Broccoli, cooked, drained, from frozen, chopped	1 cup	50	94
Collards, cooked, drained, from frozen	1 cup	60	357
Dandelion greens, cooked, drained	1 cup	35	147
Kale, cooked, drained, from frozen	1 cup	40	179
Mustard greens, cooked, drained	1 cup	20	104
Turnip greens, chopped, cooked, drained, from frozen	1 cup	50	249
Tofu	4 ounces	86	154

Source: "Osteoporosis: Cause, Treatment, Prevention." U.S. Department of Health and Human Services.

Early in 1995, the Physicians Committee for Responsible Medicine, a national organization of more than 3,000 doctors that advocate preventive medicine among other issues, filed a complaint with the Federal Trade Commission against the dairy industry for running misleading ads promoting milk as one of the best sources of calcium. "The ad obscures the fact that loss of bone mass [in older women] is typically caused by excessive calcium loss, rather than inadequate calcium intake," the physicians noted in their complaint.

So what should you do to make sure you get enough calcium in your diet? Your best bet may be to make sure you seek out calcium from a wide variety of foods. Besides dairy products, other good sources of calcium include fish and shellfish, such as oysters, shrimp, and canned sardines and salmon; soybeans; tofu; broccoli; and dark green vegetables, such as collard, turnip, and mustard greens. (You'll find a detailed list of calcium-rich foods on page 133.) Although spinach has a high calcium content, it also contains oxalic acid, which keeps the calcium from becoming absorbed by the body. So although it's an excellent food for other reasons, spinach is not a good source of calcium.

If you are lactose-intolerant—that is, if your body has difficulty digesting milk—you should try eating yogurt, in addition to plenty of dark, green leafy vegetables, or drinking milk that has been treated with the enzyme lactase (known commercially as LactAid). This enzyme will enable your body to digest dairy foods. A few yogurts contain lactase naturally; to find out which ones, ask your grocer or write to the companies that make the yogurts.

Calcium Supplements

If it is difficult for you to reach your daily minimum requirement of calcium through your diet, you may want to use calcium supplements. Keep in mind, however, that supplements are a poor second choice to calcium-rich foods. A supplement should be used as its name implies—as a supplement to a healthful diet, not as a substitute for one.

Not all supplements are alike. To begin with, different types of calcium supplements have different amounts of elemental calcium in them. Supplements made with calcium carbonate, for example, are 40 percent calcium. In other words, 100 mg of calcium carbonate contains 40 mg of calcium.

•   •   •

"I take three or four Tums a day for osteoporosis as my doctor suggested. As I grow older I seem to experience more indigestion, so the Tums serve a dual purpose. When I am on a very careful diet, I take both a calcium and potassium supplement as well."

•   •   •

Here are the most commonly available calcium compounds and the percentage of calcium in them:

Calcium carbonate	40 percent
Calcium lactate	13 percent
Calcium gluconate	9 percent
Calcium phosphate	
Dibasic form	23 percent
Tribasic form	39 percent
Calcium citrate	24 percent or less
Chelated calcium	20 percent (varies among brands)

Read supplement labels carefully to see how much actual, or "elemental," calcium you are getting from a particular product.

Calcium supplements are usually taken in tablet form, although powders and liquids are also available. Some common antacids—such as Tums, Titralac, Chooz, and Alka 2—are also commonly used as calcium supplements because they are made from calcium carbonate. You would be wise to check with your physician before taking any kind of calcium supplement; too much calcium can cause kidney stones in susceptible people.

Here are some other tips about calcium supplements:

- One study has found that calcium carbonate supplements are less effective than chelated calcium in reducing bone loss in postmenopausal women. However, chelated calcium—supplements in which the calcium is bound to an amino acid rather than to carbonate, phosphate, or some other substance—is one of the most expensive forms of calcium. In addition, the concentration of chelated calcium varies among brands, depending on how they are manufactured. You may wish to check with your pharmacist for information about the various brands.
- If you are using antacids as your regular source of calcium, avoid aluminum-containing ones. Aluminum can keep the intestines from absorbing calcium.

- Some calcium supplements are more easily dissolved in the stomach and absorbed by the body than others. For example, in one study of calcium carbonate supplements, one-third of the supplements studied took so long to dissolve that they could not be used sufficiently by the body before being eliminated.

    Unfortunately, not all supplements have been tested for their adsorbability. In his book *Calcium and Common Sense*, Dr. Robert Heaney, a noted osteoporosis expert, suggests that consumers test a supplement's dissolvability themselves by dropping the supplement in a glass of warm water. Gently stir the solution every now and then. If the tablet has not completely disintegrated within an hour, says Dr. Heaney, you have reason to question how well the calcium in the supplement is being dissolved and absorbed in your stomach.

- Some people who take calcium carbonate supplements report unwanted side effects, most notably nausea, gas, and constipation. The nausea can often be relieved by taking the supplement with meals. If the gas and constipation persist, you may want to try one of the other forms of calcium supplements.

- Avoid taking dolomite for calcium supplementation. Although it is high in calcium, dolomite also tends to contain traces of cadmium, uranium, mercury, arsenic, and lead. In small amounts, these substances will not harm you, but if you take them regularly, particularly in large doses of one or more tablets a day, they could build to toxic levels in your body.

- Bonemeal, which consists of ground, processed animal bone, should also be avoided as a regular calcium supplement. It is often contaminated with lead.

- Significant amounts of lead and aluminum have also been found in calcium carbonate supplements labeled "oyster shell" or "natural source." Avoid using these products as your regular source of calcium.

Vitamin D—Calcium's Helper

You need vitamin D to get calcium out of your digestive system and into your bones, particularly as you grow older and your body becomes less efficient at absorbing dietary calcium. In fact, vitamin D appears to play an important role in keeping bones strong. In a 1993 study, researchers at Tufts University divided 250 postmenopausal women into two groups. One group was given daily supplements of 377 mg of calcium and 400 IU of vitamin D. The other group received the calcium supplement and a placebo. After one year, the women taking only the calcium supplement experienced no change in their bone density, but the women taking vitamin D along with the calcium gained significant bone mass.

You need only a modest amount of vitamin D to ensure optimum calcium absorption. The recommended daily dosage is 400 IU (international units). Through the greater part of our adult life, most of us can easily meet this requirement by eating a normal diet and by spending ten to fifteen minutes out in the sun several times a week. Exposure to sunlight activates a compound in the skin that the kidney and liver then convert to an active form of vitamin D.

By the time we reach our sixties, however, our bodies become less adept at manufacturing vitamin D from sunlight. To ensure an adequate supply of the vitamin, therefore, we must either eat more foods rich in vitamin D or take a vitamin D supplement. Good food sources include milk fortified with vitamin D, fortified breakfast cereals, egg yolks, canned sardines, canned tuna, saltwater fish, and liver.

A word of warning about vitamin D supplements: They can be dangerous, even deadly, in high doses. Symptoms of an overdose include loss of appetite, nausea, abdominal pain, excessive thirst, excessive urination, and headaches. According to the National Institutes of Health's Consensus Panel on Osteoporosis, women should take no more than 600 to 800 IUs daily without a doctor's recommendation.

Some calcium supplements contain added vitamin D. If you are also taking a multiple vitamin daily, you may be getting an overdose of vitamin D. Read supplement labels carefully. In addition, avoid calcium supplements that contain vitamin D unless your doctor specifically recommends them.

FOOD FOES OF CALCIUM

Protein

As noted earlier, if you eat more protein than your body needs (and most Americans do), you will lose excess amounts of calcium in your urine. (To find out how much protein is too much, see chapter 7.) To preserve calcium in your bones, reduce meat in your diet as much as possible.

Caffeine

Caffeine increases the amount of calcium lost in urine. The more caffeine you put into your body, the more calcium you lose. So if you can't give up your coffee or caffeinated soft drink habit, be sure you get extra calcium in your diet.

Alcohol

This drug reduces the intestinal absorption of calcium. Again, the more you drink, the less calcium absorbed.

Salt (Sodium)

Salt causes more calcium to be washed out of the body in urine. This gives you yet another good reason to throw away your salt shaker and to read food labels carefully for sodium content.

Fiber

Fiber moves food through the digestive system more rapidly, thus providing less time for calcium to be absorbed through the intestines. However—and this is a big however—the anticancer and other health benefits of a high-fiber diet far outweigh the increased loss of calcium. So don't give up fiber; just add a little more calcium to your diet.

Phosphorus

Some osteoporosis researchers believe that if the phosphorus levels in a person's diet greatly exceed the amount of calcium in the diet, bone loss will result. Other scientists think this concern about phosphorus is unwarranted. They point out that although phosphorus does increase the amount of calcium lost during digestion, it also *decreases* the amount of calcium lost in urine.

All this concern about the phosphorus-calcium ratio stems from the fact that the modern American diet is low in calcium and high in phosphorus, thanks primarily to the excess phosphorus in red meat and soft drinks. If you increase the amount of calcium-rich foods in your diet and cut back on—or, better yet, eliminate—red meat and soft drinks (which aren't all that healthful for you anyway), you won't have to worry about your phosphorus-calcium ratio at all.

TREATING OSTEOPOROSIS WITH
ESTROGEN

Estrogen replacement therapy (ERT) has been shown to be an effective preventive therapy against bone loss. Studies have revealed that women who start estrogen therapy within a few years of menopause maintain their bone density and have fewer hip and wrist fractures later in life than women who do not take estrogen. In one 1995 study that included more than 9,700 women 65 years of age or older, researchers found that women who began taking estrogen within five years of menopause and who continued to take it had about a 50 percent reduction in the risk of all nonspinal fractures and about a 60 percent decrease in the risk of hip fractures. The protective effect was seen whether the women were taking estrogen alone or in combination with progesterone. Even women who started estrogen replacement therapy after five years experienced a drop of 25 percent in their risk of having a nonspinal fracture.

Estrogen appears to prevent bone loss by inhibiting the cells that tear down, or resorb, bone. In other words, it keeps those cells from becoming overly efficient at their job. In addition, estrogen appears to help get calcium absorbed through the intestinal tract and to help conserve calcium in the bones. It also may interact positively with other hormones that affect bone. Yet estrogen alone can not be depended on to prevent bone loss. Exercise is needed to stimulate the building of bone, and calcium is needed to provide the raw materials. Only then can estrogen do its job and keep existing bone strong and intact.

Still, the situation concerning the connection between a drop in estrogen and brittle bones remains confusing. Approximately 15 percent of women taking estrogen lose bone density anyway. And a recent study found no difference after age 75 in the bone density between long-term previous users of estrogen and never-users.

You should also be aware that when you stop taking estrogen, bone loss will begin again, and at the same rapid pace as at menopause. For this reason, estrogen treatment for osteoporosis is a lifetime commitment. Given the health risks associated with estrogen (see chapter 3), the decision to use estrogen therapy to maintain bone should be made only after careful consideration of all of the hormone's risks and benefits.

To lower the health risks, doctors recommend that you take the lowest possible dose of estrogen. The smallest dose usually prescribed to maintain bone density is .625 milligrams per day. Researchers at the Kaiser Permanente Medical Center and University of California Medical Center in San

Francisco, however, have found that a lower daily dose of .3 mg will also slow bone loss—if taken in conjunction with 1,500 mg of calcium daily. Recent research also suggest that treatment with a combination of both estrogen and calcium (1,000 mg daily) may be more effective in preserving bone mass than either of the two agents alone.

Until very recently, scientists believed that women had to begin taking estrogen soon after menopause—and then continue it for the rest of their lives—for it to prevent the fractures in old age that can lead to disability and death. New research has revealed, however, that estrogen therapy can help increase bone density and reduce the risk of fractures even if begun in old age. You would still have to stay on the hormone for the rest of your life, but by starting the treatment at, say, 65 rather than 50, you greatly reduce the number of years of exposure to estrogen and thus significantly reduce your risk of developing estrogen-related breast cancer. Be sure to discuss this option with your physician, especially if your diet and lifestyle are healthful and a bone-density assessment shows you have good bone density.

Before you decide to take estrogen, you should first assess how great is your risk for osteoporosis. If, for example, you are white, petite, of Northern European heritage, and experienced menopause before age 45, or if you are a smoker with a sedentary lifestyle that you refuse to change, you are at high risk for osteoporosis and may benefit greatly from hormone therapy. If, on the other hand, you are a tall, active woman and menstruated until your early fifties, you may wish to try more natural methods of preventing osteoporosis, such as continuing to exercise and making sure to eat a healthful diet rich in calcium and vitamin D. Regardless of other risk factors, you should also take steps as you age to reduce your chances of falling. Taking estrogen has not been shown to have any beneficial effect on muscle strength or neuromuscular function and will not reduce your risk of falling. Be sure to discuss your risk factors and all treatment options with your physician.

OTHER TYPES OF TREATMENT

In addition to estrogen, several other drugs are currently being studied by researchers for their effectiveness against osteoporosis. Two, alendronate and calcitonin, have been approved by the Food and Drug Administration for the treatment of osteoporosis.

Alendronate (Fosamax)

In 1995, alendronate, which is marketed under the brand name Fosamax, became the first nonhormonal drug approved by the Food and Drug Administration for the treatment of osteoporosis. Alendronate is a type of drug known as a bisphosphonate. It works by blocking the action of osteoclasts, cells whose regular job is to take away, or resorb, worn out bone cells. The removed bone cells are usually replaced, but if the osteoclasts do their job too aggressively, bone can be resorbed too rapidly, resulting in brittle bone. Alendronate coats the excess osteoplasts, thus helping bones stay stronger.

In a series of studies involving more than 1,800 women aged 41 to 85, researchers showed that alendronate increased bone strength in the spine and hip by about 8 percent. Women in a comparison group who took only a placebo experienced a decline in bone density of about .65 percent. The women using alendronate also suffered about half the number of spinal fractures as those taking the placebo.

Alendronate is administered in pill form and should be taken each morning 30 to 60 minutes before eating breakfast. Side effects are reported to be mild, but include nausea, heartburn, gas, and abdominal pain. You should know, however, that no research has been done on the long-term use of this drug. Some scientists are concerned that Alendronate may interfere with the remodeling as well as the resorption of bone, thus eventually causing bones to become brittle.

Calcitonin

A hormone produced by the thyroid gland, calcitonin conserves calcium in bone, thus slowing bone loss. Calcitonin levels in the body decrease with age; they are also lower in women than in men. The Food and Drug Administration approved the use of calcitonin as a treatment for osteoporosis in 1984. It is usually given by daily injection in conjunction with 1,500 mg of calcium and 400 IU of vitamin D. In its injected form, calcitonin is expensive to use. A less expensive, inhaled form of the hormone was approved under the brand name Miacalcin Nasal Spray to treat osteoporosis in women, beginning five years after menopause. Two studies have shown that daily use of the spray increases bone mass in the spine. The drug did not improve bone mass in the forearm or hip, however, nor has the drug been shown to prevent fractures.

Common side effects of the inhaled calcitonin include inflammation of the membranes in the nose, nosebleeds, and sinusitis. If you use this drug, you will need to have your nasal passages examined periodically for ulceration or irritation.

Slow-Release Fluoride and Calcium

For a while in the 1980s, it looked as if supplements of sodium fluoride, the mineral that protects teeth from decay, could actually increase bone mass in the spine. In one early study, for example, women taking fluoride and calcium showed a 10 percent increase in spinal bone compared to a 3 percent increase for those taking calcium alone.

Early in 1990, however, the Mayo Clinic reported the results of a four-year study of fluoride as a treatment for spinal osteoporosis. More than 200 women with spinal osteoporosis took part in the study, which was the most comprehensive study of its kind to date. All the women received 1,500 mg of calcium daily; half also got 72 mg of fluoride.

The findings were surprising: the two groups of women experienced a similar number of vertebral fractures, but the group receiving the fluoride had three times as many fractures in bones elsewhere in the body. The fluoride group also reported twice as many side effects from their treatment, most notably nausea and acute pain in their legs.

Although fluoride did stimulate the formation of bone, it appeared that the newly created bone was not of normal strength. The authors of the Mayo study concluded that fluoride therapy was neither safe nor effective for the treatment of osteoporosis.

A few years later, however, a group of Texas researchers reported that daily doses of a slow-release fluoride combined with calcium citrate appeared to increase bone mass—normal, healthy bone—and reduce fractures in women with osteoporosis. In their four-year study, which involved 110 postmenopausal women who had all suffered severe bone loss, the researchers found that the fluoride-calcium formula increased spinal bone density by more than 4 percent annually and hip bone density by 2.4 percent annually. It also reduced spinal fractures by about two-thirds. The patients reported only minor side effects.

Slow-release fluoride pills are not available for general use, although the company that developed the drug has applied to the Food and Drug Administration for approval to market the product. Stay tuned.

Etidronate Disodium (Etidronate)

A chemical compound known to slow down the resorption of bone, etidronate has been used for more than a decade for the treatment of Paget's disease, a chronic disease in which bones become enlarged, weak, and deformed. Two studies, one conducted in Denmark and the other in the United States, indicate that etidronate may also prove useful in treating osteoporosis.

In the Danish study, 66 women with postmenopausal osteoporosis were divided randomly into two groups. One group was treated with etidronate tablets; the other group took a placebo. Neither the women nor the researchers knew which women received the etidronate and which received the placebo. Both groups received supplements of calcium and vitamin D as well.

At the end of the three-year study, the group receiving etidronate therapy experienced a significant decrease in the rate of new vertebral fractures.

The American study, which involved more than 400 women, showed similar results: The group of women in the study who took etidronate experienced half the rate of new vertebral fractures compared to that of the other women. In addition, the bone in their spines increased in density by as much as 5 percent.

Recent reports, however, have begun to question the long-term efficacy of etidronate. More studies are needed.

Etidronate has been released for the experimental treatment of osteoporosis. Its use requires physician supervision and should be reserved for special cases where more natural therapy with vitamins and calcium have not worked.

Calcitriol

Also known by the tongue-twisting names of 1,25 dihydroxyvitamin D and 1,25 dihydroxycholcalciferol, calcitriol is the body's working form of vitamin D. The vitamin D that we take in through our food or that is made when the sun strikes our skin is converted into calcitriol by a two-step process in the liver and the kidney. Only in the final form of calcitriol can vitamin D be effective in our bodies.

Our bodies make less calcitriol as we age. Some scientists believe that if we can keep calcitriol levels from falling, we may also keep bones from weakening. Although the studies are conflicting, calcitriol appears to increase calcium absorption and decrease fracture rates in osteoporosis patients. In one study, patients who took calcitriol had 50 to 75 percent fewer spinal fractures than those who took placebos. More research is needed, however, to establish calcitriol's role in treating osteoporosis.

Progesterone

Some evidence indicates that the hormone progesterone may, like estrogen, help protect against bone loss. However, most research suggests that a progesterone taken alone, without estrogen, is *not* effective as a treatment for osteoporosis. It should not be used in place of estrogen for the treatment of osteoporosis.

DETECTING OSTEOPOROSIS

New screening techniques that attempt to determine bone density can be helpful in diagnosing osteoporosis. Most techniques involve taking an x-ray or other radiographic image to determine the density of a woman's bones. Bone-screening tests, therefore, expose patients to very small amounts of radiation. Although such exposure does, theoretically, subject women to a slightly increased cancer risk, no case of cancer has been attributed to bone density measurements, and, like mammograms, these tests can save lives and decrease hospitalization.

In recent years, some physicians have begun recommending that women who are not on HRT begin regular bone-density screenings beginning right after menopause. They argue that screenings done at menopause and every two to three years afterward can help determine which women are losing bone too rapidly and therefore are at greatest risk of developing osteoporosis. This first test will provide a baseline for future comparison, and if a woman's bones show signs of serious deterioration, she can then begin prompt treatment, usually estrogen therapy, to stop the loss. Thus regular bone screenings, argue the doctors who advocate their use, would result in fewer women on estrogen because the screenings would identify only those women who are truly at risk of developing osteoporosis.

Other physicians, however, do not believe in routine bone screening for all women. They point out that no study has shown that bone screening done around menopause—or age 50—accurately predicts whether or not a woman will suffer bone fractures later in life. This may be partly due to the fact that the average age is 80 for a hip fracture and 66 for a wrist fracture—too far in the distance to be predicted at age 50 with any accuracy. Also, bone loss tends to be more rapid right after menopause and then becomes slower as a woman ages, sometimes even ceasing altogether. Each woman's pattern of bone loss is different. Thus a measurement of bone around age 50 may not reflect what will happen to a particular woman's bone as she ages. Furthermore, even the best screening instruments have a 1 to 2 percent margin of error—which is about the annual rate of bone loss commonly experienced right after menopause. So a loss in bone during this time could be missed or it could seem much larger than it actually is. Bone-density screening may, however, be more accurate at predicting a woman's future risk of fracture if the screening is done when the woman is several years past menopause. In studies showing screening to be effective, the women were an average of 65 years old.

●　　●　　●

"Thank God I'm not likely to get osteoporosis. My mother, who is 82 and who has fallen a number of times because she's always in a hurry, has never even fractured a bone. I'm banking on the fact that it's mainly heredity and I won't have the problem."

●　　●　　●

Should you undergo regular bone screening? That's something you will need to discuss with your physician. Women with special medical conditions that place them in a high-risk category for osteoporotic fractures—those who had their ovaries removed at an early age, for example, or who have used corticosteroid medications for a long time, may benefit from having their bone density measured every one or two years. Other women may also wish to have a "baseline" measurement taken right after menopause to use later for comparison. If your only risk factors for osteoporosis are age, race, or having gone through menopause, however, you probably will not need routine bone screenings. Nor do you need bone screenings while you are taking HRT, as the estrogen in your supplement should be protecting your bones against loss.

If you do have a screening, be sure to ask your physician for your results in relation to those of *other women your age*. As noted earlier in this chapter, comparing your bone density to other women your age is more revealing of your risk of suffering a bone fracture than comparing it to women half your age.

145

It should be noted that the diagnosis of *significant* osteoporosis can be made from nearly any x-ray. If you have had an x-ray performed during the last year or two, ask your physician to call the radiologist to review the films. She or he can determine if osteoporosis is present from these films. Unfortunately, by the time osteoporosis shows up in an x-ray, the disease will have already progressed to an advanced stage. That's because bone must lose about one-third of its density before it looks weak on an ordinary x-ray. Regular x-rays, therefore, are not useful tools for the early screening of osteoporosis, but only for incidentally observing the presence of significant bone loss.

The screening methods discussed in the following sections are currently being used to detect osteoporosis.

Single-photon Absorptiometry

Single-photon absorptiometry exposes the person having the screening to about 15 mrem of radiation. (By comparison, one chest x-ray gives a radiation dose of 20 to 50 mrem.) Most researchers question, however, the usefulness of this technique, citing studies that show that it cannot predict the bone density at two of the most critical fracture sites: the spine and the hip.

Dual-photon Absorptiometry (DPA)

This technique, which directs two different beams of radioactive iodine at a bone, can be used to measure bone density in all areas of the body, including the spine and hip. It is also relatively low in radiation (less than 5 mrem per test), but can be off in its measurements by as much as 8 percent.

Dual Energy X-ray Absorptiometry (DEXA)

This is an advanced form of dual-photon absorptiometry. It is a faster and more precise technique, and, like DPA, emits less than 5 mrem of radiation per test. Most research centers studying osteoporosis employ this technique because it offers a 1 to 2 percent error rate and is most useful for following an individual's changing bone density over time. Further information on DEXA is available in Appendix B.

Quantitative Computerized Tomography (QCT)

This technique uses "pinpoint" x-ray beams to measure trabecular bone—the porous, spongy interior part of the bone. It is often used to measure bone density of the spine, where changes in bone mass can happen more quickly than elsewhere in the body. Exposure to radiation is much greater with QCT—about 200 to 400 mrem per test—than with other bone-screening methods.

Computerized Axial Tomography (CAT Scan or CT Scan)

The CAT scan offers the most detailed analysis of bone density. It can determine the density of either the entire bone or just the spongy, inner part, which is where bone weakening usually first begins.

CAT scans are expensive and time-consuming, however. They also expose you to a much higher dose of radiation than the other techniques. If you have had a CAT scan in the last year or two for other medical reasons, your physician should ask that these films be reevaluated for signs of osteoporosis. If these films reveal evidence of the disease, another, special kind of scan—one that is cheaper and shorter than the usual CAT scan—can then be ordered to further evaluate the density of your bones.

SOME FINAL WORDS

Obviously, prevention is the key with osteoporosis. Your aim should be to build the strongest bones possible by midlife and then to keep them strong through weight-bearing exercise, proper diet, and other healthful lifestyle habits (such as not smoking).

If you have already been diagnosed with osteoporosis, you can still take steps to keep the disease from progressing any further. Follow the same precautions as you would for preventing the disease. Make sure, however, that your exercise is vigorous enough to build strong bones, but not so vigorous that you risk fracturing them.

Also, find ways to minimize hazards in your home that might lead to a fracture. (Refer to the earlier section in this chapter, "Take Steps to Prevent Falling.") You should also be careful about how you lift objects. Do not lift while bending forward, as it can put too much stress on your spine and lead to a vertebral fracture. Instead, bend your knees, keep your spine upright by lowering your hips, and, using your leg muscles, lift the weight straight up. If your spine is very weak, your doctor may advise you not to lift heavy objects at all.

Finally, be sure you keep up to date on the latest osteoporosis treatments. New research on both existing and potential treatments is constantly being reported in the press. You may also wish to contact the National Osteoporosis Foundation periodically for information about new treatments (for the foundation's address, see the Resources section at the end of the book). As scientists learn more about osteoporosis, they may be able to come up with safer and more effective ways to prevent, diagnose, and treat the debilitating fractures that often result from it.

7

TAKING CHARGE:
Eating for Health

Certainly the effort to remain unchanged, young, when the body gives so impressive a signal of change as the menopause, is gallant; but it is a stupid, self-sacrificial gallantry, better befitting a boy of twenty than a woman of forty-five or fifty. Let the athletes die young and laurel-crowned. Let the soldiers earn the Purple Hearts. Let women die old, white-crowned, with human hearts.

—Ursula K. Le Guin
"The Space Crone,"
Dancing at the Edge of the World

What you eat—and don't eat—has a major impact on how you look and feel during your menopausal years. In fact, if there ever was a time in your life to pay attention to what you eat, now is that time.

To begin with, the foods you eat can affect how your body reacts to the hormonal changes of menopause. By avoiding certain foods, for example, you may be able to lessen the severity and frequency of your hot flashes.

A healthful diet can also help slow down the aging process. The cells throughout your body become less efficient at regenerating and repairing themselves as you grow older. Eating well can provide a greater reserve of vitamins and nutrients for your cells, thus helping to ensure your body of the healthiest and strongest cells possible. As a result, you'll feel, look, and function better as you pass through and beyond your middle years.

Finally, a healthful diet can help your body fight off many of the chronic illnesses—such as cancer, heart disease, arthritis, and diabetes—that become a real threat during the middle and older years of our lives.

There's no doubt about it: This is the time to get your act together when it comes to food and health. This chapter takes a look at what a good diet for the menopausal years—and beyond—is all about.

THE NEED FOR FEWER CALORIES

As you have no doubt already noticed, it is much more difficult to keep weight under control in your forties and fifties than it was in your twenties. That's because your basal metabolic rate—the rate at which your body burns energy—has slowed down. Older bodies just don't burn up as many calories as younger ones, even for the same activities. We get more efficient as we age. The average 120-pound woman, for example, needs 2,100 calories a day at age 20, but only 1,800 calories a day at age 50.

•　　•　　•

"I'm fairly slim usually, but since the radiation treatments, when I stopped menstruating, my weight seems more distributed around my middle, which never was that way before. I feel like my metabolism has really slowed down."

•　　•　　•

One of the reasons for this slower metabolism is a change in the proportion of the body that is made up of "lean tissue," which consists of organs, bone, and muscle. As we age, we lose lean body mass and gain a greater proportion of body fat. During daily maintenance of the body, fat tissue burns fewer calories than the same weight of muscle tissue because its only function is the storage of fat. We also tend to become less physically active as we grow older, which also means that we burn fewer calories. (Of course, these two factors can each be partially reversed if you exercise—see chapter 8.)

Most people gain, on average, one pound a year after age 25. The extra weight is amassed not by eating more, but simply *by not eating less.* Just taking in ten more calories a day than you burn off—the amount found in a single stick of chewing gum—can make you put on a pound a year!

Gaining *some* weight as you age is not necessarily bad, however. In fact, recent research by the Gerontology Research Center of the National Institute on Aging suggests that for the sake of your health and longevity you need not try to maintain at 45 or 50 the weight you carried around at 25. The key, of course, is to keep weight gain within healthy limits. (To find out the Center's suggested weights for various heights and ages, see the chart on page 152.)

Obesity is by far the biggest nutritional problem in the United States, particularly among people in their middle and later years. About a third of the women between the ages of 45 and 65 are overweight. Excess weight can lead to a host of health problems, including high blood pressure, hardening of the arteries (arteriosclerosis), diabetes, gallbladder disease, hernias, heart disease, and arthritis. Obesity has also been significantly associated with an increased risk of cancer of the breast, colon, uterus, and gallbladder. In addition, being overweight increases your chance of developing painful arthritis.

To help prevent these health problems, the World Health Organization recommends that moderately active people reduce their calories by 5 percent during their forties, by another 5 percent during their fifties, and then by 10 percent during their sixties. In other words, by age 70, you should be eating 20 percent fewer calories than you did at age 40.

Of course, that's a lot easier said than done! Counting calories can be difficult at any age, but particularly now when your metabolism is slowing down. With careful diet planning, however, it can be done—if you're truly willing to put some effort into it. You'll be well rewarded for your efforts. Keeping your weight at a healthful level will help you prevent or reduce the severity of many health threats—and that will mean a more comfortable and enjoyable life during your middle years and beyond.

Tips for Maintaining a Healthy Weight

- The key to losing—and keeping off—weight is to do so gradually. Aim for dropping no more than a pound or two a week. That may sound terribly dull and slow, but study after study has shown that gradual weight loss is the best way of guaranteeing *permanent* weight loss. It's also the healthiest way of slimming down, because it won't deplete your body of important stores of nutrients, as a crash diet will.
- Adopt a permanent eating plan—one that you will be able to follow for a lifetime, rather than just while you're "on" a diet. That doesn't mean you have to give up every food you like forever—an impossible task for even the most disciplined of us. But it does mean learning how to be sensible about your food choices—and learning how and why you make unhealthful choices. For example, *plan* to have your favorite dessert once a month. This way you know when you will next be enjoying such a treat and will thus "splurge" less often.
- Another key to maintaining a healthy weight is to exercise. In fact, not incorporating exercise into a weight loss plan is almost sure to doom it to failure. Besides making your body burn more calories, exercise also decreases your appetite. Whether it does this by simply improving your self-esteem (thus giving you more willpower to monitor what you eat) or by a more complex physiological change is unclear—and ultimately unimportant. All you really need to know is that exercise helps you eat more sensibly.

Regular exercise is also important for a host of health reasons during the midlife years, from mitigating the effects of hot flashes to protecting against heart disease (see chapter 8). If you are not already following an exercise program, sit down with your physician and devise one that will suit your health needs and lifestyle. Be sure to start your exercise program slowly, then gradually work up to more intense workouts. Exercise that is erratic or overly intense can lead to broken bones, torn muscles, joint pain, and even heart trouble.

- Finally, invest in some good healthy-eating books—ones that stress losing weight gradually and permanently through lifestyle changes rather than through a get-thin-quick scheme. Avoid any diet that restricts your caloric intake to fewer than 1,000 calories a day or that relies on only a few foods or groups of foods.

WHAT YOU SHOULD WEIGH

The following weight ranges for men and women were developed by the National Institute on Aging's Gerontology Research Center. They assume that you are wearing no shoes or clothes. The lower figure in each range is for people with small physical frames; the higher is for those with large frames. Also, keep in mind that these figures apply to healthy men and women, those who are free of chronic diseases, such as high blood pressure, arthritis, diabetes, or even elevated blood cholesterol.

Expected Weight Ranges for Men and Women (in lbs.)

Height	Age 25	Age 35	Age 45	Age 55	Age 65
4'10"	84-111	92-119	99-127	107-135	115-142
4'11"	87-115	95-123	103-131	111-139	119-147
5'0"	90-119	98-127	106-135	114-143	123-152
5'1"	93-123	101-131	110-140	118-148	127-157
5'2"	96-127	105-136	113-144	122-153	131-163
5'3"	99-131	108-140	117-149	126-158	135-168
5'4"	102-135	112-145	121-154	130-163	140-173
5'5"	106-140	115-149	125-159	134-168	144-179
5'6"	109-144	119-154	129-164	138-174	148-184
5'7"	112-148	122-148	133-169	143-179	153-190
5'8"	116-153	126-163	137-174	147-184	158-196
5'9"	119-157	130-168	141-179	151-190	162-201
5'10"	122-162	134-173	145-184	156-195	167-207
5'11"	126-167	137-178	149-190	160-201	172-213
6'0"	129-171	141-183	153-195	165-207	177-219

Source: National Institute of Aging, Gerontology Research Center.

• • •

"I've put on quite a bit of weight since my hysterectomy. Part of it is certainly my sedentary lifestyle, but I think it's also because my metabolism has shifted."

• • •

THE NEED FOR NUTRIENTS

Although you need fewer calories as you grow older, your overall need for nutrients—the chemical elements essential to human health: proteins, carbohydrates, fats, minerals, and vitamins—does not decrease. A body at 50 still requires the same basic nutritional material as it did at 20. A good diet, therefore, is essentially the same at any age, with only a few minor changes.

However—and this is a key point to remember—*because you need fewer calories during your menopausal years, it is extremely important that the foods you do eat have a greater concentration of nutrients and a lower concentration of calories than some of those you used to eat.* You can no longer afford, nutritionally speaking, to eat foods that are empty of nutrients. Sorry, but that's a fact of growing older.

Scientists have identified about fifty chemical elements as the nutrients we need to stay healthy. These nutrients provide the body with energy and the raw materials necessary to build, repair, and maintain healthy tissues. Some of these nutrients help to regulate biochemical reactions within the body. We must get nearly all of these nutrients from the food we eat; our bodies cannot manufacture most of them on their own, at least not in amounts sufficient to meet our needs.

Nutrients have been divided into six main groups: protein, carbohydrates, fats, water, vitamins, and minerals. Because they are needed by the body in relatively large amounts (grams), protein, carbohydrates, fats, and water are known as *macronutrients*. Vitamins and minerals, which the body needs in smaller amounts (milligrams and micrograms) are called *micronutrients*. It's important that you get enough of each nutrient—but not *too* much—to look, feel, and function in a healthy way.

PROTEIN: OVERDOING A GOOD THING

General Guidelines

- Reduce your protein intake to no more than 15 percent of your total caloric intake.
- Get more of your protein from vegetable sources and less from animal sources.

Most Americans eat two to four times more protein than they actually need for good nutrition. And most of that protein comes from animal sources—meat, poultry, eggs, fish, and dairy products—which also tend to be high in the unwanted fat that can clog arteries and the calories that can cause obesity.

That's not to say that you don't need protein. You do. Protein, after all, is a vital part of every cell and plays an essential role in building, maintaining, and repairing the body's tissues. But the amount of protein your body requires to keep it running smoothly is much less than you are probably getting. Nutritionists recommend that protein constitute only 10 to 15 percent of our daily calories. For the average 130-pound American woman, that comes out to about 45 grams of protein each day—about the amount of protein found in two cups of cottage cheese or one and a half 4-ounce hamburgers.

Now, think back on all the meat, fish, poultry, eggs, and milk products you've eaten during the previous twenty-four hours. You have probably consumed much more than the protein equivalent of two cups of cottage cheese. And that doesn't include all the *nonanimal* sources of protein in your diet—the protein found in some vegetables, grains, beans, nuts, and seeds.

Too much protein—particularly animal protein—can be harmful to your health. Excess proteins are broken down by the body into nitrogen waste products and sugars. Most animal protein is also very high in fat, which has been linked to heart disease, some kinds of cancer, and a host of other health problems. (See the section on fat on pages 161–163.) A high-protein diet also poses a specific health risk for women during the menopausal years: It promotes urinary excretion of calcium from the blood, resulting in the depletion of calcium from bones, and thus may accelerate bone loss. It also accelerates atherosclerosis, or plaque formation in the arteries, which can lead to heart attacks and strokes.

Tips for Eating Protein Foods

- Eat red meat only rarely—if ever. Your heart will thank you for it. If you must eat red meat, buy the leanest cut possible and trim all visible fat from it. Serve it as a smaller side dish rather than the main course.
- Substitute chicken, turkey, and fish for red meat. They contain less fat than red meat and have more nutrients important for a long, healthy life. Be sure to remove the skin from poultry before eating it. That's where you'll find most of the fat, a fat that is known to be particularly adept at forming plaques and clogging arteries.
- When you do eat meat, keep portion sizes small—a three-ounce serving is plenty for most adults. Serve more vegetables and fruits on the plate to make the meat look appetizing.
- Work more vegetarian meals into your weekly menus. Try recipes that call for beans, grains, rice, or low-fat dairy products instead of meat. Many excellent vegetarian cookbooks are on the market today.

CARBOHYDRATES: UNJUSTLY MALIGNED

General Guidelines

- Eat more complex carbohydrates, such as whole grains, breads and pastas, beans, nuts, rice, vegetables, and fruits.
- Eat less sugar and fewer foods containing large amounts of sugar.
- Eat more food rich in fiber.

Carbohydrates have long had the unjust reputation of being fattening, when, in fact, they are no more caloric than proteins and about one-half as caloric as fats. Potatoes, pasta, bread, and other starchy foods are often passed over by people watching their calories in favor of meat. They are unaware of the hidden fat in red meat, which raises the calorie per gram value of meat to a level higher than that of potatoes, vegetables, or rice. A 5-ounce baked potato, for example, has 110 calories (or 145 calories if you add a pat of butter); a 5-ounce T-bone steak has 550! In addition, the potato contains significant amounts of a variety of vitamins and minerals (including 50 percent of the average adult's requirement of vitamin C), as well as a small but significant amount of high-quality protein.

When offered a second helping of steak and potatoes, you would thus do best to take the potato and leave the steak.

Nutritionists recommend that we eat more carbohydrates. In fact, they suggest that at least 60 percent of our daily calories come from carbohydrates. Currently, the average American woman gets only about 45 percent of her calories from carbohydrates.

Carbohydrates are important because they provide the body with its main source of energy. During digestion, carbohydrates are converted into blood sugar, or glucose, which fuels the brain, the nervous system, and the muscles.

Not all carbohydrates are alike, however—or even good for you. Carbohydrates basically fall into three groups: refined or simple sugars, starches, and fiber. When nutritionists recommend eating more carbohydrates, they are referring to the starches and fibers. We do not need sugar in our diets because the liver can manufacture blood glucose from most other foods. The average American already consumes about 130 pounds of sugar annually. Imagine storing thirteen 10-pound bags of sugar in your kitchen! That's how much you put into your body each year.

The Perils of Sugar

Sugars are known as "simple carbohydrates" because of their simpler molecular structure. Most of the sugar found in the American diet is sucrose, or table sugar, which is purified, or refined, from sugar cane or sugar beet. Two other sugars—fructose and dextrose—are derived from fruits and other plants, and one—lactose—is found in milk.

•　　•　　•

"Certain foods increase hot flashes for me. Cheese, for instance, and sugar. If I eat sugar, which I don't often, I'm going to flash automatically."

•　　•　　•

Sugar is, by far, the most common food additive. It is, of course, added to many of the foods we identify as sweets, such as candies, cakes, jams, and soft drinks. In addition, however, it is also "hidden" in a wide variety of other processed foods, from soups to salad dressings, from crackers to cured meats. A single tablespoon of some brands of ketchup, for example, contains one teaspoon of sugar.

We don't even need sugar in our diet. Our bodies can easily convert starches to sugar in the blood, or glucose, for all the energy we need. Sugar also offers our bodies no vitamins or minerals, with the possible exception of molasses, which has small amounts of calcium, iron, potassium, and B vitamins. Contrary to popular belief, honey does *not* offer any significant amounts of nutrients. In fact, as the consumers' watchdog group, Consumers Union, has pointed out, you would have to eat 91 tablespoons of honey to get one day's worth of the daily requirement for potassium and 267 tablespoons for the daily requirement of phosphorus!

Although sugar has been blamed for a wide variety of health problems, only a few have been documented solidly. The strongest case against sugar involves tooth decay and obesity. Sugar definitely causes cavities, or dental caries, even in adults. You can minimize this danger by eating sweets only with meals and by flossing and brushing your teeth regularly.

Sugar can also make you fat. When the body's organs have used up enough calories to run on, any leftover sugar in the blood is converted into fat for storage in fat cells. The same is true, of course, of other foods. Any time you take in more calories than your body uses, you will put on weight as fat. The calories in sugary, or "junk," foods are also densely packed, usually with fats, in a relatively small volume of food. Thus when eating sweets, especially fatty sweets like chocolate, you're likely to go over your calorie limit long before your stomach feels full. Also, sugar stimulates a chemical reaction in your body that can quickly make you feel hungry again.

Although eating sugary foods does not cause diabetes or hypoglycemia (low blood sugar), people with these disorders must usually restrict their consumption of sweets to avoid wide swings in blood sugar. Some specialists claim a connection between a diet high in sugar and heart disease, but the research supporting this view is weak, except for people who are genetically prone to developing high blood fats while on sugary diets.

Finally, a word about sugar and a specific menopausal complaint: postmenopausal vaginitis. Eating too much sugar can create an alkaline environment in the vagina, leaving the vagina more susceptible to the disease organisms that cause vaginitis. So if you are having problems with vaginitis, you may want to look at your sugar consumption. (For more information about postmenopausal vaginitis, see chapter 5.)

So what's the bottom line on sugar? Avoid it as much as possible. It does your body little good and can do it considerable harm, particularly in large doses. Sugar appears to be an acquired taste—in other words, the more you eat it, the more you want it. Fortunately, the opposite is also true: You can cut down your desire for sugary foods simply by eating fewer of them. You may experience fewer mood and energy swings as well.

Tips for Eating Less Sugar

- When you have a craving for something sweet, reach for fresh fruit or fruit frozen in water. Gradually, you'll notice a decrease in your desire for sugary snacks—and an increase in your appreciation for the natural sweetness of fruit.

- Avoid artificial sweeteners. Substituting artificial sweeteners for sugar is not a healthful choice. Questions about the cancer risks of saccharin remain unanswered, as do concerns about the health effects of the artificial sweetener, Aspartame. Products with these sweeteners usually contain other unnatural and potentially harmful chemicals as well. Also, artificial sweeteners do nothing to reduce your desire for sweets; in fact, they can perpetuate it.

- Bake your own cakes, pies, and cookies and cut the amount of sugar called for in the recipes by a third or more. Also, when baking desserts, try recipes that contain nutritious ingredients, such as fruits and vegetables, whole grain flours, and cereals, along with a minimum of sweetener, such as zucchini bread, carrot cookies, banana cake, apple turnovers, and sweet potato pie.

- Experiment with "sweet" spices and herbs, such as cinnamon, cardamon, coriander, nutmeg, ginger, and mace, to enhance the flavoring of foods.

- When buying processed foods, be alert for "hidden" sugars. Look for the following on food labels: corn syrup, corn sweetener, honey, maple syrup, sorghum, dextrin, mannitol, and words ending in *ose*—sucrose, lactose, maltose, dextrose, and fructose. All are types of sugar.

- Eliminate soft drinks from your diet, including diet soda. The ultimate "empty" food, soft drinks provide about one-fourth of the sugar in the average American's diet. Read the label for contents: They contain nothing nutritious—only sugar, water, artificial coloring, artificial flavoring, and a few other nonnutritious goodies, such as preservatives. Some, most notably the cola drinks and Dr. Pepper, also contain caffeine, which, among other concerns, can trigger hot flashes and enhance your chances of caffeine addiction.

  Some companies are now making more healthful soft drinks by mixing real fruit juice and mineral water. Read labels carefully, however, to make sure nothing else has been added. Of course, you can also make these "natural" sodas yourself at home. Try adding a tablespoon or two of orange or grapefruit juice to an 8-ounce glass of sparkling mineral water. This combination soda is light, refreshing, healthful, and delicious!

Starches: One of the "Good" Guys

Starches are known as "complex" carbohydrates because, although they are made of similar elements, they have more complex molecular structures than sugars. They contain far fewer digestible calories than sugars and thus are less likely to add unwanted pounds to your weight. Starches are found principally in cereal grains, such as wheat, rice, corn, oats, barley, and millet, and they form the substance of most fruits and vegetables.

Eat more starches! They are generally rich in vitamins and minerals and, along with fiber, are one of the two food components without a single "negative" side.

Fiber: For Good Digestion—and More

Dietary fiber—the parts of plants that humans cannot digest—is a type of complex carbohydrate. Despite the fact that it travels essentially intact from the mouth to the large intestine without breaking down into nutrients for the body to absorb and use, fiber still plays a very important role in human nutrition. It provides "roughage"—the bulk that both satisfies the appetite and helps the digestive system move food along and work properly. Fiber is found in fresh fruits, vegetables, and unrefined grains.

Fiber offers the body many possible health benefits. It softens stools by retaining more water and adding volume, making them easier to pass. Fiber can relieve such problems as diarrhea, constipation, and hemorrhoids. It is also helpful in preventing and treating diverticulosis, a common condition in which the colon develops little sacklike out-pockets that, if blocked by hard stool, can become inflamed and infected. Some 40 percent of people in their middle years are believed to suffer from this condition, which can result in frequent hospitalization and even surgery.

By reducing the amount of time cancer-producing chemicals are exposed to the intestinal lining, fiber may also help prevent colon cancer, which is the third leading cause of cancer death in midlife women. In addition, some types of dietary fiber—most notably the pectin found in fruits, the guar gum found in beans, and the fiber in oat bran and carrots—appear to help lower blood cholesterol and blood sugar levels, providing possible protection against heart disease and diabetes.

Fiber must, however, be ingested carefully. A sudden large increase in dietary fiber can cause diarrhea, bloating, and the formation of intestinal gas. These symptoms are usually temporary, however, and can be prevented in many cases by increasing the amount of fiber in a diet gradually, rather than suddenly. Adding excessive amounts of fiber can also interfere with the body's absorption of important nutrients, such as protein, calcium, and iron. This happens only rarely; still, don't go overboard on a high-fiber diet.

What's a safe balance? Most of us could easily double or even triple our daily consumption of fiber with no ill effects. A reasonable goal is about 40 grams of fiber a day—or the amount found in two cups of 100 percent all-bran cereal. Other sources of fiber are not as concentrated. One cup of rolled oats, for example, has 4.5 grams of fiber; one slice of whole-wheat bread, 2.4 grams; one medium-sized carrot, 3.7 grams; and a half cup of cooked peas, 3.8 grams. As you can see, it's unlikely that you will get excessive amounts of fiber from foods other than bran. So, unless you are overdoing it with bran additives, eating too much fiber-rich food should not be a concern.

•   •   •

"I noticed my energy level is so much higher now that I'm not hemorrhaging every month. It seemed like all my energy was devoted to making blood before my hysterectomy, and now, I get to use that energy!"

•   •   •

HOW TO RECOGNIZE *REAL* WHOLE WHEAT

People are often fooled into thinking they are buying whole wheat bread, when they are actually purchasing ordinary white bread that has been dyed with caramel coloring to make it *look* like whole wheat.

How can you avoid this mistake? Read bread labels carefully. Make sure the type of flour listed first on the ingredient label is "whole wheat." If it just says "wheat flour," it is not whole wheat bread—no matter what its color.

Tips for Eating More Fiber

- Eat a wide variety of fibrous foods. Remember, different types of fiber offer different health benefits. Whole grains, for example, can help with constipation, and pectin and gums (found in fruits and vegetables) are important for lowering blood cholesterol. All fibers will help you keep your weight under control.
- Drink plenty of liquids. Fiber needs water to move smoothly through the

digestive tract. Without water, fiber can have a constipating rather than a laxative effect on your system.

- Include raw fruits and vegetables in your daily diet. They have more useful fiber than fruits and vegetables that have been cooked, pureed, juiced, or otherwise processed. In addition, their natural vitamins will remain more active if eaten uncooked.
- Look for "whole-grain" products. This means these foods contain both the bran (the outside) and the germ (the inside) part of the grain, which is where most of the fiber is found—as well as most of the vitamins and minerals.

FATS: LESS IS BEST

General Guidelines

- Reduce your total fat intake to no more than 25 to 30 percent of your total caloric consumption.
- As you decrease your total fat intake, increase the ratio of "good fats" (polyunsaturated) to "bad fats" (saturated).

The typical American eats far too much fat. Currently, about 40 percent of our calories come from fat. The National Academy of Sciences has recommended that we reduce our dietary fat to 30 percent of calories, and recent research suggests that even that number may be too high.

Our overindulgence with fatty foods is one of the major reasons we carry so much *body* fat around with us. Fat is the most concentrated source of calories in our diet. Gram for gram, pure fat contains more than *twice* as many calories as pure protein or carbohydrates.

Eating less fat is one of the surest ways of keeping your weight under control. Reducing the fat in your diet can also bring you many other important health benefits, for the fat in our foods has been linked to a number of chronic health problems, including heart disease, other vascular problems, and cancers of the colon, breast, and uterus—important concerns for women during the menopausal years.

However, although we need to reduce drastically the fat in our diets, we shouldn't cut it out completely. A very *small* amount of fat is essential for our health. Fat helps carry the fat soluble vitamins—A, D, E, and K—through our digestive system and into the blood. Dietary fat is also our only source of linoleic acid, which is essential for normal growth and healthy skin.

Just how much fat do you really need? Only about one tablespoon a day. You can meet this requirement simply by eating a healthful diet with no added fat, for all the essential fatty acids we need can be found in a typical well-balanced diet. If you are like the average American, however, you are probably getting six to eight tablespoons of fat a day—far more than necessary for good health.

In addition to watching the total amount of fat in your diet, you should also be concerned with which type of fat you are eating. Fat is made up of three types of fatty acids: saturated, polyunsaturated, and mono-unsaturated. Each fatty acid has a different chemical makeup and, as a result, a different effect on the body, so it's important to learn how to distinguish among the three.

Saturated fatty acids are believed to do the most damage to the circulatory system. That's because they tend to raise blood cholesterol, which in turn can clog and damage blood vessels (see the box on pages 164–165). Saturated fats are found mostly in animal foods, such as beef, ham, pork, butter, whole milk, eggs, and cheese. They occur in only a few plant products, most notably palm and coconut oils, and in hydrogenated vegetable oils, which are unsaturated oils that have been changed via a chemical process into saturated fats. Hydrogenated vegetable oils are often used in making preprocessed foods in order to give the foods a longer shelf life. Beware of premade, prepackaged foods sold in grocery stores!

Polyunsaturated fatty acids are believed to protect against heart disease by helping to reduce cholesterol in the blood (although they are only half as effective in reducing cholesterol as saturated fats are in raising it). Most vegetable oils, such as corn oil, sunflower oil, sesame oil, and soybean oil, are high in polyunsaturated fats. Some fish are also sources of polyunsaturated fats.

Monounsaturated fatty acids appear to neither raise nor lower blood cholesterol levels. Peanut oil and olive oil have a high proportion of this type of fatty acid, as do avocados, olives, and cashews.

For the benefit of your heart, you should pay particular attention to the amount of saturated fat in your diet. Try to eat as little of it as possible, substituting margarine for butter and vegetable oils for lard.

Because of its ability to lower blood cholesterol, it might seem to make sense to eat more polyunsaturated oil. However, there are two factors to consider. *All* fats have been implicated in cancer, particularly cancers of the breast, colon, and uterus; and all fats are twice as fattening as any other food source. So, although you should substitute a polyunsaturated fat for a saturated one whenever possible, it is also important to cut down on *all* types of fats in your diet.

Tips for Eating Less Fat

- Eat less meat, particularly high-fat meats such as bacon, sausage, and heavily marbled steaks and roasts.
- Use a polyunsaturated or monounsaturated vegetable oil for frying in place of lard or bacon fat.
- Eliminate hot dogs and bologna from your diet. Eighty percent of their calories come from fat, and both contain nitrates, which are unsafe additives.
- Drink skim milk (0 percent fat) or 1 percent milk. Whole milk contains about 3.5 percent butterfat.
- Instead of frying foods, try steaming, poaching, baking, or oven-broiling them. If you must fry, use as little fat as possible—or, better yet, do it in a nonstick frying pan that requires no added fat at the stove. Use only vegetable oils—read the labels to be sure.
- Use herbs and spices rather than sauces, butter, or margarine for seasoning vegetables.
- When a recipe calls for sour cream or mayonnaise, substitute plain lowfat yogurt, blender-whipped lowfat cottage cheese, or buttermilk.
- Use margarine instead of butter in baked goods and, when possible, use oil instead of shortening. But choose your margarine carefully. Make sure the first ingredient on the label is a *liquid* vegetable oil, such as safflower, soybean, or corn. Don't buy a margarine if the first ingredient is "partially hydrogenated" or "hardened." That means it's highly saturated. In general, don't use a fat that is solid or hard at room temperature, as these tend to be more plaque-forming in your body.
- Read the labels on processed foods carefully. Avoid those foods that contain coconut oil, palm oil, or animal fat, or those that list "vegetable oil" on the label without specifying which one.
- Read some of the many available low-fat cookbooks for further tips and low-fat recipes.

WATER: THE NEGLECTED NUTRIENT

Although it is not often thought about as a nutrient, water is the most important nutrient of all. We can live much longer without food than without water. Even two or three days without water can be fatal for some.

Our bodies contain more water than anything else. The average adult body is about two-thirds water—about 60 percent water for women, about 70 percent for men. The difference is due to the larger proportion of fat that women carry on their bodies. Fat holds less water than lean tissue.

CHOLESTEROL: FAT'S COMPANION

Cholesterol is a waxy, white, fatlike substance that can play havoc with your circulatory system if you get too much of it. Cholesterol does its dirty work by lodging itself on the walls of your arteries and clogging them up until they become so narrow and hard that blood has difficulty flowing through them properly. Known as *atherosclerosis* (*athero* = grainy plaque; *sclerosis* = hardening), this dangerous condition can eventually result in a complete blockage of the artery and cause a heart attack or stroke. If the vessel leads to the muscles in the heart, this condition can cause a heart attack. If the blocked vessel leads to the legs, it can cause foot and leg pain and difficulty walking. The plaque can also become dislodged and travel to other areas of the body, such as to the brain, where it can cause a stroke or blindness.

Some cholesterol is vital for health. The body needs it to make cell membranes, hormones, bile acids for digestion, and the protective sheaths around nerve fibers. However, the liver makes all the cholesterol the body needs—about 1,000 milligrams a day. Cholesterol from food sources is *not* necessary; yet the average American consumes between 400 and 700 additional mg of cholesterol from food each day.

The cholesterol in our diet comes exclusively from animal foods, such as meat, poultry, eggs, butter, milk, and cheese; plant foods contain no cholesterol. The amount of cholesterol in animal foods varies widely, from 5 mg of cholesterol in a cup of skim milk to 275 mg in a medium-

---

Water performs a wide range of vital jobs in the body. It is the body's great transporter, helping to carry nutrients, oxygen, hormones (including estrogen), disease-fighting cells, and waste products to and from body organs via the bloodstream and the lymphatic system and into the cells of each organ. It also lubricates body joints, keeps skin and mucous membranes moist, helps eliminate waste from the blood into the urine, and helps the bowels clean out their waste as well.

Through the process of perspiration, water also serves as the body's natural cooling system. For perspiration to evaporate into vapor, the body must release some of its own internal heat. Perspiration, therefore, enables your body to keep your internal organs from overheating.

You need about two or three quarts of water each day to replace the amount you lose through urine, feces, skin, and lungs. Half of the water we consume comes from food. Most fruits and vegetables contain an astonishingly large amount of water: Bananas are 76 percent water; carrots,

sized egg yolk to a whopping 2,668 mg in a 3-ounce serving of calf brains. The American Heart Association recommends we limit the cholesterol in our diet to no more than 300 mg a day. Studies have shown that eliminating all sources of animal fat from our diet results in the lowest rates of cancer and heart disease and leads to the fewest number of hospitalizations.

Besides eating less food high in cholesterol, we must also watch our total dietary fat intake if we want to keep our blood cholesterol levels down. Cholesterol is the carrier of fat in the bloodstream. The less fat to carry, the less cholesterol needed. Saturated fat appears to induce the liver to make more cholesterol, whereas polyunsaturated fat tends to lower the cholesterol levels in the blood (see page 162). Replace the saturated fats in your diet with unsaturated ones. In addition, eat more fiber-rich foods, particularly legumes and oat bran, which also tend to have a lowering effect on blood cholesterol.

Finally, have your fasting cholesterol checked. That's your cholesterol levels after you have not eaten for eight hours. If your low-density lipoprotein (LDL) level is elevated over 110, then consider taking additional steps to reduce the fats in your diet. (LDL is the "bad" cholesterol associated with increased heart attack and stroke risk.) To have your fasting cholesterol checked, talk to your physician.

88 percent; and zucchini, 95 percent. Meats and poultry are one-half to two-thirds water. Even bread is one-third water.

To supplement the water we get from food, nutritionists recommend that we drink six to eight 8-ounce glasses of water each day. That water can come straight from the tap (if you have a clean water supply), or it can be in the form of fruit juices or low-fat milk. Beverages containing caffeine or alcohol are not good choices for replenishing water because they act as diuretics and increase the amount of water lost through urine. Nor should sodas be considered good water replenishers; the sugar in them can actually increase your body's need for water.

On days when you are physically active or when it is hot, you should drink even more than the recommended six to eight glasses of water. If you are experiencing hot flashes, you should also drink extra amounts of water, as your body will be using up more water in its attempt to cool off after the flashes.

DON'T FORGET YOUR PHYTOESTROGENS!

As noted in chapter 2, soybeans and other food products made from soy (such as tofu and soymilk) and many other foods are rich in *phytoestrogens*, compounds that resemble the hormone estrogen. Not only may these compounds help reduce hot flashes, they may also protect against heart disease, osteoporosis, and cancer. Researchers have found for example, that animals raised on a high-soy diet have a reduced risk of cancer. Humans who eat a lot of soy foods also appear to be at reduced risk. Phytoestrogens appear to help protect against heart disease by reducing cholesterol. Scientists believe phytoestrogens may help protect against cancer either by directly inhibiting cancer cells from multiplying or by taking up space in the breast tissue or uterus normally occupied by human estrogen, which is believed to stimulate the growth of certain cancers.

For a list of foods rich in phytoestrogens, see page 36.

To cool your body quickly, drink cold, rather than warm, liquids. Cold drinks absorb body heat from within as they warm to body temperature. They also leave your stomach faster, which means the water will get to your blood and alleviate dehydration faster, too.

In general, if your urine frequently appears to be concentrated and dark yellow (excluding the yellow caused by B vitamin supplements), you are not drinking enough water. You should drink water in amounts that make your urine a pale yellow color—at least one quart a day.

VITAMINS AND MINERALS:
SMALL BUT ESSENTIAL

Although our bodies need them in very small amounts—altogether, less than a teaspoon a day—vitamins and minerals are essential for good health. They perform a myriad of crucial tasks, from helping the body process other major nutrients (fats, carbohydrates, and protein) to assisting in the formation of hormones, blood cells, and even genetic material.

Because of their important role in helping the body repair itself, vitamins and minerals may influence the aging process itself. For example, vitamins A, C, E, B1 (thiamine), B6 (pyridoxine), and B5 (pantothenic acid) appear to be dietary antioxidants that can protect cells from the damage of abnormal internal oxidation. In addition, several micronutrients—most notably, A, E, and B vitamins—appear to have a direct impact on the physiological changes related to menopause.

Recent studies also indicate that even small deficits of nutrients—most notably, vitamins C, B1, B12, and folic acid—can interfere with brain function as we get older and can impair our memory and ability to think abstractly.

Although all vitamins and minerals are essential for good health, a few are especially important to women during their midlife years. These nutrients are described in depth in the following pages.

Vitamin A: For Healthy Skin   10,000

Vitamin A has several forms. *Retinol* is the vitamin A found in animal foods; it is in a form ready for immediate use by the body. *Carotene* (or beta-carotene) is a substance found almost exclusively in plant foods; it must be converted by the body into vitamin A and may have an anti-cancer effect that retinol lacks.

Vitamin A is necessary for healthy skin, hair, and eyes. It keeps skin elastic and smooth and can sometimes help with the dry skin conditions of midlife. Vitamin A also helps repair the body's internal soft tissues, including the linings of the uterus, cervix, vagina, and urinary tract. In addition, vitamin A has key antioxidant properties. That means it helps keep certain harmless chemicals in the body from becoming harmful ones. Research studies have shown that beta-carotene in particular may help prevent the development of cancer-causing chemicals in the body.

The adult recommended daily allowance (RDA) for vitamin A is 5,000 IU (International Units); however, some nutritionists recommend taking up to 20,000 IU. The need for Vitamin A increases with body weight. Taking estrogen supplements may also increase your need for this vitamin, as high estrogen levels have been shown to inhibit vitamin A's ability to function within the body. You should never take more than 25,000 IU of Vitamin A daily; excessive amounts can lead to headaches, loss of hair, blurred vision, emotional disturbances, and a host of other problems.

The best natural sources of beta-carotene can be found in dark green leafy vegetables, such as spinach, collard greens, beet greens, and mustard greens; in yellow vegetables, such as carrots, sweet potatoes, and winter squash; and in orange fruits, such as cantaloupes, apricots, and papayas. Fish oils, such as cod liver oil, contain retinol. Liver is an excellent source of vitamin A but should be eaten in moderation because of the chemical toxins that tend to accumulate in it.

Vitamin E: For Hot Flashes

Like vitamin A, vitamin E is a major antioxidant in the body. It helps protect other nutrients from becoming destroyed by oxidation. It may also play an important role in cancer prevention, although much more research is needed to confirm the few studies pointing to this conclusion.

Grand claims have been made about vitamin E's ability to slow the changes of the aging process by slowing the deterioration of cells. These have not been substantiated. There is some evidence, however, that vitamin E may be useful in treating fibrocystic breast disease, PMS symptoms, and several rare medical conditions.

Vitamin E also plays an important role in the production of sex hormones, which may explain why it seems to provide many women with relief from the hot flashes of menopause. Before you start stocking up on cases of vitamin E supplements, however, you should know that no scientific data exists to support this claim. The only evidence so far has been anecdotal. Still, because the doses of vitamin E recommended for relieving hot flashes are easily tolerated by most adults and because taking vitamin supplements poses fewer health risks than hormone therapy, you may want to give vitamin E a try if hot flashes are a problem for you. Good food sources of vitamin E include cold pressed oils, wheat germ, eggs, molasses, organ meats, sweet potatoes, and leafy vegetables.

For specific information about taking vitamin E for hot flashes, see chapter 2.

Vitamin C: For General Well-Being

Probably no other vitamin has been heralded for so many health benefits as vitamin C. Unfortunately, many of the claims made about vitamin C—that it prevents cancer, for example, or that it protects against heart disease—have yet to be proven. Nor has it be proven that it can prevent the common cold, although it *can* lessen the severity of cold symptoms in some people.

Vitamin C does, however, perform many crucial jobs in the body. In fact, it's one of the most versatile vitamins around. Here are just a few of vitamin C's varied duties that are particularly important during midlife:

- It acts as an antioxidant.
- It helps form collagen—the protein necessary for healthy skin, blood vessels, muscles, and bones.

- It promotes healthy adrenal glands (where estrogen is produced after menopause).
- It helps heal wounds and broken bones.
- It helps fight infections.
- It aids iron absorption.
- It promotes healthy gums and teeth.

The adult RDA for vitamin C is 60 mg. That's about the amount found in four ounces of orange juice or half a cup of broccoli. If you are experiencing stress, if you smoke cigarettes (or regularly inhale the smoke from someone else's cigarettes), or if you have recently undergone surgery, you may need more of this vitamin. Many nutritionists also recommend that women who are taking estrogen increase the amount of vitamin C in their diet.

The best natural sources of vitamin C are citrus fruits and dark green leafy vegetables, such as broccoli, spinach, and collard greens. Strawberries, cantaloupes, tomatoes, peppers, and potatoes are also good sources. The vitamin C in food, however, is very unstable and can be destroyed easily by heat from cooking, light, air, and water. That's one of the reasons many nutritionists recommend taking vitamin C supplements in addition to eating a balanced diet.

If you should decide to take a supplement, be sure not to overdo it. Although side effects from vitamin C supplements are rare, some have been reported, including diarrhea, abdominal cramps, fatigue, and heartburn. Large doses taken over a long period of time have also been linked— although not yet conclusively—to the development of kidney stones and a drop in blood copper levels.

How much, then, is too much? As noted nutritionist Patricia Hausman argues convincingly in her book, *The Right Dose*, a good, safe, long-term dose of vitamin C is 500 mg daily. People who take daily supplements of more than 1,000 mg of vitamin C, Hausman stresses, should have their blood copper levels checked periodically. In addition, she adds, people should take megadoses of the vitamin—2,000 mg or more—only under medical supervision.

Also, avoid chewable vitamin C tablets. They can damage the enamel on your teeth.

The B Vitamins: For All-Around Health

The eight B vitamins that make up the B-complex play a key role in maintaining health during the menopausal years. They are necessary for strong adrenal glands, a healthy nervous system, and the conversion of carbohydrates into the glucose we need for energy.

The B vitamins that have the most direct effect on midlife health are thiamine (B1), riboflavin (B2), niacin, pyridoxine (B6), and folic acid. *Thiamine* keeps mucous membranes—including those of the vagina—healthy. It is also an antioxidant, especially when it works with vitamin C.

Riboflavin is essential for the release and activity of a variety of hormones, including estrogen. It also helps keep skin, nails, and hair healthy.

Niacin helps with the body's production of estrogen and other sex hormones. In addition, it reduces blood cholesterol and dilates blood vessels, which is why it is sometimes prescribed to prevent premenstrual headaches.

Pyridoxine is a natural diuretic and thus is effective against water retention and perhaps the depression and other symptoms associated with premenstrual syndrome (which may be related, in part, to water retention). With vitamin C, pyridoxine also helps make serotonin, a brain chemical associated with calm moods and restful sleep. In addition, pyridoxine interacts with estrogen in the body, although this interaction is not yet clearly understood.

Folic acid helps the body manufacture and use estrogen. It also promotes the formation of healthy red blood cells, which is why a deficiency of this vitamin can lead to anemia.

The B vitamins are usually found together in the same foods. The best sources of these vitamins are whole wheat breads and cereals, oatmeal, and dried beans. Brewer's yeast is another excellent source of all the B vitamins except B12. Liver, nuts, eggs, and seeds are rich in B vitamins, although because of health concerns noted elsewhere in this chapter, these foods should be eaten only in moderation. In addition, the white meat of poultry and fish, especially that of chicken and tuna, are good sources of niacin, pyridoxine, and folic acid.

Because taking estrogen appears to deplete the body of some of the B vitamins—most notably, pyridoxine and folic acid—some nutritionists recommend that women on hormone replacement therapy take supplements of some or all of the B vitamins. It is theorized, for example, that the more severe hot flashes experienced by some women when they give up estrogen may be the result of a depletion of folic acid caused by having taken the hormone. Some doctors also prescribe a B-complex supplement along with vitamin E for relief from hot flashes for women who are not on HRT.

If you do take a supplement of any of the Bs, be sure to take 100

THE RDAs FOR THE B VITAMINS

Thiamine (B1)	1.0 mg
Riboflavin (B2)	1.2 mg
Niacin (B3)	13.0 mg
Pantothenic acid (B5)	4 to 7 mg*
Pyridoxine (B6)	2.0 mg
Folic acid (B9, folate, or folacin)	400 meg
Cyanocobalamin (B12)	3 meg
Biotin	100 to 200 meg*

* No RDA has been established. This is the estimated "safe and adequate" range established by the Food and Nutrition Board of the National Academy of Sciences.

---

percent of the RDA for all the others to maintain a correct balance of these vitamins in your system. (For a list of the RDAs for all the B vitamins, see the box above.) Also, make sure the niacin you take is in the form of *niacinamide*. Other forms of niacin dilate the blood vessels, which can cause flushing and exacerbate your hot flashes—exactly the effect you *don't* want!

Calcium: For Strong Bones

The body's most abundant mineral, calcium is well known for its crucial role in developing strong bones and teeth. A high-calcium diet, or calcium supplementation, may even prevent or slow the bone-deteriorating disease of osteoporosis.

Calcium performs other essential tasks in the body as well, including helping blood to clot and enabling muscles, including the heart muscle, to contract and relax. Recent studies also suggest that a calcium-rich diet may lower blood pressure for some people and may also help prevent colorectal (colon or rectal) cancer.

Milk and other dairy products are the richest natural sources of calcium, yet some doctors have recently expressed concern that the protein in dairy foods may deplete the body of calcium, thus negating at least some of the value of these foods as a calcium source. Broccoli and green leafy vegetables also contain calcium in smaller, but significant amounts. For a list of foods rich in calcium and a full discussion of the relation between calcium, estrogen, and osteoporosis, see chapter 6.

Vitamin D: For Strong Bones

It was once believed that only calcium was needed for strong bones. Now vitamin D has been recognized as an important player in building and maintaining a healthy skeleton. Vitamin D not only helps the body absorb calcium, but also keeps it from losing calcium too rapidly.

The average person needs about 400 to 800 IUs of vitamin D daily. The most natural way of getting vitamin D is through direct exposure to sunlight. Ten minutes in the sun with face and hands exposed each day is enough for young and middle-aged people to meet the daily requirement. However, as you age, your skin becomes less adept at making vitamin D. An 80-year-old's skin makes only half as much vitamin D as a 20-year-old's. Thus older people may benefit from vitamin D supplements. Do not, however, take more than 800 IUs daily without consulting your doctor. This vitamin can be toxic at doses not much higher than the RDA. Some calcium supplements contain vitamin D, so if you are taking calcium daily, you may not need an additional vitamin D supplement.

One final note: You can't get too much vitamin D from sunlight—but you can damage your skin. So don't overdo it.

Iron: For Preventing Anemia
from Heavy Periods

Iron is an essential component of hemoglobin, which is the oxygen-carrying chemical in the red blood cells. Too little iron in the body means that your heart has to work harder to deliver more blood to the tissues, and that can result in the tissues getting less oxygen. This condition, known as anemia, is characterized by extreme fatigue and susceptibility to stress and illness. Iron deficiency from a poor diet is the most common nutritional deficiency in the United States; as many as one out of four Americans is estimated to suffer from it. Because iron is lost through bleeding, women are considered at greatest risk during their menstruating years, particularly if they are experiencing heavy monthly flows. Women approaching menopause sometimes have heavy flows, which means they are at a special risk of iron deficiency and thus of anemia.

The RDA for iron is 18 mg for women who are still menstruating and 10 mg for those who have stopped. The best natural sources of iron are foods rich in protein, such as liver, meats, poultry, fish, beans, and dark green leafy vegetables. Eating foods rich in iron along with ones rich in vitamin C can greatly enhance your body's absorption of the mineral. Using iron pots for cooking is another good way of adding to your iron intake.

Manganese: For Strong Bones

Recent studies indicate that manganese deficiency may be an important factor in osteoporosis. In one Belgian study, for example, women with severe osteoporosis were found to have in their blood only a quarter of the manganese found in the blood of age-matched women without osteoporosis.

Some researchers now believe that the current RDA for manganese, 2.5 to 5 mg daily, is too low. They recommend that at least 3.8 mg be consumed daily to prevent the body from depleting its stores of the mineral.

Ironically, the richest natural sources of manganese—wheat bran, tea, and spinach—also contain other ingredients, such as the tannins in tea, that make the manganese unavailable to the body. Better sources of this mineral are nuts, vegetables and fruits, meats, milk, and eggs; the amounts of the mineral in these foods are smaller but are much more available to the body.

SOME SPECIAL INGREDIENTS

Salt, caffeine, and alcohol are three ingredients in your diet to which you should pay special attention during your menopausal years. All three can trigger hot flashes and can contribute to several midlife health problems.

Salt

It may look innocent enough as you sprinkle it onto your food at the dinner table, but those white crystals we know as salt can have a significant effect on your health during the menopausal years.

To begin with, salt—or, more specifically, the sodium that is in salt—is a major cause of high blood pressure, a condition that has a tendency to worsen with advancing age, leading to kidney failure, stroke, and heart disease. Salt causes the body to retain excessive amounts of water. In addition to its link to high blood pressure, water retention has been implicated as a possible factor in triggering hot flashes. It is also theorized to aggravate many of the symptoms of premenstrual syndrome, such as headaches, irritability, and depression.

Our sensitivity to the effects of salt increases with age. As we get older, kidney function tends to slow down and our bodies become less adept at excreting sodium. As a result, more of the sodium we eat stays in our bodies, and that means we have a greater potential for developing high blood pressure and other sodium-related problems.

It's important, therefore, that you now eat less salt and salty foods. The Food and Nutrition Board of the National Academy of Sciences recommends a range of 1,100 to 3,300 mg of sodium daily, with an average consumption of 2,200 mg. That's one-half to one-fifth of the sodium that the average American woman now gets in her diet. So start throwing out your salt shakers, or at least put them in a cabinet where they are difficult to reach!

The taste for salt is acquired: The more of it you eat, the more you want. Fortunately, the opposite is also true; if you gradually use less salt, your desire for it will diminish.

Tips for Eating Less Salt

- Gradually reduce the amount of salt you use in cooking and baking. Instead, flavor your foods with herbs, spices, garlic powder (not garlic salt), onion powder (not onion salt), lemon juice—anything rather than salt.
- Limit the amount of presalted foods you buy and eat, such as potato chips, pretzels, salted nuts, cured meats, and pickled foods. Also, ask for unsalted popcorn at the movie theater.
- Read food labels carefully for hidden sodium. Salt is the leading food additive after sugar and is hidden in a wide variety of processed and packaged foods, including cheeses, breads, canned soups, and breakfast cereals. Find low-sodium products and use them instead of the high-sodium ones.

Caffeine

Found in coffee, tea, chocolate, some cola drinks, and aspirin-type pain killers, caffeine is a powerful drug with a stimulating effect on the brain and a diuretic effect on the kidneys. In small doses, caffeine can be an effective pick-me-up, producing clearer thinking, sharper sensory awareness, and a quicker reaction time. In large doses, however—or even in small doses in people who are particularly sensitive to the drug—caffeine can lead to "coffee nerves," an anxious, jittery feeling associated with drinking too many cups of coffee.

If you are experiencing hot flashes, any amount of caffeine can be a problem. By causing constriction or tightening of the blood vessels in the skin, caffeine can elevate body temperature, cause high blood pressure, and possibly trigger hot flashes. Caffeine is also a diuretic and can deplete the body of vitamin C, several B vitamins, calcium, potassium, and zinc—much needed nutrients during the midlife years. In addition, caffeine encourages the pancreas to release more insulin, which can cause your blood sugar to drop, making you more drowsy and hungry. And that can hurt your attempts to keep your weight under control.

It's easy to become psychologically and physically dependent on caffeine. As few as three or four cups of coffee a day will do it. Because of caffeine's addictive qualities, going "cold turkey" and excluding all caffeine from your diet can lead to withdrawal symptoms, including headaches, nausea, depression, constipation, and drowsiness. For that reason, experts recommend that you wean yourself from caffeine gradually—say, by reducing the number of cups of coffee you drink by one each day over a period of a week or more. Even on this gradual program, you can expect to feel tired or irritable—or both—for a few days as your body adjusts to being caffeine-free. Make sure your diet is rich in fiber and drink plenty of water to reduce constipation. Get plenty of exercise, too. But stick with it; in the long run, you'll feel a lot better.

Tips for Reducing Caffeine

- When brewing coffee, use a mixture of both regular and decaffeinated coffees, then gradually increase the decaf component until you have eliminated the caffeinated part. Be aware, however, that even decaffeinated coffee contains small amounts of caffeine. If you want to eliminate caffeine entirely from your diet, you'll need to give it up, too.
- Try one of the several grain-based coffeelike beverages on the market today. They may taste strange to you at first—but probably not any stranger than your very first cup of coffee tasted all those years ago!
- You can also substitute hot or cold herbal teas for caffeinated beverages. Be sure, however, that you drink herbal teas in moderation. Some herbal teas, such as those made from senna leaves or buckthorn bark, can cause severe diarrhea; others, including teas from chamomile, goldenrod, and yarrow, can cause severe allergic reactions in people sensitive to ragweed and related plants. Chamomile and valerian root tea can cause drowsiness, and some packaged herbal teas also contain caffeine. Read the label carefully.

Alcohol

Alcohol has two very distinct sides. When consumed in moderation—one or two glasses of wine or beer a day or one or two shots (1.5 ounces each) of hard liquor—alcohol can actually be good for some people. Studies done on men have shown that moderate drinkers live longer than abstainers or light drinkers. Scientists believe this longevity is due to the fact that moderate levels of alcohol raise high-density lipoproteins (HDLs), the blood proteins that protect against heart disease. Many scientists have applied this and other research done solely with male subjects to women. However, no data proves this effect in women, and women have a very different metabolism than men. Several studies are finally currently underway to determine these effects on women.

•   •   •

"I've accepted lots of things in life, and one of them is getting older. So that's why I try to stay healthy, because if you're not healthy, that's when your attitude toward life begins to suffer. Diet, exercise, not smoking, and being very careful about alcohol are very important. I drink little or nothing now. I do think I have some blessings—I have good health and tend not to get sick."

•   •   •

Alcohol has, however, a less pleasant side. It is an antinutrient, depleting the body of vitamin C, calcium, and several B vitamins, most notably niacin, thiamin, and folic acid. It can cause depression and insomnia and can impair your body's immunological response, making you more susceptible to bacterial and other infections. Heavy alcohol drinking is also a risk factor in many cancers and can lead to potentially fatal liver damage. And although moderate amounts of alcohol raise the beneficial HDLs, heavy amounts can lead to high blood pressure, which can cause heart disease.

Midlife women should also be aware that alcohol is a known trigger of hot flashes. It is also a powerful oxidant in the body, which can lead to premature wrinkling of the skin. It can greatly aggravate the symptoms of premenstrual syndrome.

If you like to drink alcohol, be sure you do so in moderation. Also, remember that alcohol is essentially an empty calorie food, providing 7 calories per gram (more than carbohydrates and protein) and only meager amounts of nutrients.

HOW TO EAT FOR HEALTH

The key to a healthful diet is balance and moderation. This is true at any time of life but particularly now, at midlife, when your body is experiencing so many changes. By making a purposeful effort to eat well now, you can greatly ease your transition through the menopause years.

Here are some general guidelines to help you on this journey:

- Eat a variety of foods, with a special emphasis on fruits, vegetables, and whole grains.
- Make sure you get enough calcium in your diet.
- Cut down on total fat in general and saturated fats and cholesterol in particular.
- Make sure your diet is rich in fiber.
- Go easy on refined sugars and empty calorie junk food.
- Avoid too much sodium.
- Cut down on your caffeine intake.
- If you drink alcoholic beverages, do so only in moderation.

Changing eating patterns can be difficult, especially if you are living in a household with other people who may not want to change their habits. Some changes are relatively easy—such as cutting back on sodium or getting more calcium. Other changes are more difficult because they involve entirely new ways of looking at food and at your relationship with it. "I realized that I ate the worst kinds of food when I was under the most stress," says one woman. "I had to stop and recognize what I was doing and then consciously change my eating habits—and that wasn't easy."

•　　•　　•

"I used to gain weight every time I got upset because eating made me feel better at the time. Then I'd be stuck with all that weight! Now I just exercise harder, which helps me release my frustrations and keeps weight off."

•　　•　　•

It is often best to take one small step at a time. "One of the main things I did after my hysterectomy was give up oils and butter," say another woman. "That was mainly because of my skin. I noticed that having too much oil on something instantly made my skin break out above my lip. It hadn't done that before the operation. Then, a couple of years later I gave up coffee, because of the caffeine, of course, but also because it made me want to eat. I was slowly realizing that weight was now becoming a problem."

Changing to a healthful diet sometimes requires outside, professional help, particularly if you are extremely overweight or have a chronic illness. But for most of us, changing our eating habits is something we can accomplish on our own. For the changes to happen, however, we must first recognize the impact diet has on our mental and physical health and then make a personal commitment to actively alter our diet in positive, life-giving ways.

Eating well is one of the most important things you can do for yourself during midlife. So start today!

8

TAKING CHARGE:
Exercising

I feel stronger than ever before. I am confident about myself and my mental capacity. I feel I can do just about anything. But after twenty years of training and fulfilling many of my goals, maybe I'm not hampered as much by aging as by the need to find new challenges and a more diversified life.
—Former Olympic figure skater JoJo Starbuck

Many women who begin an exercise program at midlife report that it is the best thing they've ever done for themselves.

"It's changed my whole attitude," says one 54-year-old woman who walks two miles with a friend each morning and swims three evenings a week. "I used to feel so much of my life was out-of-control. But now, because I've been able to discipline myself to stick with an exercise program, I feel more in control of other aspects of my life as well."

"Before I started running," says another woman who took up the sport at age 42, "I used to want to take a nap every afternoon. It was incredible how sleepy I would get. Now I have much more energy. And, ironically, I seem to sleep better at night, too."

If you are not already following a good, regular exercise program, now is the time to get started. Regular exercise can help you become physically fit, and that means you'll enjoy significant health advantages during your midlife and later years.

In fact, if you are looking for a "youth pill," a good exercise program is undoubtedly the best one around.

Exercise's ability to slow down the aging process can not be overstated. Study after study has shown that many of the physical and mental changes we associate with aging—and with menopause—are really the result of inactivity.

In this chapter, we'll take a look at the benefits of exercise, particularly during midlife. We'll then explore the three basic types of exercise, why each is important at midlife, and how you can incorporate all three into your daily and weekly schedules.

WHAT EXERCISE CAN DO FOR YOU

Exercise is truly a magic potion. It can instill a vitality in your life that no medicine can match.

The next sections tell you why.

More Stamina and Energy

Being physically fit will enable you to perform at your best, both mentally and physically. Your mind will be more alert, your body less likely to complain with aches and pains at the end of the day. You'll also have a greater store of strength and energy to call upon for those crisis times in your life when you are under added physical and emotional demands.

The extra stamina comes primarily from a strengthened cardiovascular system. Regular exercise conditions the heart, enabling it to pump more efficiently. Exercise also increases lung capacity. As a result, more oxygen reaches the muscles—and that means that the body becomes less tired.

A Healthier Heart

A long-term exercise program also offers protection against heart disease, the risk of which increases after menopause. Exercise raises the level of HDLs, the blood proteins that protect the arteries from becoming clogged with fatty deposits. It also helps lower blood pressure. In fact, exercise therapy is sometimes all that is needed to control high blood pressure.

Recent studies have shown an impressive lowering of heart disease and cancer risk from even modest physical activity. A 1995 study of 73,029 women involved in the ongoing Nurses Health Study revealed that regular exercise reduced the risk of heart attack and stroke by as much as 40 percent. Another recent study of more than 1,100 women with an average age of 67 found that walking just 30 to 45 minutes three times a week lowered the risk of heart disease by 50 percent. Women who engaged in even more physical activity had as much as a 60 percent drop in heart attack risk.

Help for Hot Flashes

Exercise tunes up the hormonal system, ensuring that the adrenal and ovary glands stay healthy and function efficiently. It may even help lessen the frequency and intensity of hot flashes by reducing stress and improving the regulation of body temperature through sweating.

In one Swedish study, investigators found that 79 menopausal women in a gymnastics group experienced half as many severe hot flashes as did women in a randomly chosen control group. Although the study's authors do not claim that exercise will reduce the incidence of hot flashes, they stress that it is a strong possibility and call for further research.

Also, by getting you accustomed to sweating, exercise may help you accept hot flashes with more equanimity and less embarrassment.

Stronger Bones and Joints

As noted in chapter 6, regular weight-bearing exercise (the kind that puts stress on your bones) can help protect against osteoporosis, especially when coupled with a calcium-rich diet. Exercise also helps build strong supporting muscles and ligaments for the joints and the back, making it less likely that you will injure yourself either while exercising or during everyday activities.

A Natural Antidepressant and Sedative

Exercise can help ease depression and anxiety. It's a way to work off tension, dissipate anger and frustration, relieve boredom, and build self-confidence. In fact, some studies have shown that exercise is at least as effective as therapy in treating moderate depression. In addition, exercise improves sleep, particularly deep, restful sleep, which can become more elusive as we age.

Exercise may even make you more creative. In one study of 120 women, researchers found that women who had just completed 20 minutes of aerobic dance were able to solve problems more originally and creatively than their sedentary peers. The researchers theorize that the endorphins and adrenaline released during exercise help people activate the creative right side of the brain.

The Best Defense Against Middle-aged Spread

Regular exercise can also help you achieve and maintain your weight goal and avoid middle-aged spread. Studies have shown that active women weigh 30 percent less than sedentary women, *even though both groups eat about the same amount of food!* The reason for the weight difference is simple: Exercising uses up calories and burns unwanted fat from the body. This calorie loss doesn't stop when you're done with your daily workout; the body burns extra calories for several hours after vigorous exercise. In addition, exercise helps keep blood sugar levels stable, which means that you won't feel as hungry as often during the day. And it speeds up the digestive process, which means that the body has less time to convert food supplies into fat.

Even when they weigh the same, active people often appear trimmer than their sedentary counterparts. That's because a greater percentage of their weight is made up of muscle rather than fat, and muscle is denser than fat.

Smoother, Healthier Skin

Exercise increases blood circulation to your skin, giving it better color and a healthy natural "glow." Exercise also helps your skin produce more collagen, the fibrous protein that enables skin to bend and stretch and then return to normal shape. The more collagen cells you have, the thicker, firmer—and potentially less wrinkled—your skin. Don't expect miracles, however. Exercise cannot undo the effects of years of exposure to sunlight, which is the main cause of wrinkles (see chapter 9).

Increased Libido

Exercise can greatly enhance our sexuality. By easing stress and mild depression, exercise can make us more open to sexual enjoyment. It can also make us more fit for sex, providing us with more physical energy and suppleness.

In one study, for example, researchers found that recreational swimmers over the age of 40 had sex lives as active as those reported by many people in their twenties and thirties. An overwhelming majority of the swimmers—94 percent—reported that they continued to enjoy sex a lot.

Physical activity, therefore, can play an important role in enriching our sexual lives.

And More

As if all of the above weren't enough, exercise also offers a host of other health benefits. It helps your body make better use of nutrients, particularly protein, vitamin C, vitamin B6, and iron. It aids digestion and elimination. It prevents arthritic joints from becoming stiff. And it can help control diabetes, a disease that often occurs in midlife and is associated with obesity.

As you can see, the question of whether you should exercise is really moot. You cannot afford *not* to exercise. It's essential for your health and well-being.

•   •   •

"I've always been athletic and I've always taken care of myself. I eat the right foods. I don't smoke. I don't drink. I do all of these things right and there was a big part of me that said, 'And this is the thanks I get? Hot flushes?' "

•   •   •

BEFORE YOU START

To protect your heart, you should consult with your physician before you start an exercise program, even if you have no prior history of heart disease. Some cardiovascular diseases, such as high blood pressure and aortic stenosis (the blockage of one of the heart valves) can exist without showing any symptoms, particularly in sedentary people. You may have a "silent" heart disease without knowing it. Starting a vigorous exercise program without consulting your physician may therefore put you at great risk.

In addition to a general routine physical, your physician may want you to undergo a cardiac stress test before giving you the okay to begin a vigorous exercise program. For the test you will be asked to walk on an automated treadmill or ride a stationary bicycle while attached by electrodes to an electrocardiogram machine (ECG), a device that records the

---

THE "I DON'T NEED TO EXERCISE, I'M ALREADY ACTIVE" SYNDROME

Many people tend to perceive their lives as being more active than they actually are. They may believe that because they are on their feet all day at work or because they spend a great deal of their time at home with household chores, they are getting plenty of exercise.

A hectic lifestyle, however, is not the same as a physically active one. Most of us overestimate the amount of physical exertion we expend as we go about our everyday activities.

For a more realistic appraisal of exactly how much exercise you get each day, try keeping an "activities journal" for three days. Write down exactly how much time you spend standing, sitting, and moving about. Or wear a pedometer—a device that records distances walked—for a few days. One nurse who wore such a device found that the five or six miles she thought she walked each day at work turned out to be only about a mile!

---

heart's electrical activity. Pulse rate, blood pressure, and other signs of possible malfunctions of the heart and blood vessels will also be monitored during the test. The tilt and speed of the treadmill or the speed and resistance of the bicycle will be increased gradually until by the end of the test you will be walking rather quickly up a slight incline or pedaling vigorously. A stress test generally takes no more than 15 minutes. Its results should give you and your doctor a good idea of how your heart will react to the extra stress of exercise.

If you should have a special health condition, such as heart disease, high blood pressure, or diabetes, don't let it deter you from beginning an exercise program. In fact, people recovering from heart attacks are now encouraged to start a regular exercise program as part of their rehabilitation therapy. And exercise is an important component in the treatment of diabetes. You'll just want to begin more slowly and under the careful guidance of your physician.

CHOOSING AN EXERCISE PROGRAM

Designing a good exercise program involves more than just choosing a specific activity, such as running or bicycling, and then going out and doing it. A good exercise program must work the entire body. That means that it should include all three components of physical fitness—flexibility, strength, and cardiovascular endurance.

Any single activity may include one, or perhaps two, of these fitness components, but seldom all three. Running, for example, develops cardiovascular endurance and lower body strength but does nothing for strengthening the upper body or improving flexibility. Tennis can be good for strength but not for endurance. Yoga is a superb choice for improving flexibility but does little for strength or endurance. The only two activities that come close to being all-around conditioners are cross-country skiing and swimming.

The best plan is to choose as your primary method of exercise an activity that builds cardiovascular fitness. Then supplement that activity with strengthening and flexibility exercises.

AEROBICS: THE HEART OF THE MATTER

Exercises that build cardiovascular fitness are known as *aerobic* activities. *Aerobic* means "with oxygen." An aerobic activity is one that requires a steady supply of oxygen for sustained periods of activity. This means that the heart and respiratory rates are much above normal for a sustained period. Running is a good aerobic exercise. So is bicycling, if you pump your legs hard and don't spend a lot of time coasting. Playing tennis is usually not aerobic for the novice—there are too many pauses in the action. The same is usually true of lifting weights, no matter how much poundage you press.

Aerobic activities are the best ones for getting and staying in shape. They are the activities that condition your heart to pump efficiently in order to transport oxygen to muscle cells more efficiently. And that's what gives you endurance, energy, and that overall good feeling that comes with exercising.

As we age, we gradually lose some aerobic power as our heart, muscles, lungs, and blood vessels experience normal changes. But by engaging regularly in aerobic activities, you can restore much of the fitness that had been lost. You may even find yourself feeling more fit at 50 than you did at 30!

Know Your Pulse Rate

For an aerobic exercise to be beneficial, it must be done with an intensity that gives your heart and lungs a reasonable workout. Just what is "reasonable"? You can determine that by measuring your pulse rate. During a good aerobic workout your pulse should be beating at a rate that is between 70 and 85 percent of its maximum rate. This is called your *training heart rate* and it should be your goal.

To determine your training heart rate, do the following simple calculations:

- Find your maximum heart rate by subtracting your age from the number 220. If you are 50 years old, for example, your estimated maximum heart rate is 170 beats per minute.
- Now multiply your estimated maximum heart rate by both .70 and .85. Those figures will give you the lower and upper ranges of your training heart rate. In other words, if you are 50, your pulse should beat during your aerobic workout at a rate of 119 (.70 × 170) to 144.5 (.85 × 170) times per minute.

If you've been sedentary for a long time, you should aim for a training heart rate of only 70 percent, or even lower. Work your way toward the upper figure slowly, over a period of several months.

The best way to check the intensity of your workout is to measure your pulse rate immediately after finishing. Take your pulse for 10 seconds, then multiply this number by six to determine how fast your heart was beating during the workout. You can use either the pulse in your wrist or the one in the carotid artery in your neck (between the windpipe and the large neck muscles).

If this sounds too complicated, there's another, less scientific way of knowing whether your aerobic workout is actually conditioning your heart: If you have worked up a sweat and feel slightly out of breath for about 15 minutes after completing the activity, you can probably assume that you reached your training heart rate. You can also use the "conversation" test: If during your workout you can keep up a conversation with a partner (or sing out loud to yourself)—but just barely—you are probably within your target range. (This test is not recommended for swimmers!)

Thirty Minutes, Three to Five Times a Week

For aerobic exercise to do you any good, you must keep your pulse rate up for a good 15 to 30 minutes. The brisker the exercise, the more strenuous the workout for your heart—and the less time you need to spend doing it to reap some cardiovascular benefits. If you want to lose weight, longer workouts—a minimum of 40 to 60 minutes—are necessary. The body doesn't start to burn significant amounts of fat until you've been exercising strenuously for at least half an hour.

You must also schedule your aerobic workout at least three times a week, preferably five, for it to be beneficial. Don't overdo it, however. Extending the frequency of aerobic workouts to more than five days a week will not significantly improve your aerobic power, but it will increase the possibility of injury.

Choosing Aerobic Activities

Convenience is the major factor to consider when determining which aerobic activity you want to pursue. Remember, you need to have an aerobic workout at least three times a week. If the activity isn't convenient—say, you have to drive half an hour each way through heavy traffic to get to an indoor pool—you're likely to start skipping sessions.

You'll also want to keep cost in mind. Some activities have an initial high expense, such as the purchase of a bicycle; others may be costly over time, such as keeping up a membership in a health club. Running, walking, and rope skipping are probably the least expensive aerobic activities, although you will need to invest periodically in a good pair of shoes.

The best aerobic activities are listed below. Although you may want to concentrate at first on a single activity, you may eventually find it more interesting—and easier on your body—to alternate among two or three activities. You may decide, for example, to alternate your aerobic workouts between walking and swimming, or to substitute cross-country skiing in winter for running. This is known as "cross training" and helps ensure against both mental and physical burnout.

Walking is the easiest, most natural, and safest aerobic activity you can do. It requires no special equipment—except comfortable shoes—and can be done just about anywhere. Besides getting the heart in shape and helping to shed pounds (a mile of walking uses up as many calories as a mile of running, although it takes longer), walking improves circulation in the legs. Walking also helps with constipation by stimulating elimination. And it's a great mental tonic, relieving tension and anxiety. Walking does little to strengthen the upper body, so you should supplement it with other activities or exercises.

Walking must be done at a brisk, arm-swinging pace for it to do any good. If you've been sedentary, start slowly and gradually increase both speed and distance.

Running   gets you in shape the fastest with the least investment in time. You must start very slowly, however, to give your body time to adjust to the added stresses. The best way to begin is with a walk/run program in which you alternate every few minutes between walking and running. High-quality running shoes are essential for avoiding injuries. Be sure you have a pair before starting.

Running, like walking, strengthens the muscles of the lower body but does little to develop the upper body and should be supplemented with another activity that requires upper body muscles. Running is not good for knees because of the high impact on this joint. If you have had any kind of knee trouble, consult your physician before starting a running program, or consider walking or swimming instead.

Swimming   has been described as the "perfect" sport. Besides building cardiovascular endurance, swimming develops all major muscles in the body—arms, legs, back, abdomen, and chest. It is also great for improving flexibility. Swimming puts no stress on bones, joints, or muscles, which makes it an ideal activity for people who are obese or who have back or joint problems, such as arthritis. Because it is not a weight-bearing exercise, however, you should alternate it with a walking, running, or weight-lifting program to keep your bones strong and reduce your risk of osteoporosis.

Bicycling,   when done vigorously and regularly, can equal running for cardiovascular conditioning. It strengthens your thighs, hips, and, to a lesser extent, your calves. Bicycling does nothing for your upper body strength, however; nor does it help with flexibility.

Bicycling can be done outdoors—preferably on a bicycle path—or indoors on a stationary bicycle. Not only will you avoid gas fumes and bad weather on an indoor bike, but you can also read, watch television, or listen to music while you pedal. Stationary bicycles also require no balancing skills.

Rope skipping   doesn't raise the heart rate as consistently as running, but it is still an excellent way of improving cardiovascular fitness. You can substitute it for walking or running during bad weather or while traveling. If you are out of shape, go slowly. Rope skipping accelerates the heart rate to near maximum levels very quickly and can be very hard on the knees. It's best to start by mixing rope skipping with walking until, over a period of two or three months, you can skip continually for 30 minutes. Be sure to wear well-cushioned shoes and avoid skipping on asphalt or other hard surfaces.

Aerobic dancing, or "exaerobics," can be great fun and a good conditioner for your heart. A well-choreographed aerobic dance routine can also improve flexibility and strengthen both upper and lower parts of the body. The workout, whether choreographed by an aerobic dance instructor in a class setting or on a video tape you follow at home, should include a warm-up, at least 30 minutes of vigorous movements, and a cool-down session at the end.

Rowing builds strength and cardiovascular endurance. It uses most of the large muscle groups of the body yet doesn't put a great deal of stress on joints. If you have easy access to open water where you live and want to row outdoors, your best bet is to join a rowing club. Most clubs offer lessons and make boats available for use by members. The great majority of people who row for exercise, however, use indoor rowing machines that simulate the water's resistance with tension devices.

Cross-country skiing, whether done indoors on a machine or outdoors on a snow trail, requires more oxygen than almost any other sport and is an excellent aerobic conditioner. It's also easy on your knees and other joints. It's a good winter alternative to walking or running.

Ice skating and roller skating can also be good aerobic conditioners—if you're skilled at them and can keep moving at a steady, vigorous pace for 30 minutes or more.

Racket sports such as tennis, racquetball, squash, and handball will help you use up calories and build muscles but will give your cardiovascular system an aerobic workout only if the ball is kept in play for sustained periods.

Remember, your best bet is to do a variety of aerobic activities. Not only will that approach cut down on injuries, but it will also make exercising more interesting. And boredom is the major reason people cite for giving up exercising.

WEIGHT TRAINING:
FOR BUILDING STRENGTH—
AND BONES

From lifting laundry to lugging a stuffed briefcase home from work, many of our daily activities require strong muscles. Yet, unless we make a point of exercising our muscles, we can expect to lose 3 to 5 percent of muscle tissue with the passage of each decade of our adult lives. Such a loss can turn once-routine tasks into overwhelming obstacles. It can lead to fatigue and joint stiffness, limiting our activities and making us feel old before our time.

You can stop or even reverse this trend by making muscle-strengthening activities part of your weekly exercise routine. These are exercises that work muscles against gradually increasing degrees of resistance. The idea is to overload the muscles by making them work extremely hard during the workout. The muscles respond to the demand put on them by becoming larger and stronger.

• • •

"I read about all the studies that say that weight-bearing exercise can decrease bone mass loss, so I switched my training program. I'd been running a lot, but I increased my mileage even more and cut back on the swimming, which didn't do that much for my bones. I also watch my diet. I'm very careful about the amount of calcium I take. I even take calcium supplements."

• • •

To rebuild themselves, muscles need at least a 48-hour rest period between workouts—so be sure to schedule your weight training sessions accordingly. Many women find it helpful to do their aerobic and weight training exercises on alternate days.

If you are worried that weight training will lead to a bulging, masculine physique, don't be. The hormone testosterone is responsible for those big muscles that men develop when they lift weights. Women secrete only 5 to 20 micrograms of testosterone daily, whereas men secrete 30 to 200 micrograms a day. So although you can strengthen and tone your muscles lifting weights, it's highly unlikely that you'll develop a physique resembling that of Charles Atlas.

You will look better, however. Weight training tightens and improves the shape of the body. And, as noted earlier, it encourages weight loss because muscle tissue uses up more calories than fat tissue.

Weight Training and Osteoporosis

Besides building stronger muscles, weight training exercises also build stronger bones and thus help reduce the risk of developing osteoporosis after menopause. When muscles contract during exercise, they appear to stimulate underlying bones to conserve calcium, which makes the bones denser and stronger. A tennis pro, for example, will not only have bigger muscles in her playing arm than in her nonplaying arm but will have thicker bones as well.

Walking, running, and other aerobic activities build muscles and bones, but usually only in the lower part of the body. It's important that you also build strength in your shoulders, chest, back, and arms so that all your bones remain strong as you pass through menopause. Establishing a weight training program will do that for you.

If you have already experienced bone fractures as a result of osteoporosis, you should consult with your physician before beginning weight training exercises. You will first need to do other exercises to strengthen your muscles and bones.

How to Begin Strength Training

Your best bet is to join a YWCA or YMCA or other health facility with weight resistance training rooms. These rooms will have a variety of free weights (the traditional barbells and dumbbells) and elaborate machines that help you work on one isolated muscle group at a time. If you are new to weight lifting, start with the machines; they are easier and safer to use. Be sure to have a trained instructor show you how to use the machines before beginning.

If you prefer more privacy during your workouts, you can buy your own equipment and lift weights at home. A home gym, however, takes space and an initial investment of several hundred dollars. Also, you won't have an instructor available to answer your questions or help you evaluate your progress. And lifting weights alone can be dangerous, particularly as you lift heavier weights. It is safe, however, to start a program of light weight training at home. Start with a 2.5-pound set of dumbbells (those little barbells meant for one hand). With the weights in hand, flex the various sets of your upper body muscles. Flex repeatedly until you feel a slight burning sensation in the muscles being worked and then move on to another muscle set. These kinds of flexing repetitions build muscle endurance, unlike heavier weights that build muscle bulk.

Strength-building exercises can be done, of course, without any special equipment. Simple resistance exercises, like pushing against a door or lifting a book or chair, will help you develop strong muscles and bones. Most good exercise books include these kinds of resistance exercises as part of their workout program. Find a book—and a program—you like.

THE NEED FOR FLEXIBILITY

Flexibility exercises that make our bodies bend, stretch, and reach are important for combating the muscle stiffness that begins in midlife. The stiffness is caused by chemical linkages, or side chains, that form around muscle tissue. When we are young and growing, these side chains are constantly being broken. As we age, however, physical movement is needed to break the chains. The chains can develop literally overnight—which is why our bodies often feel so stiff upon awakening in the morning.

To keep our joints healthy, it's important that we periodically move and stretch our muscles and break the chemical linkages that cause stiffness. Otherwise, the action of our joints may become so limited that the cartilage within the joints become permanently damaged.

Hatha yoga exercises are among the best for improving flexibility. You can begin either by taking a class in yoga or by reading one of the many excellent books on the topic. Aerobic dance workouts also incorporate yogalike stretching exercises as part of their warm-up and cool-down sessions. So do most standard dance workouts, from ballet to belly dancing. In fact, any strenuous exercise or dance workout should begin with warm-up stretches and end with cool-down stretches. Try to include at

---

DON'T FORGET YOUR ABDOMINAL MUSCLES

Strong abdominal muscles are important—and not just because they make your stomach look flatter. A strong abdomen also means more support for your internal organs and your back. And that can mean fewer problems with bladder control and backaches.

To tighten your abdominals, do modified bent-knee sit-ups. First, lie on your back with your knees bent and your hands behind your head. Tucking your chin to your chest, curl forward into a sitting position, reaching with your elbows toward your knees. Then lower your body slowly to the starting position. Repeat the exercise nine more times. Gradually try to work your way up to doing fifty of these sit-ups each day.

---

least 15 minutes of flexibility exercises as part of your daily routine. They will help stretch out muscles that have become tightened by aerobic or weight training activities and thus will lower your risk of injury. In addition, you'll experience fewer muscular aches and pains. You'll also find that flexibility exercises are a great way of releasing stress-related tension. Do them in the morning to get your day off to a good start and again in the evening to help you relax and sleep.

You may also want to think about signing up for a class in the ancient Chinese martial art of Tai Chi. This gentle form of exercise, which involves slow, controlled movements, has been shown in one study to help elderly people improve their balance and experience fewer falls. Falling is the leading cause of fractures in the elderly.

KEEPING AT IT

To avoid burnout and injuries, begin your exercise program at a fairly slow pace. Go easy at the beginning. Avoid pushing your body too hard too fast. Your best bet is to write out a one-month program. Keep an exercise journal to track your progress. Then, at the end of the month, reevaluate your program and make any necessary adjustments.

Be realistic about results. No program will make you physically fit overnight. Usually, it takes about six weeks before any measurable results appear. Nor can you expect to lose weight immediately. In fact, you may actually see a small weight *gain* at the beginning as your muscles get stronger and gain mass. (But that doesn't mean you'll look bigger; muscle tissue has a smaller volume than fat tissue.)

•   •   •

"Walking is all I can do. I guess I've smoked so much all my life that my lungs are damaged, but I get good and tired from a fifteen-minute walk. So I do that every day now."

•   •   •

You can expect to experience some stiffness and soreness at first. After all, you'll be asking your muscles to do things they haven't done in years! A few weeks into your program, however, the workouts should get easier and you should begin to feel much better—stronger, more limber, and much more energetic.

"I started my walking program in May," says one woman. "I was so

---

GOOD POSTURE IS GOOD FOR YOU

Posture affects not only how you look but also how you feel. Poor posture can interfere with digestion and elimination and can lead to problems with hernias, hemorrhoids, and bladder control. It can contribute to arthritis of the spine. Pay attention to your posture, while sitting as well as while standing. Also, be sure to include as part of your regular workout routine exercises that will strengthen your abdominal, back, and chest muscles. Those are the muscles that help you stand tall.

---

overweight and out of shape that I could barely walk half a mile without huffing and puffing. By the end of the summer I was doing three miles a day, and I couldn't believe how much better I looked and felt. Now I'm thinking about getting some running shoes."

Whatever specific types of exercises you decide upon, be sure they give your entire body a workout. Here's a simple schedule to follow:

- *Aerobic activities* (minimum of 30 minutes)—four days a week
- *Strength exercises* (minimum of 30 minutes)—three days a week (alternating with aerobic activities)
- *Flexibility exercises* (minimum of 15 minutes)—daily

Staying in shape is really not a complicated matter. All it requires is a little effort and determination, and the patience to stick with a program long enough to reap the benefits. Those benefits, as you've seen in this chapter, are both numerous and profound. Not only can regular exercise add years to your life but it can also help you retain a youthful vigor throughout your menopausal years. So get up and get going!

9

TAKING CHARGE:
Skin Care

*Anyone who frees himself or herself from the denial and the dread that's caused
by this obsolete age mystique is then free from trying to hold on to youth or deny
age. Surprising things emerge, strengths that as yet have no name.*

— Betty Friedan

Our skin is the packaging in which we present ourselves to the world. It's
not surprising, therefore, that we worry about how that packaging looks.
Each year, Americans spend almost $3 billion on moisturizers, soaps,
cleansing lotions, and other skin-care products. Millions more are spent
on cosmetic surgery to lift and smooth out saggy skin.

Unfortunately, in today's youth-oriented culture, too much emphasis
is put on having clear, fresh, firm, *young* skin. Yet it would be foolish to
expect your skin to look the same at age 50 as it did at age 20. After all,
you've put 30 years of living into the intervening three decades! Even if
you've had a relatively easy life, your skin will still reflect the normal wear
and tear of daily living.

Your goal, therefore, should not be young skin, but healthy skin—skin
that radiates vitality in both its texture and its tone. You should also, of
course, aim to keep your skin from aging prematurely—primarily by
keeping out of the sun. This chapter examines what happens to your
skin—and hair—as you age and how those changes are related to menopause. It also looks at various medical options for women who would like
to keep wrinkles, age spots, or other midlife skin changes at bay.

• • •

"I don't use any makeup anymore, except when I get really dressed up. Then I might use blush-on and mascara and maybe a bit of lip gloss. I think not using makeup comes with a sense of being more comfortable with yourself, and I think that comes with age. Most of the people I know who are older and who feel good about themselves don't use makeup."

• • •

SOME SKIN BASICS

To understand the changes your skin is experiencing as you age—and how you can minimize those changes—you must first have some basic knowledge about your skin's anatomy. Skin has two main layers—the thin, outer *epidermis* and the thicker, underlying *dermis*. The epidermis constantly regenerates itself. Its deepest cells slowly migrate to the surface, where they die and dry out and then are rubbed, washed, or flaked away. Within the epidermis are the pigment-making cells known as melanocytes that determine the color of your skin and cause you to tan (more about tanning in a minute).

The dermis, which makes up 85 percent of the thickness of skin, contains a complex network of nerve endings, blood vessels, sweat glands, oil glands, and hair follicles. It is made up mostly, however, of collagen and elastin fibers. Collagen, an abundant body protein found throughout the body, gives skin its strength and keeps it from becoming torn when overstretched. Elastin, another protein, makes it possible for stretched skin to snap back to its original shape. Together, collagen and elastin keep the skin taut, smooth, and resilient.

HOW YOUR SKIN CHANGES

As you grow older, the collagen and elastin fibers in your skin deteriorate, losing their elasticity. The dermis also becomes thinner and less able to retain water. Less body fat is stored under the facial skin with advancing age, contributing to a thinner and more wrinkled appearance. The sweat and oil glands within the dermis slow down, producing less moisture and oil. The result: a gradual drying, wrinkling, and sagging of the skin.

These changes seem inevitable with age. But are they? Yes and no, say scientists. For although some drying and wrinkling of the skin is a natural outcome of the aging process, most of the changes we see in our skin as we grow older are the direct result of a single damaging factor: exposure to the sun. In fact, dermatologists estimate that as much as 70 percent of skin damage comes from the sun. The damage is cumulative, beginning in youth. If we had kept our skin shielded from the sun during our younger years, most of us would have smooth, clear, wrinkle-free skin well into our sixties—the kind of skin you can still find on protected areas of your body, such as the underside of your breast or the underside of your upper arm.

•   •   •

"I've always had dry skin, but recently, in the last ten years, it's been really dry. I use a lot of grease on my face now."

•   •   •

Some women mistakenly blame menopause for wrinkles, primarily because both tend to occur during midlife. Although estrogen does seem to have some influence on the biological structure of skin, most scientists point out that estrogen's effect on the aging of skin, if any, is minimal compared to changes evoked by the sun and other environmental factors. Taking estrogen, therefore, will not keep your skin youthful. The Food and Drug Administration even requires estrogen manufacturers to state that fact in their labeling literature.

HOW THE SUN HARMS YOUR SKIN

It's the sun's ultraviolet rays that wreak havoc on skin. They break down collagen and elastin fibers, which, over time, makes it more difficult for skin to snap back into place after being stretched. The skin becomes loose—and wrinkled. Repeated tanning and burning of the skin also causes skin cells to thicken, which eventually gives the skin a hard, leathery texture. Sun exposure can also cause permanent brown blotches, called *lentigos* by scientists (and *age spots* or *liver spots* by the rest of us), to form on the skin.

More important, ultraviolet rays can damage the skin's DNA, or genetic material, which can eventually lead to the formation of cancerous cells. Sun exposure is the primary cause of basal cell carcinoma and squamous cell carcinoma, the two most common types of skin cancer. About 500,000 people in the United States develop one of these cancers each year. Fortunately, both cancers are usually curable if treated early.

SUNBURN AND HOT FLASHES

When your skin is sunburned, hot flashes may feel even more uncomfortable. The reason? Sunburned skin has more trouble regulating heat. In fact, it may not sweat normally again for about two weeks, or until it is completely healed.

So if you're having trouble with hot flashes, don't get burned. It might just make things worse.

Other skin cancers are more deadly, especially malignant melanoma, which strikes about 23,000 Americans each year and has a 40 to 50 percent fatality rate. About 40 percent of melanoma cases are believed to have been caused by sun exposure.

You should take the risk of skin cancer very seriously. Your chances of getting some form of the disease increases as you age. Some people are at greater risk than others. It depends on your skin type and on how readily you tan. Light-skinned people who freckle or burn easily are more likely to develop skin cancer than black or olive-skinned people, because they have less melanin, the pigment that protects skin from the sun's harmful ultraviolet rays. Some women also find that they burn more easily as they grow older. Everyone, however, should take precautions when out in the sun.

HOW TO PROTECT YOUR SKIN

Your best protection against premature aging of the skin and skin cancer is to stay out of the sun as much as possible. If you have been a sun worshipper all your life, you may consider such advice heresy. Getting a "healthy" tan, after all, has become a rite of summer for millions of people. It is also, however, the reason that the incidence of skin cancer has doubled in the United States since the 1960s, and why our skin looks old long before its time.

If you insist upon getting a tan, here are a few steps you can take to give your skin at least some protection:

- Don't let yourself get burned. Avoid basking in the sun between 10 A.M. and 2 P.M. standard time, when ultraviolet rays are at their strongest.
- Although no amount of tanning is safe, if you must be in the sun, build your tan slowly. Expose yourself to the sun for only 15 minutes the first

few days, as it's during this first exposure that you're most likely to burn. Once your tan develops, you can increase the exposure by 30 minutes per day. Be sure to include time spent in the water as exposure time; ultraviolet rays can easily penetrate water. Even wearing a tee-shirt won't completely protect you. A wet cotton tee-shirt permits 20 to 30 percent of ultraviolet radiation to reach your skin.

- Avoid tanning lamps and booths. Many proprietors of tanning salons claim that their lamps filter out almost all of the dangerous ultraviolet light rays, leaving only the safe "tanning rays." *But there are no safe rays.* Furthermore, without the protection of goggles, tanning lamps can do permanent and serious damage to the corneas of your eyes.

- Use a good sunblocking agent or sunscreen. Sunblocking agents are opaque creams or pastes containing zinc oxide or titanium dioxide. They physically block sunlight from reaching the skin. Although a bit messy to use, sunblocks are extremely useful for the nose, lips, and other particularly sun-sensitive areas of the body. Sunscreens are oils, lotions, or creams containing chemical compounds that filter out ultraviolet rays. Contrary to popular belief, however, sunscreens do not prevent tanning; they simply slow down the process.

    Most dermatologists recommend that people choose a full-spectrum sunscreen product with an SPF (sun protection factor) of at least 15. That number simply means that you can remain in the sun without burning fifteen times longer, on average, than if you didn't use the sunscreen. Be sure to apply sunscreen frequently and liberally. If you swim or sweat a lot, choose a sunscreen that is waterproof or water-resistant. And don't forget to use a sunscreen when you're skiing or doing other outside winter activities; the winter sun can also burn.

OTHER WRINKLING FACTORS

Sunlight isn't the only cause of premature wrinkles. Repeated exposure to wind and heat can also damage skin. Overweight people who rapidly lose significant amounts of weight may also develop wrinkles because their skin, which became stretched when they were overweight, is not able to conform completely to the new contours of their bodies.

Repeated facial movements, such as squinting or furrowing the brow, can cause wrinkles—particularly in skin that has been damaged by the sun. People who smoke often develop tiny permanent creases around their mouths—the result of pursing their lips while inhaling. And some people develop a "sleep crease" from sleeping with their face scrunched up in the same position against a pillow night after night.

Facial expressions can create wrinkles because muscles in the face are directly attached to the skin rather than to tendons and bones, as they are in other areas of the body. Whenever you contract a facial muscle, the skin attached to it folds. Young skin will spring back easily to its original position once the underlying muscle relaxes. Older skin, however, has more difficulty snapping back, especially if its collagen and elastin have been damaged by the sun. Gradually, after many years and millions of muscle contractions, the temporary folds of the skin become permanent wrinkles.

• • •

"I think my skin has changed since my hysterectomy. There seems to be a dryness around my eyes that I never had before, and I find my skin is sagging a little more."

• • •

Of course, this doesn't mean that you should suddenly become stone-faced just to avoid wrinkles! Faces that are animated and expressive have character, personality—and beauty. You can take some steps, however, to avoid or delay at least some of the wrinkles caused by facial movement:

• Stop smoking. You'll avoid those pucker wrinkles around the mouth.
• If you notice creases in your skin when you awaken in the morning, try sleeping in a different position—or without a pillow.
• Wear a hat or sunglasses (or both) when outside to avoid squinting, which can hasten the formation of "crow's feet" wrinkles around the eyes.
• Avoid facial exercises. Contrary to the advice found in some beauty books, facial exercises do not offer protection against wrinkling. In fact, the opposite is true. Besides throwing skin into folds, facial exercises can cause skin to stretch as the underlying muscles get bigger. As you grow older, and the bones and muscles in your face become slightly smaller, the skin will stay stretched and eventually sag.

KEEPING SKIN MOIST

Dry skin does not cause wrinkles, but it can make them more noticeable. Some women have dry skin all their lives. For others, dry skin becomes noticeable only as they reach midlife. Shifting hormone levels may be partly responsible for this late-life drying of the skin, although it should be noted that a man's skin also becomes dryer as he ages.

What can you do to help keep your skin moist and soft-looking and to avoid the itchiness and discomfort of dry skin? Several things. First, avoid frequent showering and bathing. Excessive washing can dry the skin by removing essential oils. Second, use soap sparingly; it strips the skin of both oil and water. As many dermatologists note, soap is really needed to wash only the armpits and between the legs, the two areas that secrete carbohydrates, fats, and proteins in their sweat. Other sweat glands on the body secrete only salts and minerals, which can easily be rinsed away with water. Superfatted and low-alkaline soaps are the best for dry skin. Because soap manufacturers are not required by law to list their ingredients on their products' labels, you may need your pharmacist's help in picking out the right brand for you.

Dermatologists also recommend that people with dry skin use a moisturizer. Moisturizers work by creating a seal over the skin that keeps water from evaporating from the stratum corneum, the very top layer of dead cells of the epidermis. The more water you can retain in your skin, the softer and smoother it will appear.

The best time for applying a moisturizer is after you have bathed or showered, while your skin is still damp. Moisturizers that have more oil than water work better than those with more water than oil. Unfortunately, oil-rich moisturizers, such as petroleum jelly and lanolin, are also the messiest to use. Some women use them at night and use less oily moisturizers during the day.

When choosing a moisturizer, don't be fooled by the price. According to a *Consumer Reports* study, price has little to do with a moisturizer's effectiveness; some of the best products are the least expensive. Also, don't be taken in by fancy claims or ingredients. No cream or lotion—whether it contains collagen, elastin, vitamin E, or some other special ingredient—can penetrate the stratum corneum and "heal," "nourish," "rejuvenate," or otherwise repair damaged skin. And that's exactly what a product would have to do to stop or repair the aging process in skin.

•   •   •

"After menopause, my face stopped breaking out. That was one great benefit."

•   •   •

WHAT TO DO ABOUT AGE SPOTS

Age spots are sometimes called *liver spots*, although they have nothing to do with the liver. A more appropriate name for them would be *sun spots*, for they are a direct result of repeated exposure to the sun. They are usually found on the face, hands, and V-area of the neck, the most sun-exposed areas of the body. Flat to the touch, age spots are light brown or tan in color and round or oval in shape. They come in all sizes.

Some women who go on hormone replacement therapy also develop areas of hyperpigmentation, or excess darkening, on their skin. These brownish blotches, like age spots, are permanent unless treated.

Age spots can be "removed" by freezing them with liquid nitrogen, which inhibits the skin's melanocyte cells from producing excess pigment. Or they can be "bleached" with a bleach or fade cream containing hydroquinone, which also causes the melanocytes to produce less pigment. Some dermatologists also recommend alpha hydroxy acid (AHA) creams or ointments to diminish age spots. None of these processes works overnight. It can take a month or more for liquid nitrogen to work its wonders and three or four months for fade or AHA creams to produce results. You must continue to use fade creams after the spot has faded, or the spot will redarken.

ERASING WRINKLES

When it was suggested to her that she have a face lift, one famous actress retorted, "What? And erase sixty years of living!"

Many women share that actress's view. "I would never, never let a doctor tamper with my face," says a 50-year-old woman. "Whether or not you feel good about yourself depends on something within yourself, not on your face. My mother, who's 81, has extremely wrinkled skin, but she has such a vibrant personality that she is often taken for a woman in her sixties. Feeling beautiful or ugly is a state of mind. Some older women have beautiful skin, beautiful figures, but they feel ugly anyway."

Still, many women find it difficult to accept the changes they see in their faces as they pass through midlife, particularly in a society that puts so much emphasis on the youthful appearance of women. They see each sag and crevice as an unwelcome sign of age—a sign they would like to erase.

If you feel this way, you should know that several techniques are available today that can improve the appearance of aging skin. The following pages describe these techniques. You should also know that each of these techniques carries with it certain risks—and no guarantees. Be sure to educate yourself thoroughly about each procedure. And shop around for a physician who is both skilled and experienced.

Tretinoin (Retin-A)

Retin-A, the trade name for tretinoin, is one of a group of vitamin-A-like compounds called retinoids. Although approved by the Food and Drug Administration (FDA) in 1971 for the treatment of severe acne, tretinoin emerged as a potential wrinkle-remover only in 1988, after a study published in the *Journal of the American Medical Association* reported that the drug had rejuvenating effects on the skin. In that study, 30 patients, aged 35 to 70, rubbed tretinoin into one forearm and a placebo cream into the other once a day. Four months later all of the treated arms had fewer fine wrinkles and rosier skin. Half of the study's subjects also applied tretinoin to their faces with similar, yet much less significant, results. Most of the improvement from tretinoin seems to be in "fine wrinkling." Wrinkles on the face tend to be more deeply etched.

• • •

"A year ago I started using Retin-A. I had noticed that my skin was getting really, really dry. It would get to the point where my face felt really tight and shriveled. I went to my dermatologist and he suggested I try Retin-A. The first two weeks were really tough. My skin became red and raw. When I exercised, the sweat would feel like acid. It burned that much. It took two or three weeks, then I was fine. My skin softened up. The wrinkles around my eyes and forehead went away, and the dryness, the flakiness went away, too. My skin got really smooth."

• • •

Although the study's findings are promising, many questions remain to be answered. Scientists do not know how long the drug's benefits will last or whether long-term use presents any health hazards. Also, tretinoin has side effects—redness, blistering, swelling, and peeling—that can be severe in some patients. These side effects can last from two weeks to several months.

Nor do scientists have a clear idea of how tretinoin repairs damaged skin, although it appears to stimulate new growth of tiny blood vessels, which may encourage damaged skin cells to regenerate.

Because of all the unanswered questions about tretinoin, the FDA h̄ not yet approved the drug for treating aging skin. The agency wants to see further studies. Doctors can, however, prescribe an approved drug for an unapproved use, and many doctors are doing just that with tretinoin. If you choose to use Retin-A, be sure to follow your doctor's instructions carefully. It is especially important that you stay out of the sun while using the drug, as its use may greatly increase your risk of sunburn—and, thus, skin cancer. Do not use Retin-A during pregnancy, as it can cause birth defects.

Finally, don't confuse Retin-A with vitamin A. Some cosmetic companies are trying to cash in on the publicity surrounding Retin-A by marketing over-the-counter face creams containing vitamin A. These creams will do nothing more for your skin than any other moisturizing lotion—but they may put a bigger dent in your makeup budget.

Alpha Hydroxy Acid Creams and Ointments (AHAs)

AHAs are the hottest new development in wrinkle-removing, although whether they deliver or not may be in the eye of the beholder. AHAs basically work as exfoliators—they peel off the skin's dead surface cells. Their active ingredients include various acids, such as lactic acid from milk, glycolic acid from sugar cane, and tartaric, citric, or malic acid from fruits. Because they smooth and penetrate skin, they are great moisturizers. Now some dermatologists believe AHAs can also be effective in erasing fine lines and age spots.

AHA products vary widely in their concentrations of alpha hydroxy acid. Some products contain as little as 2 percent of the active ingredient, others as much as 70 percent. Those with high concentrations can be dangerous, warn dermatologists, as they may result in serious burns.

If you want to try an AHA cream or lotion, start with one that has a low concentration of AHA—perhaps somewhere in the 4 to 8 percent range. You will have to use the product for six to eight weeks for it to reach its maximum effectiveness. If at that point the product does not seem to be working, try another brand.

Injection Treatments

Although rubbing collagen cream into your skin will do nothing for your wrinkles, having collagen injected under your skin will. Approved by the FDA in 1981, collagen injection treatments are used primarily to erase forehead furrows and deep laugh lines that stretch from the nose to the lips. The collagen fills in the space behind and around the wrinkles, puffing up the skin, much like air puffs up a balloon. The treatment, which stings slightly, generally takes less than half an hour. Afterward, your face may throb and be red for about a day.

The collagen used for injections is derived from the hides of cows. About 7 percent of patients are allergic to it and develop severe adverse reactions to its repeated use, including beef allergy, facial welts, abscesses, and scars lasting more than six months. For this reason, an allergy test is a prerequisite for the treatment. Even if you pass the test, you may experience a delayed allergic reaction to the shots and develop tiny bumps that can take up to six months to disappear. Women with eczema, psoriasis, thyroid disease, or with a history of an autoimmune disease, such as rheumatoid arthritis or lupus, may also have a bad reaction to collagen. In fact, some critics believe that collagen has the potential of *causing* autoimmune diseases in susceptible people.

Collagen injections are only a temporary solution for wrinkles, lasting from six to eighteen months. Eventually, the collagen breaks down and becomes absorbed by the skin. Many people return for follow-up injections, which increases the cost and health risks associated with the treatment.

Another technique that is growing in popularity is called microlipoinjections, or fat injections. For this procedure, excess body fat is removed from the patient's stomach or buttocks and then injected into facial creases. Because the patient's own tissue is used, allergic reactions are less of a concern than with collagen injections. However, this treatment also has its risks, primarily infection and overinjection, which can leave the skin lumpy. And, like collagen injections, fat injections provide only temporary improvement.

The only permanent injectable for smoothing out wrinkles is liquid silicone. However, serious concerns over silicone's safety have been raised, and the FDA does not approve its use for this purpose.

Chemical Peels (Chemabrasion)

Peeling the outer layer of the skin to get at the less weathered and wizened skin below is an ancient practice. The early Egyptians used alabaster, pumice, salt, and extracts of animal oil for their skin-peeling formulas. Today, dermatologists usually use the chemical phenol in a solution of distilled water, croton oil, and liquid soap. The phenol burns the superficial layers of the skin, which causes them to peel. After the peeling is complete and the skin has completely healed, a clearer, less wrinkled complexion is revealed.

Although often extremely successful in softening wrinkles, chemical peels should not be undertaken without careful thought. The procedure which, after all, involves a second-degree burn—has several adverse side effects. The absorption of phenol into the body can cause temporary heart-beat irregularities and has been reported to have caused cardiac or respiratory arrest. Some people have died from phenol peels. The skin may also become infected while it is healing, leading to permanent scarring. The most common unwanted side effect, however, is depigmentation: The treated area of skin emerges lighter than the skin surrounding it. Be sure to discuss all these potential problems with your physician before you proceed. In addition, ask your dermatologist about high-concentration AHA peels, which are less effective than phenol peels, but are also much safer.

Dermabrasion

Like chemabrasion, dermabrasion removes the skin's outer layers, resulting in smoother, less mottled skin. The skin is scraped mechanically with a high-speed tool that works much like an electric sander. Dermabrasion is best for treating fine lines and shallow wrinkles and for removing age spots. It is generally not as effective as a chemical peel but is safer because it poses no risk for the heart. Dermabrasion does have other risks— infection, scarring, and skin discoloration—although they are rare.

Laser Peels

This technique, which involves the use of a special laser to "resurface" the skin, is growing in popularity. Laser peels work by slightly burning the skin and are said to be especially effective in removing wrinkles around the upper lip and eyes. Because the treatment is so new, however, it is not yet known how long it works or how often it must be repeated.

Face Lifts

For sagging skin, if it really bothers you enough to want to do something about it, the only effective treatment is face-lift surgery. During this surgery, excess skin is removed, and the remaining skin is pulled up and back to make it fit more tightly over the underlying bones and muscles. The surgery takes about three hours. Patients often go home the same day the surgery is performed, although many women opt to stay overnight in the hospital. Full recovery from the operation generally takes several weeks, and your skin may not return to its normal softness for three to six months.

• • •

"I've always had a good complexion. I never use soap on my face, just cool water and a rigorous towel and a lotion. Those are the only things I've used for thirty years. Some of my friends are very wrinkled, but I'm not like that. The loose skin around my neck does bother me, and I am considering plastic surgery to tighten that up a bit. But that's just gotten bad within the last three or four years—since I turned 60."

• • •

Although complications from the surgery are rare, they can be serious, especially blood vessel and nerve damage, which can lead to blood clots or permanent facial numbness. If you smoke, you should probably not have a face lift. Smoking restricts the flow of blood and oxygen to the skin, which can inhibit healing. Studies have shown that smokers are ten to twenty times more likely than nonsmokers to have their incisions heal poorly after a face lift, with resulting wide scars and skin discolorations.

Successful face-lift surgery requires a skilled plastic surgeon. Be sure to shop carefully for a surgeon. Your best guarantee is to choose one who has been certified by the American Board of Plastic Surgery. To receive this certification, doctors must have completed four years of medical school, three to five years of general surgery training, and at least two years of training in an approved plastic surgery residency program. Then they must pass rigorous written and oral examinations. Only about 3,400 physicians in the United States are currently board-certified. To get a list of board-certified plastic surgeons in your area, write to the American Society of Plastic and Reconstructive Surgeons at 444 E. Algonquin Road, Arlington Heights, Illinois 60005, or call (800) 635-0635 toll-free.

HAIRY CHÁNGES

Around the menopausal years, many women begin to notice changes in hair growth all over their bodies. These changes are truly paradoxical: Hair on the scalp and in the pubic area seems to thin while excess hair begins to appear on the chin, lip, and sometimes on the neck and around the nipples of the breasts.

The excess hair growth appears to be related to hormonal changes: When estrogen levels drop, as, of course, they do during the menopausal years, there is less estrogen available to counter the hair-growing effects of the "male" hormone testosterone made in the ovaries. As a result, hair may begin to appear in places that used to be hair-free—such as on the upper lip. The development of this type of hair is not as pronounced in women who have had their ovaries surgically removed before menopause.

The thinning of scalp and pubic hair, on the other hand, appears to be related not to hormonal changes but instead to the natural aging process. In fact, the hair of everyone—men and women—begins to thin after the age of 25. In the past, estrogen drugs applied locally or taken internally were believed to stop hair loss in women. Newer studies have shown, however, that such treatment rarely helps. Hair loss appears to be more hereditary than hormonal.

Finally, menopause should not be blamed for causing gray hair. The loss of hair pigment—and that's what graying is—is inherited, as is baldness in men. You can't stop the graying process once it has begun.

GETTING RID OF UNWANTED HAIR

For centuries women have tried to rid their bodies of unwanted hair. Ancient remedies included using sharpened clam shells as tweezers and concocting herbal depilatories laced with arsenic.

Today, fortunately, you don't have to hone shells or smear yourself with arsenic to remove unwanted hair. Still, modern hair-removal techniques are not altogether pleasant. Here are your current options:

Shaving is quick and easy. Although most women are comfortable shaving their legs and underarms, many balk at the idea of using the same method for removing facial hair, thinking it too masculine. Dermatologists, however, say there is no reason women should not shave unwanted hair from their faces. The old belief about hair growing back thicker and coarser after it is shaved is simply not true. It just looks thicker because you see only the blunt end of the hair when it begins to grow back in.

Tweezing or plucking hairs out individually is a slow and sometimes painful process. It's best used for removing a few, select hairs. Repeated tweezing can stunt the regrowth of hair, making it take longer for the hair to reach the surface of the skin—an effect, of course, that is usually desirable for unwanted facial hair.

Waxing involves applying melted wax to the skin and then pulling it quickly away once it has solidified, thus removing any underlying hair that has become enmeshed in it. Although this process keeps skin hair-free for several weeks, it is usually not recommended for the face, as it also removes the upper layers of skin. If the wax is not properly cooled or removed, it can burn or tear the skin, which may result in permanent scarring. Waxing can also cause hair to become ingrown, leading to infections. In addition, the hairs must be allowed to grow out sufficiently between treatments for the waxing to work, which means you cannot keep your face completely hair-free at all times.

Depilatories—creams that cause the chemical bonds of hair to disintegrate so that they can be wiped away—are also not usually recommended for the face, unless a product specifically states otherwise on its label. The skin in this area of the body is often too sensitive to the chemicals. Even if a product says it can be used on the face, you should test it first on a small area of skin on your leg.

Electrolysis is the only technique that will remove hair permanently. A thin wire thread is inserted into the hair follicle, and then an electric current is sent through the wire, destroying the hair root deep within the follicle. Electrolysis is slow and expensive. Much of the success of the treatment depends upon the skill of the practitioner; be sure to select a licensed electrolysist. Even with a trained and experienced practitioner, 40 to 60 percent of the treated hairs are likely to grow back, so be prepared to return for many follow-up treatments.

CARING FOR YOUR SKIN FROM WITHIN

"There is nothing to beautify the complexion of the face so much as frequent excursions into the mountains, climbing hills, which cause thorough perspiration and breathing; simple diet without alcohol or meat, but rather sweet fruits and sleeping in air huts," wrote Anna Fischer-Dueckelmann, a doctor in the early 1900s.

What was good advice then is good advice now. The best way of caring for your skin during the menopausal years is to simply take care of the rest of you. That means following the basics: Eat well, exercise, and get plenty of rest. (Although you don't necessarily need a mountain hut for a good night's sleep!)

In particular, be sure to eat foods rich in vitamin A, vitamin C, and riboflavin, one of the B vitamins. (See chapter 7 for information about which foods are good natural sources of these vitamins.) You should also drink plenty of water; it helps keep skin moist.

Finally, be aware that both alcohol and smoking can lead to premature wrinkling. If you like to drink, do so only occasionally. And throw the cigarettes out!

•　•　•

"People's expectations are so strange. I had a birthday not so long ago. I turned 49. People would say, 'You don't look like you're 49.' And I would say, 'I got news for you. This is what 49 looks like.' For me, at least. For somebody else, it's going to look different. Where is this thing that says that if you're 49 you're supposed to look a certain way, and if you're 35, you're supposed to look a certain way? Where does that come from? It comes from advertising, it comes from people not objecting to advertising, and it comes from people buying into it, and it comes from movies and from TV. But it's stupid, and it's wrong, and it's a lie."

•　•　•

APPENDIX A
Hormone Replacement Therapy Decision Flowchart

Katherine A. O'Hanlan, M.D.

You may find the following flow chart helpful in making your decision about whether hormone replacement therapy (HRT) is a good choice for you. This is a very individualized decision, so use the flow chart to see if hormone therapy offers you a significant quality of life or health benefit, and be sure to note the following:

- First, be sure you are doing all you can to maintain a healthy diet and lifestyle. Prevention of bone loss and heart disease is always the most important and safest way to a long and healthy life. The only side effect of a good diet and exercise is a long life!
- If you develop significant symptoms at menopause, try the natural herbal and vitamin remedies that have been listed in this book. There do not appear to be any side effects from these remedies, so they make a safe first choice. If you find the symptoms are not alleviated by these methods, be assured that short-term use of HRT (less than 5 years) does not appear to cause increased rates of breast cancer. Use hormones for as long as you need them to feel like your normal self, but go off the hormones for a week or so every year to see if the symptoms have abated. Most women have hot flashes for only the first two or three years after their periods lighten or cease.
- If your only bothersome symptom is vaginal dryness and the natural remedies and vaginal moisturizers do not work, then try vaginal estriol or estrogen cream. The estrogen doses used for vaginal skin health are extremely low and thus do not carry the risks of the higher doses.

- Some women cannot exercise or may have other factors such as diabetes, obesity, or an unfavorable cholesterol profile which puts them at high risk for heart disease. A cardiologist may be able to give you the best advice for balancing the lifelong use of estrogen to benefit the heart against the increased risk of developing breast cancer. Women who must take estrogens for cardiac reasons should use a natural progesterone to protect the lining of the uterus.
- Similarly, the decision to use HRT to maintain bone density must be carefully weighed against the attendant risk of developing breast cancer. Preventive measures such as exercise, calcium supplements, and not smoking are best started by age 30, and should be carried out for life. But some women will enter menopause and find that their bones are already at a very low density because of their heredity, diseases of calcium metabolism, kidney disease, or treatments of other diseases with steroids that cause bone density loss. Women entering menopause with a very low bone density should see a bone mineral endocrinologist before they decide on lifelong estrogens.

HORMONE REPLACEMENT THERAPY
DECISION FLOWCHART

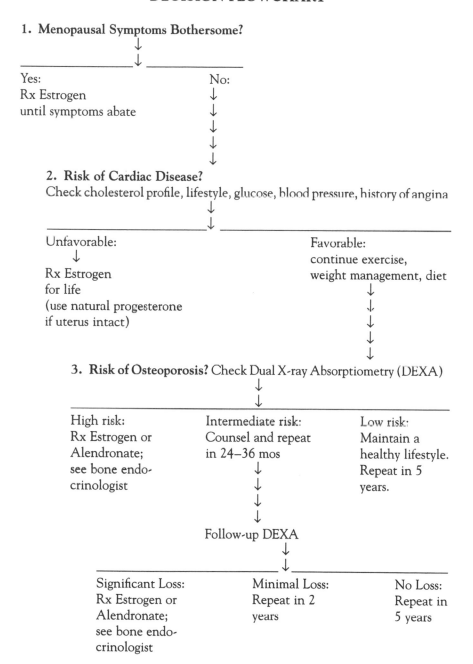

1. Menopausal Symptoms Bothersome?

Yes:
Rx Estrogen
until symptoms abate

No:

2. Risk of Cardiac Disease?
Check cholesterol profile, lifestyle, glucose, blood pressure, history of angina

Unfavorable:

Rx Estrogen
for life
(use natural progesterone
if uterus intact)

Favorable:
continue exercise,
weight management, diet

3. Risk of Osteoporosis? Check Dual X-ray Absorptiometry (DEXA)

High risk:
Rx Estrogen or
Alendronate;
see bone endo-
crinologist

Intermediate risk:
Counsel and repeat
in 24–36 mos

Low risk:
Maintain a
healthy lifestyle.
Repeat in 5
years.

Follow-up DEXA

Significant Loss:
Rx Estrogen or
Alendronate;
see bone endo-
crinologist

Minimal Loss:
Repeat in 2
years

No Loss:
Repeat in
5 years

APPENDIX B
Interpreting Your Bone Density Report

Katherine A. O'Hanlan, M.D.

The Dual X-ray Absorptiometry (DEXA) machine provides unparalleled accuracy and precision in reading bone density, so, while other methods are available, this is the only bone density assay I recommend. It has been shown to be able to predict which women are at high risk for developing fractures from thinning bone, called osteoporosis, and which women are relatively protected from fractures due to osteoporosis. It is usually not necessary to perform yearly DEXA tests except in the beginning of the menopause when bone loss is most rapid. After that, as long as you maintain your healthy diet and exercise lifestyle, you may need one only every few years. This is safe because the small amount of radiation involved is far less than even a mammogram uses. It is also essential to monitor your bone density in order to avoid osteoporosis. There are usually no symptoms to warn about osteoporosis until the first fracture occurs, and at that time reversal of bone loss is only minimally possible, while prevention of further loss is essential. Thus it is understandable that many doctors are suggesting that all women take hormones to prevent osteoporosis. However, many women will not need it, as indicated by testing of their bone density. If a woman elects to test her bone density and decides hormones are not necessary for her, she must remember to obtain follow-up DEXA assays to be sure she is maintaining her density. The following information will help you understand the DEXA computations, and can help you use this information to keep strong healthy bones.

The computer that reads your bone density prints the data in a graphic form and in numbers. An example follows. By looking at the graph you can see the normal range of densities over a range of years from 20 to 80. The normal range covers a wide area and decreases over time. None of the women who were used in the creation of this "normal" chart were advised to do all the measures that maintain bone density, so their bone densities decreased over time. Your bone density does not have to drop as you age, if you are eating a healthy diet, moderating amounts of protein, supplementing your dietary calcium to receive at least 1,500 mg of calcium daily, living a healthy lifestyle free of cigarette and alcohol abuse, and performing weight-bearing exercise for at least 30 minutes, four times weekly.

Two areas are studied in the DEXA assay because they are the most frequent sites of fracture: the neck of the hip joint and the lower vertebrae of the backbone. Under each graphic display of your bone density is a numerical chart that lists each of the sites of the bone assessed in the second column. The third column lists the absolute density of that site of your bone in grams of calcium observed by the computerized x-ray per square centimeter of area viewed (g/cm^2).

The fourth column, the T-Score, contains a computerized comparison of your bone density with that of an average 30-year-old woman to give you an idea of how much bone you may have lost over the years. This is to enable you to see the long-term effects of your lifestyle and habits so that you can then try to predict how your bone density will change over the next multiple years using your same diet and lifestyle. This value is given in statistical language as a "standard deviation (SD)" from the average. The exact average would be no change from the average, or 0.0. The usual range of bone density readings is from -2.9 to $+2.9$, with very few women scoring above or below these figures. A large decrease since age 30 would give a negative T-Score number such as -2.0. A gain in density would be a positive number, such as 0.86 (the "$+$" symbol is not routinely used, but is implied when no "$-$" symbol is used). This reading may also be accompanied by a percentage figure, which would indicate the percent of bone density you have now compared to what an average 30-year-old has.

The sixth column is the Z-Score, also reported in standard deviation format. This reflects how you differ from a group of "normal" women who are your age. As before, a negative number means less than average density, and a positive number means higher density than average, with the same range. Each reduction of 1.0 in the Z-Score is associated with an increased likelihood of bone fracture of 1.5 to 3 times an average woman's risk. The Z-Score number may also be accompanied by a percentage comparing your density with that of other women your age.

In the example, Jane has a T-Score of $-.88$ and a Z-Score of 1.53. Although she may have lost some density since age 30, she still has an average bone density for her age group. Her percentage of bone compared to women her age might be 98 percent, because she has very near the expected average density. This would be an excellent report. If she had just started her menopause, she would not need hormones specifically for purposes of maintaining her bone density, but it would be important to prove that she can maintain it with her healthy lifestyle and diet, calcium supplementation, and exercise. She should obtain another DEXA in 3 to 5 years. If that study shows a loss greater than 2 percent yearly, she should reevaluate her diet and lifestyle for methods of improvement, make the improvements, and repeat the DEXA again in 1 to 2 years. If she continues to lose more than 2 percent yearly, she should be evaluated by an endocrinologist subspecializing in bone mineral maintenance. If her bone density stabilizes, then she should repeat the DEXA every few years to be certain her bones remain strong.

A second example, Mona, has a T-Score of -2.8, a Z-Score of -1.7, a percentage of 22 percent. This suggests she has lost significant bone density over the years since age 30 and now is well below average, but still in the normal range. She needs to be careful about maintaining her bone density and should be strongly supported to make all the necessary diet and lifestyle changes she can. If she cannot make these changes, or, if, a year or two later her DEXA shows continued bone density loss, then she should consider starting hormones. She also should get follow-up DEXA assays to be certain she does not need both the hormones and Alendronate (see page 141).

Two other women, Phyllis and Maria, are 60 and 65, respectively, and have been taking estrogen prescribed by their physicians since their menopause at age 53. Both want to stop taking the hormones if they don't need them, and both have good diet and exercise programs and take a calcium supplement. Phyllis might safely stop and check her bone density in a few years, because she could enter the normal range if she maintains the density she currently has, but Maria should see an endocrinologist subspecializing in bone mineral maintenance who will likely recommend continuing the hormone therapy for life, and may prescribe a few other tests, as well. Beth has such a great bone density that she need not get further tested, but she still needs to continue all the important steps to maintain her density.

Women who are in menopause who find they do not need hormones for troublesome symptoms such as hot flashes or insomnia and who have no cardiac reasons for taking hormones should be certain their bones are strong and remain so, by requesting a DEXA from their primary care providers. Not all providers know how to interpret the data from a DEXA, but you can request a copy of the computerized printout for your own observation and files, and see a specialist if needed.

DEXA GRAPHIC DISPLAY OF BONE DENSITY

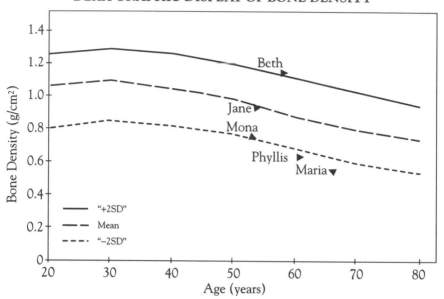

	Age	Spinal Region	Density (g/cm²)	T-Score	Age-matched Comparison	Z-Score
Jane	52	L2-L4	1.03	−0.88	98%	1.53
Mona	52	L2-L4	.81	−2.8	22%	−1.7
Phyllis	60	L1-L3	.70	−2.2	30%	−2.1
Maria	65	L1-L4	.61	−2.9	8%	−2.3
Beth	58	L1-L4	1.21	−0.02	131%	2.01

APPENDIX C
Measuring Your Cardiac Risk

Katherine A. O'Hanlan, M.D.

It is useful to know your cholesterol levels in order to assess your risk of developing heart disease. The National Cholesterol Education Program (NCEP) recommends that all adults over age 20 be tested to determine their cholesterol count. Remember, you can change your risk for heart disease by exercising and eating a low-fat, fresh, vegetable-rich diet supplemented by vitamin B (niacin, folic acid) and vitamin E.

You should fast for 12–16 hours before having your blood drawn for a cholesterol assay. Do not drink alcoholic beverages for the two days previous to the test, and abstain from vigorous exercise that morning. Sit for 5–10 minutes before having your blood drawn. Drink plenty of water to keep from getting dizzy or weak, and plan a breakfast or snack for after the assay.

Total cholesterol (TC) is the sum of the "good cholesterol" or high-density lipoproteins (HDL) which you want to be high, and the "bad cholesterol" or low-density lipoproteins (LDL) which you want to be low. The following values for LDL apply to women:

Age	Desirable	Borderline	High	Very high
30-49	<130	131-159	160-189	>220
50+	<130	131-159	160-189	>190
If two risk factors*	<130		>130	>130
If heart disease	<100		>100	>100

* A risk factor includes the following: a family history of heart disease or high cholesterol; hypertension; diabetes; or if you are a smoker.

When the LDL is high, significant dietary changes are needed, and drug therapy should be started if the numbers do not improve when remeasured in six weeks. The LDL can usually be lowered by exercising and reducing the saturated fats in your diet. This includes dairy and animal fats and the "tropical oils" such as coconut oil used in many food items. Low-fat dairy foods such as 1% milk, cottage cheese, and low-fat cheeses are delicious sources of calcium and protein without the unhealthy fats. Most red meats have fat interspersed with the muscle, making these a poor choice for frequent consumption. Many fish and chicken without the skin are low in fats. Try to devise a diet plan that rarely uses red meats and dairy fats. Remember, you don't need a meat at every meal as most of us were taught long ago. Combining grains, fruits, vegetables, and legumes can give you all the dietary essentials you need.

The HDL is worrisome for women of all ages when it is less than 50, and ideal when it is over 60, according to the Lipid Resource Center (LRC). It is improved, or raised, by regular exercise, by weight loss if you are overweight, by quitting smoking, and by limiting yourself to one alcoholic beverage daily.

If your cholesterol profile is in the borderline range and cannot be reduced by modification in lifestyle and diet, drug therapy should be started if you have two of the following: a family history of heart disease or high cholesterol; hypertension; diabetes; or if you are a smoker. The first drugs to consider are hormone therapy and vitamins if you are in menopause, but other prescription drugs may be necessary to reduce your risk of heart disease.

Resources

Keeping up to date on research concerning menopause will help you through this important passage in your life—and help you make informed decisions concerning your health care. The following organizations are good resources for this kind of information. Many of them publish regular newsletters or other publications. For information about the cost of membership or subscriptions, contact each individual organization.

American Cancer Society
1599 Clifton Road N.E.
Atlanta, GA 30329
(800) ACS-2345

For the latest information about cancer research, call the American Cancer Society's toll-free number listed above. A representative will either read you the information over the phone or mail it to you.

American Heart Association
7320 Greenville Avenue
Dallas, TX 75231
(214) 373-6300

The American Heart Association (AHA) can provide you with the latest information concerning heart disease and its relation to menopause and hormone replacement therapy. For the local AHA chapter nearest you, check your telephone directory or call the national center listed above.

Boston Women's Health Book Collective
465 Mt. Auburn Street
Watertown, MA 02172
(617) 625-0271

A nonprofit organization devoted to education about women and health, the Boston Women's Health Book Collective conducts many projects and services, including a Women's Health Information Center, which is open to the public, and distribution (for a nominal fee) of health-related materials to women. The collective has published two classic women's health books: The New Our Bodies Ourselves *and* Ourselves, Growing Older, *which deals extensively with menopause.*

A Friend Indeed
Box 515
Place du Parc Station
Montreal, Canada H2W 2P1
(514) 843-5730

Devoted entirely to information of particular interest to women in menopause or midlife, this rather informal eight-page newsletter is published ten times a year by founder/editor Janine O'Leary Cobb. It includes a lengthy section of letters from readers who describe their own menopausal experiences.

HERS (Hysterectomy Educational Resources and Services)
422 Bryn Mawr Avenue
Bala Cynwyd, PA 19004
(215) 667-7757

This organization provides information and counseling for women who are considering a hysterectomy or who have already had one. It publishes a quarterly newsletter and sponsors conferences around the country.

Melpomene Institute for Women's Health Research
1010 University Avenue
St. Paul, MN 55104
(612) 642-1951

Founded in 1981, the Melpomene Institute focuses on the link between physical activity and women's health. They are currently doing research in the area of menopause and exercise. Annual membership includes the Melpomene Journal, *published three times a year.*

Midlife Woman
5129 Logan Avenue South
Minneapolis, MN 55419
(800) 886-4354
(612) 925-0020

*This informative bimonthly newsletter publishes practical, easy-to-read articles o
health and other topics of interest to women of midlife and beyond.*

National Osteoporosis Foundation
2100 M Street NW
Suite 602
Washington, DC 20037
(202) 223-2226

*For information about the latest treatments for osteoporosis, contact the National
Osteoporosis Foundation. This organization will also give you the most current
research concerning prevention of the disease.*

National Women's Health Network
1325 G Street NW
Washington, DC 20005
(202) 347-1140

*A national public-interest organization dedicated solely to women and health, the
National Women's Health Network sponsors many educational and research
projects concerning all areas of women's health, including menopause. The organization has published a booklet on hormone replacement therapy and also offers a
highly informative newsletter,* The Network News.

Older Women's League (OWL)
730 Eleventh Street NW
Suite 300
Washington, DC 20001
(202) 783-6686

*OWL, which has chapters in almost every state, is an advocacy group that focuse
on issues of concern to middle-aged and older women, including health issue
The organization publishes special reports and a bimonthly newsletter,* The O·
Observer.

Public Citizen Health Research Group
2000 P Street NW
Suite 605
Washington, DC 20036
(202) 833-3000

Founded by consumer advocate Ralph Nader, the Public Citizen Health Research Group fights for protection against unsafe foods, drugs, and workplaces and for greater consumer control over personal health decisions. The organization has published a variety of excellent books and also produces the bimonthly publication, Public Citizen, *and the monthly* Health Letter.

Resources for Midlife and Older Women, Inc.
226 East 70th Street
Suite 1C
New York, NY 10021
(212) 439-1913

A nonprofit social service agency for midlife and older women, Resources offers quick information and referral to agencies providing services in such areas as personal financial management, legal rights, employment, and health.

Selected Bibliography

Introduction

Bart, Pauline B., and Marlyn Grossman. "Menopause." *Women and Health* 1, no. 3 (May–June 1976): 3–11.

Dege, Kristi, and Jacqueline Gretzinger. "Attitudes of Families Toward Menopause." In *Changing Perspectives on Menopause*. Austin: University of Texas Press, 1981: 60–69.

McKinlay, Sonja M., and John B. McKinley. "The Impact of Menopause and Social Factors on Health." In *Menopause: Evaluation, Treatment, and Health Concerns*. (Proceedings of the National Institutes of Health Symposium held in Bethesda, Maryland, April 21–22, 1989.) Edited by Charles B. Hammond, Florence P. Haseltine, and Isaac Schiff. New York: Alan R. Liss, 1989: 137–61.

MacPherson, Kathleen. "Menopause as Disease: The Social Construction of a Metaphor." *Advances in Nursing Science* 3, no. 2 (January 1981): 95–113.

Neugarten, Bernice L., Ph.D., and Ruth J. Kraines, Ph.D. " 'Menopause Symptoms' in Women of Various Ages." *Psychosomatic Medicine* 27 (1965): 266–73.

Paley, Grace. "The Long-Distance Runner." *Enormous Changes at the Last Minute*. New York: Farrar, Straus, and Giroux, 1974.

Chapter 1
What Is Menopause?

Allen, Patricia, M.D., and Denise Fortino. *Cycles: Every Woman's Guide to Menstruation*. New York: Pinnacle Books, 1983.

Bell, Susan. "Changing Ideas: The Medicalization of Menopause." *Social Sciences and Medicine* 24, no. 6 (1987): 535–42.

Brambilla, Donald, and Sonja McKinlay. "A Prospective Study of Factors Affecting Age at Menopause." *Journal of Clinical Epidemiology* 42, no. 11 (1989): 1031–39.

Kaufert, Patricia, and Penny Gilbert. "Women, Menopause, and Medicalization." *Culture, Medicine and Psychiatry* 10 (1986): 7–21.

LaRocco, Susan A., and Denise F. Polit. "Women's Knowledge about the Menopause." *Nursing Research* 29, no. 1 (January–February 1980): 10–13.

MacPherson, Kathleen. "Menopause as Disease: The Social Construction of a Metaphor." *Advances in Nursing Science* 3, no. 2 (January 1981): 95–113.

Madaras, Lynda, and Jane Patterson, M.D. *WomanCare*. New York: Avon Books, 1981.

Martin, Emily. *The Woman in the Body: A Cultural Analysis of Reproduction.* Boston: Beacon Press, 1987.

The New Our Bodies, Ourselves. Written and edited by the Boston Women's Health Book Collective. New York: Simon and Schuster, 1984.

Padus, Emrika. *The Woman's Encyclopedia of Health and Natural Healing.* Emmaus, Penn.: Rodale Press, 1981.

Pedersen, Bonnie, and Elaine Pendleton. "Menopause: A Welcome or Dreaded Stage of Development." *Journal of Nurse-Midwifery* 23 (Fall 1978): 45–51.

Phillips, Pat. "Menopause: A Complete Medical Report." *McCall's* (November 1987), 89–95.

Ransohoff, Rita M. *Venus After Forty.* Far Hills, N.J.: New Horizon Press, 1987.

Utian, Wulf H., M.D. *Menopause in Modern Perspective.* New York: Appleton-Century-Crofts, 1980.

Voda, Ann M., and Theresa George. "Menopause." *Annual Review of Nursing Research* 4 (1986): 55–75.

Chapter 2
Hot Flashes and Other Signs of Menopause

Allen, Patricia, M.D., and Denise Fortino. *Cycles: Every Woman's Guide to Menstruation.* New York: Pinnacle Books, 1983.

Bates, G. William, M.D. "On the Nature of the Hot Flash." *Clinical Obstetrics and Gynecology* 24, no. 1 (March 1981): 231–41.

Brody, Jane. *Jane Brody's Nutrition Book.* New York: W. W. Norton, 1981.

Castleman, Michael. *The Healing Herbs.* Emmaus, Penn.: Rodale Press, 1991.

Chenoy, R., et al. "Effect of Oral Gamolenic Acid from Evening Primrose Oil on Menopausal Flushing." *British Medical Journal* 308, no. 6927 (February 19, 1994): 501(3).

Cope, E. "Physical Changes Associated with the Post-Menopausal Years." In *The Management of the Menopause and Post-Menopausal Years*, edited by Stuart Campbell. Baltimore: University Park Press, 1976.

Dwyer, Johanna T., et al. "Tofu and Soy Drinks Contain Phytoestrogens." *Journal of the American Dietetic Association* 94, no. 7 (July 1994): 739(5).

Erlik, Yohanan, M.D., David R. Meldrum, M.D., and Howard L. Judd, M.D. "Estrogen Levels in Postmenopausal Women with Hot Flashes." *Obstetrics and Gynecology* 59, no. 4 (April 1982): 403–7.

Fonda, Jane, and Mignon McCarthy. *Women Coming of Age*. New York: Simon and Schuster, 1984.

Jovanovic, Lois, M.D., and Genell J. Subak-Sharpe. *Hormones: The Woman's Answerbook*. New York: Athenaeum, 1987.

Loprinzi, Charles L., M.D., et al. "Megestrol Acetate for the Prevention of Hot Flashes." *The New England Journal of Medicine* 331, no. 6 (August 11, 1994): 347–351.

Meldrum, David, M.D. "Perimenopausal Menstrual Problems." *Clinical Obstetrics and Gynecology* 26, no. 3 (September 1983): 762–68.

Murray, Michael T. *Natural Alternatives to Over-the-Counter and Prescription Drugs*. New York: William Morrow and Co., Inc., 1994.

The New Our Bodies, Ourselves. Written and edited by the Boston Women's Health Book Collective. New York: Simon and Schuster, 1984.

Pokras, R. "Hysterectomy: Past, Present, and Future." *Statistical Bulletin: Metropolitan Life and Affiliated Companies* 70 (October–December 1989): 12–21.

Schiff, Isaac, M.D. "The Effects of Progestins on Vasomotor Flushes." *Journal of Reproductive Medicine* 27, no. 8 (August 1982): 498–502.

Seaman, Barbara, and Seaman, Gideon, M.D. *Women and the Crisis in Sex Hormones*. New York: Bantam Books, 1978.

Stevenson, Dallas W., and Dennis J. Delprato. "Multiple Component Self-Control Program for Menopausal Hot Flashes." *Journal of Behavior Therapy and Experimental Psychiatry* 14, no. 2 (June 1983): 137–40.

"Study Shows Acupuncture Mitigates Hot Flashes." *Menopause News* 5, no. 3 (May–June 1995): 2.

Sturdee, D.W., K.A. Wilson, Eva Pipilli, and Ann D. Crocker. "Physiological Aspects of Menopausal Hot Flush." *British Medical Journal* 2 (July 1, 1978): 79–80.

Tataryn, I.V., P. Lomax, et al. "Postmenopausal Hot Flushes: A Disorder of Thermoregulation." *Maturitas* 2, no. 2 (July 1980): 101–7.

Wolfe, Sidney, M.D. *Women's Health Alert*. Reading, Mass.: Addison-Wesley, 1991.

Chapter 3
The Great Hormone Debate

American College of Obstetricians and Gynecologists. "Estrogen Replacement Therapy." *ACOG Technical Bulletin* 93 (April 1986): 587–91.

American Medical Association Division of Drugs. "Androgens and Anabolic Steroids." *AMA Drug Evaluations*. 5th ed. Chicago: American Medical Association, 1982, p. 918.

Antunes, Carlos M.F., Sc.D., et al. "Endometrial Cancer and Estrogen Use." *New England Journal of Medicine* 300, no. 1 (January 4, 1979): 9–13.

Barnes, Randall B., M.D., Subir Roy, M.D., and Rogerio A. Lobo, M.D. "Comparison of Lipid and Androgen Levels After Conjugated Estrogen or Depo-Medroxyprogesterone Acetate Treatment in Postmenopausal Women." *Obstetrics and Gynecology* 66, no. 2 (August 1985): 214–19.

————. "Postmenopausal Estrogen Replacement and Breast Cancer." *New England Journal of Medicine* 321, no. 5 (August 3, 1989): 319–20.

Barrett-Connor, Elizabeth, M.D. "Postmenopausal Estrogen and Prevention Bias." *Annals of Internal Medicine* 115, no. 6 (September 15, 1991): 455–56.

Bergkvist, Leif, M.D., Ph.D., et al. "The Risk of Breast Cancer after Estrogen and Estrogen-Progestin Replacement." *New England Journal of Medicine* 321, no. 5 (August 3, 1989): 293–97.

Boston Collaborate Drug Surveillance Program. "Surgically Confirmed Gall Bladder Disease, Venous Thromboembolism and Breast Tumors in Relation to Post Menopausal Estrogen Therapy." *New England Journal of Medicine* 290 (1974): 15–19.

Bremer, D.E., et al. "Postmenopausal Estrogen Replacement Therapy and the Risk of Alzheimer's Disease: A Population-Based Case-Control Study." *American Journal of Epidemiology* 140, no. 3 (1994): 262–267.

Brinton, Louise A., Ph.D., Robert N. Hoover, M.D., Sc.D., Moyses Szklo, M.D., Dr. P.H., and Joseph F. Fraumeni, Jr., M.D. "Menopausal Estrogen Use and Risk of Breast Cancer." *Cancer* 47 (1981): 2517–22.

Bush, Trudy L., et al. "Estrogen Replacement Therapy and Risk of Breast Cancer." (Letters to the editor and reply.) *Journal of the American Medical Association* 266, no. 10 (September 11, 1991): 1357(2).

"Cancer Facts & Figures—1995." American Cancer Society, Inc., 1995.

Citizen's Petition from Sidney M. Wolfe, M.D., and Public Citizen to Mark Novitch, M.D., Commissioner, Food and Drug Administration, December 8, 1983.

Clark, L.C., and K.M. Portier. "Diethylstilbestrol and the Risk of Cancer." *New England Journal of Medicine* 300 (1979): 263–64.

Colditz, Graham A., et al. "Hormone Replacement Therapy and Risk of Breast Cancer: Results of Epidemiologic Studies." *American Journal of Obstetrics and Gynecology* 168, no. 5 (May 1993): 1473(8).

————. "Prospective Study of Estrogen Replacement Therapy and Risk of Breast Cancer in Postmenopausal Women." *Journal of the American Medical Association* 264, no. 20 (November 28, 1990): 2648(6).

————. "The Use of Estrogens and Progestins and the Risk of Breast Cancer in Postmenopausal Women." *The New England Journal of Medicine* 332, no. 24 (June 15, 1995): 1589(5).

Ditkoff, Edward C., et al. "Estrogen Improves Psychological Function in Asymptomatic Postmenopausal Women." *Obstetrics and Gynecology* 78, no. 6 (December 1991): 991 (5).

Dupont, William D., et al. "Estrogen Replacement Therapy and Risk of Breast Cancer." (Letters to the editor and reply.) *Journal of the American Medical Association* 265, no. 14 (April 10, 1991): 1824(2).

"Effects of Estrogen or Estrogen/Progestin Regimens on Heart Disease Risk Factors in Postmenopausal Women: The Postmenopausal Estrogen/Progestin

Interventions (PEPI) Trial." *Journal of the American Medical Association* 273, no. 3 (January 18, 1995): 199(10).

"The Estrogen Question." *Consumer Reports* (September 1991): 587–91.

"Estrogen Therapy Reduces Stroke Risk." *Medformation* 4, no. 4 (Spring 1989): 2. (Published by Abbott Northwestern Hospital.)

Ettinger, B., et al. "Gynecologic Consequences of Long-Term Unopposed Estrogen Replacement Therapy." *Maturitas* 10 (1988): 271(12).

———. "Gynecologic Complications of Cyclic Estrogen Progestin Therapy." *Maturitas* 17 (1993): 197(8).

Fardon, David, M.D. *Osteoporosis: Your Head Start on the Prevention and Treatment of Brittle Bones*. New York: Macmillan, 1985.

Fillet, H., et al. "Observations in a Preliminary Open Trial of Estradiol Therapy for Senile Dementia—Alzheimer's Type." *Psychoneuroendocrinology* 11 (1986): 337–345.

Food and Drug Administration. "Estrogens: Another Riddle for Middle Age." *FDA Consumer* 14, no. 9 (November 1980): 13–15.

Gambrell, R. Don., Jr., M.D. "Clinical Use of Progestins in the Menopausal Patient." *Journal of Reproductive Medicine* 27, no. 8 (August 1982): 531–38.

Gambrell, R.D., Jr., M.D., et al. "Decreased Incidence of Breast Cancer in Postmenopausal Estrogen-Progestogen Users." *Obstetrics and Gynecology* 62, no. 4 (October 1983): 435–43.

Gibbons, William E., M.D., Dean L. Moyer, M.D., et al. "Biochemical and Histologic Effects of Sequential Estrogen/Progestin Therapy on the Endometrium of Postmenopausal Women." *American Journal of Obstetrics and Gynecology* 154, no. 2 (February 1986): 456–61.

Goodman, Ellen. "Medicine's Multiple Choices." *Minneapolis Star Tribune*, September 18, 1991: 14a.

Gusberg, S.B., M.D. "Precursors of Corpus Carcinoma Estrogens and Adenomatous Hyperplasia." *New England Journal of Medicine* 54, no. 6 (December 1947): 905–27.

Henderson, Brian E., M.D. "The Cancer Question: An Overview of Recent Epidemiologic and Retrospective Data." *American Journal of Obstetrics and Gynecology* 161, no. 6 (December 1989): 1859–64.

Henig, Robin Marantz. "Estrogen, In and Out of Favor." *Washington Post*, May 8, 1985: HE12a.

Hoover, R., L. A. Gray, P. Cole, and B. MacMahon. "Menopausal Estrogens and Breast Cancer." *New England Journal of Medicine* 295, no. 8 (1976): 401–5.

Kline, David. "The Power of the Placebo." *Hippocrates* 2, no. 3 (May–June 1988): 24, 26.

Kobren, Gerri. "Estrogen Said to Give Women Lifelong Edge over Men." *Minneapolis Star Tribune*, July 4, 1988: 1E.

Long, James W., M.D. *The Essential Guide to Prescription Drugs*. New York: Harper & Row, 1987, p. 360.

MacPherson, Kathleen. "Menopause as Disease: The Social Construction of a Metaphor." *Advances in Nursing Science* 3, no. 2 (January 1981): 95–113.

Madaras, Lynda, and Jane Patterson, M.D. *Womancare: A Gynecological Guide to Your Body.* New York: Avon, 1981.

Matthews, Karen A., et al. "Influences of Natural Menopause on Psychological Characteristics and Symptoms of Middle-Aged Healthy Women." *Journal of Consulting and Clinical Psychology* 58, no. 3 (1990): 345–51.

———. "Menopause and Risk Factors for Coronary Heart Disease." *New England Journal of Medicine* 321, no. 10 (September 7, 1989): 641–45.

Miller, Valery T., M.D., and John C. LaRosa, M.D. "The Effects of Gonadal Hormones on Lipoproteins: Public Health Implications." *Perspectives in Lipid Disorders* 5, no. 3 (July 1987): 4–10.

Miller, Valery T., M.D., Richard A. Muesing, Ph.D., et al. "Effects of Conjugated Equine Estrogen with and without Three Different Progestogens on Lipoproteins, High-Density Lipoprotein Subfractions, and Apolipoprotein A-1." *Obstetrics and Gynecology* 77, no. 2 (February 1991): 235–46.

National Women's Health Network. *Taking Hormones and Women's Health: Choices, Risks, Benefits.* Washington, D.C.: National Women's Health Network, 1989.

Notelovitz, Morris, M.D., and Marsha Ware. *Stand Tall! The Informed Woman's Guide to Preventing Osteoporosis.* Gainesville, Fla.: Triad Publishing Co., 1982.

"Osteoporosis Part Two: Prevention and Treatment." *Health Letter* (Public Citizen Health Research Group) 3, no. 6 (June 1987).

Paganini-Hill, A., and V.W. Henderson. "Estrogen Deficiency and Risk of Alzheimer's Disease in Women." *American Journal of Epidemiology* 140, no. 3 (1994): 256–261.

Posthuma, Ward F. M., et al. "Cardioprotective Effect of Hormone Replacement Therapy in Postmenopausal Women: Is the Evidence Biased?" *British Medical Journal* 308, no. 6939 (May 14, 1994): 1268(2).

"Research on the Menopause." *The Lancet* 2 (July 17, 1982): 137–38.

Rinzler, Carol Ann. *Estrogen and Breast Cancer: A Warning to Women.* New York: Macmillan, 1993.

Ross, Ronald K., M.D., M.S., Annlia Paganini-Hill, Ph.D., et al. "A Case-Control Study of Menopausal Estrogen Therapy and Breast Cancer." *Journal of the American Medical Association* 243, no. 16 (April 25, 1980): 1635–39.

Schapira, David V., et al. "Upper Body Fat Distribution and Endometrial Cancer Risk." *Journal of the American Medical Association* 266, no. 13 (October 2, 1991): 1808–11.

Seachrist, Lisa. "What Risk Hormones? Conflicting Studies Reveal Problems in Pinning Down Breast Cancer Risks." *Science News* 148, no. 6 (August 5, 1995): 94(2).

Seaman, Barbara, and Seaman, Gideon, M.D. *Women and the Crisis in Sex Hormones.* New York: Bantam Books, 1978.

Sherwin, B. B. "Estrogenic Effects on Memory in Women." *Annals of the New York Academy of Science* 743 (1994): 213–230.

Silberner, J. "Estrogen Use Raises Questions." *Science News* 128, no. 18 (November 1, 1985): 280.

Smith, Donald C., M.D., Ross Prentice, Ph.D., Donovan J. Thompson, Ph.D., and Walter L. Herrmann, M.D. "Association of Exogenous Estrogen and Endometrial Carcinoma." *New England Journal of Medicine* 293, no. 23 (December 4, 1975): 1164–67.

Speroff, Leon, Robert H. Glass, and Nathan G. Kase. *Clinical Gynecologic Endocrinology and Infertility.* 3d ed. Baltimore: Williams & Wilkins, 1983.

Stampfer, Meir J., M.D., Graham A. Colditz, M.B., B.S., et al. "Postmenopausal Estrogen Therapy and Cardiovascular Disease." *New England Journal of Medicine* 325, no. 11 (September 12, 1991): 756–62.

Stanford, Janet L., et al. "Combined Estrogen and Progestin Hormone Replacement Therapy in Relation to Risk of Breast Cancer in Middle-Aged Women." *Journal of the American Medical Association* 274, no. 2 (July 12, 1995): 137(6).

Steinberg, Karen K., et al. "A Meta-Analysis of the Effect of Estrogen Replacement Therapy on the Risk of Breast Cancer." *Journal of the American Medical Association* 265, no. 15 (April 17, 1991): 1985(6).

Subak-Sharpe, Genell. *Overcoming Breast Cancer.* New York: Doubleday, 1987.

Tang, Ming-Xin, et al. "Effect of Oestrogen During Menopause on Risk and Age at Onset of Alzheimer's Disease." *Lancet* 348 (August 17, 1996): 429–32.

"Update on Estrogens and Uterine Cancer." *FDA Drug Bulletin* (February–March 1979): 3.

U.S. Department of Health and Human Services, Public Health Service, National Institutes of Health. *The Breast Cancer Digest.* 2d ed. Bethesda, Md.: National Cancer Institute. NIH publication no. 84-1691 (April 1984).

———. *Osteoporosis: Cause, Treatment, Prevention.* NIH publication no. 86-2226 (May 1986).

Vandenbroucke, Jan P., M.D. "Postmenopausal Oestroen and Cardioprotection." *The Lancet* 337 (April 6, 1991): 833–34.

Wilson, Robert A., M.D. *Feminine Forever.* New York: M. Evans and Co., 1966.

Wolfe, Sidney M., M.D. Testimony before the Senate Health Subcommittee, Women's Health Hearings, August 1, 1979.

———. *Women's Health Alert.* Reading, Mass.: Addison-Wesley, 1991, p. 195.

"Women Who Take Estrogen for Several Years. . . ." The Associated Press, June 14, 1995.

Worcester, Nancy, and Marianne H. Whatley. "The Selling of HRT: Playing on the Fear Factor." *Feminist Review* 41 (Summer 1992): 1–26.

Wormser, Deborah. "Menopause, Estrogen, and Heart Disease." Article produced by the American Heart Association and distributed by the Los Angeles Times Syndicate's Health and Fitness News Service, August 1987.

Ziel, Harry K., M.D., and William D. Finkle, Ph.D. "Increased Risk of Endometrial Carcinoma among Users of Conjugated Estrogens." *New England Journal of Medicine* 293, no. 23 (December 4, 1975): 1167–70.

Chapter 4
Measuring Your Moods at Menopause

Elias, Marilyn. "Mind and Menopause." *Harvard Health Letter* 19, no. 1 (November 1993): 1–3.

Flint, Marcha, Ph.D. "The Menopause: Reward or Punishment?" *Psychosomatics* 16 (October/November/December 1975): 161–63.

Fortino, Denise. "Can Exercise Cure PMS?" *Women's Sports and Fitness*. November 1987.

Griffen, Joyce. "Cultural Models for Coping with Menopause." *Changing Perspectives in Menopause*. Edited by Ann M. Voda, Myra Dinnerstein, and Sheryl R. O'Donnell. Austin: University of Texas Press, 1981, pp. 248–62.

McKinlay, Sonja M., and John B. McKinlay. "The Impact of Menopause and Social Factors on Health." In *Menopause: Evaluation, Treatment, and Health Concerns*. (Proceedings of the National Institutes of Health Symposium held in Bethesda, Maryland, April 21–22, 1989.) Edited by Charles B. Hammond, Florence P. Haseltine, and Isaac Schiff. New York: Alan R. Liss, 1989: 137–61.

Morgan, Susanne. *Coping with a Hysterectomy*. New York: Dial Press, 1982.

Neugarten, Bernice, Ph.D., and Ruth J. Kraines, Ph.D. " 'Menopausal Symptoms' in Women of Various Ages." *Psychosomatic Medicine* 27, no. 3 (1965): 266–73.

Stein, Charlotte Markman. "Age of Enlightenment." *Ms.* (August 1988): 20.

"To Every Thing, a Season." *University of California, Berkeley, Wellness Letter* 4, no. 8 (May 1988): 7.

Weissman, Myrna M., Ph.D. "The Myth of Involutional Melancholia." *Journal of the American Medical Association* 242, no. 8 (August 24/31, 1979): 742–44.

Winokur, George, M.D. "Depression in the Menopause." *American Journal of Psychiatry* 130, no. 1 (January 1973): 92–93.

Chapter 5
How Menopause Will Affect Your Sexuality

Brecher, Edward M., and the editors of Consumer Reports Books. *Love, Sex, and Aging*. Boston: Little, Brown and Co., 1984.

Brody, Jane. "Personal Health: On Menopause and the Toll That Loss of Estrogens Can Take on a Woman's Sexuality." *New York Times*, May 10, 1990: B7.

Butler, Robert N., M.D., and Myrna I. Lewis. *Midlife Love Life*. New York: Harper & Row, 1986.

Doress, Paula Brown, Diana Laskin Siegal, and the Midlife and Older Women Book Project, in cooperation with the Boston Women's Health Book Collective. *Ourselves, Growing Older*. New York: Simon and Schuster, 1987.

Lloyd, Charles W., M.D. "Sexuality in the Climacteric." In *The Menopause:*

Comprehensive Management. Edited by Bernard A. Eskin, M.D. New York: Masson Publishing USA, 1980, pp. 100–110.

Madaras, Lynda, and Jane Patterson, M.D. *Womancare: A Gynecological Guide to Your Body.* New York: Avon, 1981.

Masters, William H., and Virginia E. Johnson. *Human Sexual Response.* Boston: Little, Brown and Co., 1966.

Morgan, Susanne. *Coping with a Hysterectomy.* New York: Dial Press, 1982.

Padus, Emrika. *The Woman's Encyclopedia of Health and Natural Healing.* Emmaus, Penn.: Rodale Press, 1981.

Reighenberg-Ullman, Judyth. "Menopause Naturally." *Natural Health* 22, no. 2 (March/April 1992): 74.

Sauer, Mark V., M.D., Richard J. Paulson, M.D., and Rogerio A. Lobo, M.D. "A Preliminary Report on Oocyte Donation Extending Reproductive Potential to Women Over 40." *New England Journal of Medicine* 323, no. 17 (October 25, 1990): 1157–60.

Schover, Leslie. *Prime Time: Sexual Health for Men Over Fifty.* New York: Holt, Rinehart and Winston, 1984.

Shapiro, Howard, M.D. *The New Birth-Control Book.* New York: Prentice Hall Press, 1988.

Weiss, Rick. "Prescription for Passion." *Health* 9, no. 5 (September 1995): 100(5).

Zussman, Leon, M.D., Shirley Zussman, Robert Sunley, and Edith Bjornson. "Sexual Response After Hysterectomy-Oophorectomy: Recent Studies and Reconsideration of Psychogenesis." *American Journal of Obstetrics and Gynecology* 140, no. 7 (August 2, 1981): 725–29.

Chapter 6
Understanding Osteoporosis

Alma, Alisa. "Osteoporosis: Background and Current Research." *CRS Report for Congress* 92-683 SPR. The Library of Congress: Congressional Research Service (September 3, 1992).

Amatniek, J.C. "Kidney Hormone May Limit Osteoporosis." *Science News* 124, no. 24 (December 10, 1983): 373.

"Bone-Bolstering Combination." *Consumer Reports on Health* 5, no. 5 (May 1993): 52(1).

"Bone Density Screen for All Women Held Unjustified." *Internal Medicine News* 19, no. 12 (June 15–30, 1986): 49.

Borner, Wilhelm, et al. "DEXA (Letter to the Editor; Includes Reply)." *Journal of the American Medical Association* 268, no. 4 (July 22, 1992): 474(2).

"Calcitriol in Postmenopausal Women with Osteoporosis." *American Family Physician* 45, no. 6 (June 1992): 2774(1).

"Calcium and Bone Density in Women Receiving Estrogen." *Nutrition Research Newsletter* 14, no. 5 (May 1995): 65(1).

Castleman, Michael. "Eat a Steak, Break a Bone." *Mother Jones* 20, no. 2 (March–April 1995): 20(1).

Cauley, Jane A., et al. "Estrogen Replacement Therapy and Fractures in Older Women." *Annals of Internal Medicine* 122, no. 1 (January 1, 1995): 9(8).

Chapuy, Marie C., et al. "Vitamin D3 and Calcium to Prevent Hip Fractures in Elderly Women." *New England Journal of Medicine* 327, no. 23 (December 3, 1992): 1637(6).

Chrebet, Jennifer. "More Ways to Keep Bones Strong." *American Health* 14, no. 5 (June 1995): 92.

"Coffee Drinkers Require More Dietary Calcium." *Better Nutrition for Today's Living* 56, no. 5 (May 1994): 22(1).

Cooper, Kenneth H., M.D. *Dr. Kenneth H. Cooper's Preventive Medicine Program: Preventing Osteoporosis.* New York: Bantam Books, 1989.

Culliton, Barbara J. "Osteoporosis Reexamined: Complexity of Bone Biology Is a Challenge." *Science* 235, no. 4791 (February 1987): 833–34.

Cummings, Steven R. "Risk Factors for Hip Fracture in White Women." *New England Journal of Medicine* 332, no. 12 (March 23, 1995): 767(7).

Dawson-Hughes, Bess, et al. "A Controlled Trial of Calcium Supplementation on Bone Density in Postmenopausal Women." *New England Journal of Medicine* 323, no. 13 (September 27, 1990): 878(6).

"Diagnostic and Therapeutic Technology Assessment (DATTA)." *Journal of the American Medical Association* 267, no. 2 (January 8, 1992): 286(8).

Doress, Paula Brown, Diana Laskin Siegal, and the Midlife and Older Women Book Project, in cooperation with the Boston Women's Health Book Collective. *Ourselves, Growing Older.* New York: Simon and Schuster, 1987.

Ettinger, Bruce, and Deborah Grady. "The Waning Effect of Postmenopausal Estrogen Therapy on Osteoporosis." *New England Journal of Medicine* 329, no. 16 (October 14, 1993): 1192(2).

"Experimental Osteoporosis Drug Slipping into Widespread Use Prematurely?" *The Back Letter* 9, no. 11 (November 1994): 124(2).

Fardon, David F., M.D. *Osteoporosis: Your Head Start on the Prevention and Treatment of Brittle Bones.* New York: Macmillan, 1985.

"Fascinating Facts." *University of California, Berkeley, Wellness Letter* 4, no. 9 (June 1988): 1.

"FDA Approves Osteoporosis Drug." Associated Press. October 1, 1995.

Greenspan, Susan, et al. "Fall Severity and Bone Mineral Density as Risk Factors for Hip Fracture in Ambulatory Elderly." *Journal of the American Medical Association* 271, no. 2 (January 12, 1994): 128(6).

Hausman, Patricia. *The Right Dose.* Emmaus, Penn.: Rodale Press, 1987.

Heaney, Robert P., M.D. *Calcium and Common Sense.* New York: Doubleday, 1988.

Heidrich, Fred. "Limitations of Bone Densitometry." *American Family Physician* 48, no. 1 (July 1993): 25(3).

Lindsay, Robert. "Fluoride and Bone—Quantity versus Quality." *New England Journal of Medicine* 322, no. 12 (March 22, 1990): 845–46.

Marino, Gigi "Update on Intake: Calcium Consumption Low." *Science News* 145, no. 25 (June 18, 1994): 390(1).

"Milk Mustache Ads Criticized by MDs." *HealthFacts* 20, no. 191 (April 1995): 1(2).

National Institute on Aging. "Exercise Increases Bone Mineral Content of Spine." *National Institute on Aging Special Report on Aging: 1987.* Bethesda, Md.: National Institute on Aging, 1987.

"New Osteoporosis Therapy (Calcitonin Salmon Nasal Spray)." *FDA Consumer* 29, no. 9 (November 1995): 2(1).

Notelovitz, Morris, M.D., and Marsha Ware. *Stand Tall: The Informed Woman's Guide to Preventing Osteoporosis.* Gainesville, Fla.: Triad Publishing Co., 1982.

"Optimal Calcium Intake." (National Institutes of Health Consensus Development Panel on Optimal Calcium Intake). *Journal of the American Medical Association* 272, no. 24 (December 28, 1994): 1942(7).

"Osteoporosis." *Consumer Reports* 49, no. 10 (October 1984): 576–80.

"An Osteoporosis Fighter." *Women's Sports and Fitness* 10 (December 1988): 14.

Ott, Susan M. "Bone Mass Measurements: Reason to be Cautious." *British Medical Journal* 308, no. 6934 (April 9, 1994): 931(2).

Pak, Charles Y.C., et al. "Treatment of Postmenopausal Osteoporosis with Slow-Release Sodium Fluoride: Final Report of a Randomized Controlled Trial." *Annals of Internal Medicine* 123, no. 6 (September 15, 1995): 401(8).

Pollner, Fran. "Osteoporosis: Looking at the Whole Picture." *Medical World News* 26, no. 1 (January 14, 1985): 38–58.

"Preventing Falls—and Fractures." *Consumer Reports on Health* 6, no. 7 (July 1994): 82.

Province, Michael, et al. "The Effects of Exercise on Falls in Elderly Patients: A Preplanned Meta-analysis of the FICSIT Trials." *Journal of the American Medical Association* 273, no. 17 (May 3, 1995): 1341(7).

Quint, Laurie, and Bonnie Liebman. "Here Are Facts Behind Calcium Hype." *Minneapolis Star-Tribune,* September 14, 1987: 3C. Column distributed by Los Angeles Times Syndicate.

Riggs, B. Lawrence, M.D., Stephen F. Hodgson, M.D., et al. "Effect of Fluoride Treatment on the Fracture Rate in Postmenopausal Women with Osteoporosis." *New England Journal of Medicine* 322, no. 12 (March 22, 1990): 802–809.

Schein, Jeff. "The Truth about Osteoporosis." *Consumers' Research* 69, no. 8 (August 1986): 11–17.

Seeley, Dana G., et al. "Is Postmenopausal Estrogen Therapy Associated with Neuromuscular Function or Falling in Elderly Women?" *Archives of Internal Medicine* 155, no. 3 (February 13, 1995): 293(7).

"Some Calcium Supplements Are Found to Be Ineffective." *New York Times,* March 27, 1987: 114.

Storm, Tommy, M.D., Gorm Thamsborg, M.D., et al. "Effect of Intermittent Cyclical Etidronate Therapy on Bone Mass and Fracture Rate in Women with Postmenopausal Osteoporosis." *New England Journal of Medicine* 322, no. 18 (May 3, 1990): 1265–71.

"Taking Hormones and Women's Health: Choices, Risks and Benefits." National Women's Health Network, 1995.

U.S. Department of Health and Human Services, Public Health Service, National Institutes of Health. *Osteoporosis: Cause, Treatment, Prevention.* NIH publication no. 86-2226 (May 1986).

Whiting, Susan J. "Safety of Some Calcium Supplements Questioned." *Nutrition Reviews* 52, no. 3 (March 1994): 95(3).

Chapter 7
Taking Charge: Eating for Health

American Health Foundation. *The Book of Health.* Edited by Ernst L. Wynder, M.D. New York: Franklin Watts, 1981.

Andres, Reubin. "Mortality and Obesity: The Rationale for Age-Specific Height-Weight Tables." In *Principles of Geriatric Medicine.* Edited by R. Andres, E. L. Bierman, and W. R. Hazzard. New York: McGraw-Hill, 1985, 311–18.

Andres, Reubin, et al. "Impact of Age on Weight Goals." *Annals of Internal Medicine* 103, no. 6 (December 1985): 1030–33.

Brewster, Letitia, and Michael F. Jacobson. *The Changing American Diet.* Washington, D.C.: Center for Science in the Public Interest, 1977.

Brody, Jane. *Jane Brody's Nutrition Book.* New York: W.W. Norton, 1981.

———. *The New York Times Guide to Personal Health.* New York: The New York Times Book Co., 1982.

Editors of Prevention Magazine Health Books. *Future Youth: How to Reverse the Aging Process.* Emmaus, Penn.: Rodale Press, 1987.

Fonda, Jane, and Mignon McCarthy. *Women Coming of Age.* New York: Simon and Schuster, 1984.

Goodwin, J. S., et al. "Association Between Nutritional Status and Cognitive Functioning in a Healthy Elderly Population." *Journal of the American Medical Association* 249, no. 21 (June 3, 1983): 2917–21.

Griffith, H. Winter. *Complete Guide to Vitamins, Minerals, and Supplements.* Tucson, Ariz.: Fisher Books, 1988.

Hager, Thomas, and Lauren Kessler. *Staying Young.* New York: Facts on File Publications, 1987.

Heaney, Robert, M.D. *Calcium and Common Sense.* New York: Doubleday, 1988.

Human Nutrition Information Service, U.S. Department of Agriculture. "Nutritive Value of Foods." Home and Garden Bulletin Number 72. 1988.

Jacobson, Michael. *Nutrition Scoreboard.* New York: Avon, 1975.

Lindsay, Anne. *The American Cancer Society Cookbook.* New York: Hearst Books, 1988.

Madaras, Lynda, and Jane Pataterson, M.D. *Womancare: A Gynecological Guide to Your Body.* New York: Avon, 1981.

National Academy of Sciences. *Recommended Daily Allowances.* Washington, D.C.: National Academy of Sciences, 1980.

Padus, Emrika. *The Woman's Encyclopedia of Health and Natural Healing.* Emmaus, Penn.: Rodale Press, 1981.

Raloff, J. "Reasons for Boning Up on Manganese." *Science News* 130, no. 13 (September 27, 1986): 199.

Root, E.J., and J.B. Longenecker. "Brain Cell Alterations Induced by Dietary Deficiency of Vitamin B6 and/or Copper." *American Journal of Clinical Nutrition* 37, no. 4 (April 1983): 540–52.

"Salt: Adjusting for Age." *University of California, Berkeley, Wellness Letter* 5, no. 2 (November 1988): 1–2.

Skalka, Patricia. *The American Medical Association's Straight-Talk, No-Nonsense Guide to Health and Well-Being After 50.* New York: Random House, 1984.

Chapter 8
Taking Charge: Exercising

American Health Foundation. *The Book of Health.* Edited by Ernst L. Wynder, M.D. New York: Franklin Watts, 1981.

Brody, Jane. *The New York Times Guide to Personal Health.* New York: The New York Times Book Co., 1982.

Galloway, Jeff. *Galloway's Book on Running.* Bolinas, Calif.: Shelter Publications, 1984.

Hammar, M., G. Berg, and R. Lindgren. "Does Physical Exercise Influence the Frequency of Postmenopausal Hot Flushes?" *Acta Obstetrica Gynelogica Scandinavia* 69: 1–4.

Harting, G.H., C. Moore, R. Mitchell, et al. "Relationship of Menopausal Status and Exercise Level to HDL Cholesterol in Women." *Experimental Aging Research* 10, no. 1 (1984): 13–18.

Kuscsik, Nina. "Aging Gracefully." *Women's Sports and Fitness* (October 1987): 16–21.

Lemaitre, Rozenn N., et al. "Leisure-time Physical Activity and the Risk of Nonfatal Myocardial Infarction in Postmenopausal Women." *Archives of Internal Medicine* 155, no. 21 (November 27, 1995): 2302(7).

Rich-Edwards, Janet W., et al. "The Primary Prevention of Coronary Heart Disease in Women." *New England Journal of Medicine* 332, no. 26 (June 29, 1995): 1758(9).

Skalka, Patricia. *The American Medical Association's Straight-Talk, No-Nonsense Guide to Health and Well-Being After 50.* New York: Random House, 1984.

Whitten, Phillips, and Elizabeth J. Whiteside. "Can Exercise Make You Sexier?" *Psychology Today* (April 1989): 42–44.

"Workouts Spur Creativity, Study Says." *Minneapolis Star Tribune,* May 15, 1990: 2E.

Chapter 9
Taking Charge: Skin Care

"All-Purpose Moisturizers." *Consumer Reports* (November 1986): 733–38.

American Health Foundation. *The Book of Health*. Edited by Ernst L. Wynder, M.D. New York: Franklin Watts, 1981.

Blumenthal, Deborah. "Coping with Unwanted Hair." *New York Times Magazine*, May 22, 1983: 71.

Brody, Jane. *The New York Times Guide to Personal Health*. New York: The New York Times Book Co., 1982.

Carter, D. Martin, M.D., and Arthur K. Balin, M.D. "Dermatological Aspects of Aging." *Medical Clinics of North America* 67, no. 2 (March 1983): 531–43.

"Fade Creams." *Consumer Reports* (January 1985): 12.

Gilchrest, Barbara, M.D. "At Last! A Medical Treatment for Skin Aging." *JAMA* 259, no. 4 (January 22/29, 1988): 569–70.

Godfrey-June, Jean. "Bye-bye, Wrinkles?" *American Health* 13, no. 6 (July–August 1994): 70(4).

Goldsmith, Marsha F. "Paler Is Better, Say Skin Cancer Fighters." *JAMA* 257, no. 7 (February 20, 1987): 893–94.

Henderson, Nancy. "Saving Your Skin." *Changing Times* (July 1988): 59–63.

Hopkins, Harold. "Tan Now, Pay Later?" *FDA Consumer* 16, no. 3 (April 1982): 9–11.

"The Latest Wrinkle." *University of California, Berkeley, Wellness Letter* 4, no. 7 (April 1988): 2.

Morgan, Elizabeth, M.D. *The Complete Book of Cosmetic Surgery*. New York: Warner Books, 1988.

Moynahan, Paula, M.D. *Cosmetic Surgery for Women*. New York: Crown Publishers, 1988.

"New Help for Wrinkles." *Health News* 13, no. 5 (October 1995): 6(2).

Padus, Emrika. *The Woman's Encyclopedia of Health and Natural Healing*. Emmaus, Penn.: Rodale Press, 1981.

"Retin-A Risky, Unproven for Wrinkles." *FDA Consumer* (May 1988): 4.

Stehlin, Dori. "Erasing Wrinkles: Easier Said Than Done." *FDA Consumer* (July–August 1987): 21–23.

Sternberg, James, and Thomas Sternberg. *Great Skin at Any Age: How to Keep Your Skin Looking Young without Plastic Surgery*. New York: St. Martin's Press, 1982.

Toufext, Anastasia. "Quick Fixes for the Face." *Time* (December 1, 1986): 76.

Weiss, Rick. "Wrestling with Wrinkles: Scientists Are Closing In on the Secrets of Skin Aging." *Science News* 134, no. 13 (September 24, 1988): 200–202.

Index